Volkswagen Scan Tool Companion 1990▸1995

Working with On-Board Diagnostics (OBD) Data for Engine Management Systems

www.
BentleyPublishers
.com

RB BENTLEY PUBLISHERS | AUTOMOTIVE BOOKS & MANUALS

Bentley Publishers, a division of Robert Bentley, Inc.
1734 Massachusetts Avenue
Cambridge, MA 02138 USA
800-423-4595 / 617-547-4170
www.BentleyPublishers.com

Information that makes the difference®

Technical Contact Information

We value your feedback. Technical comments and suggestions are helpful to us. Please send your comments and thoughts to Bentley Publishers
e-mail: tech@BentleyPublishers.com

From time to time, updates may be made to this manual. A listing of updates can be found on the web at www.BentleyPublishers.com

WARNING—Important Safety Notice

In this book we have provided Volkswagen scan tool diagnostic information using examples and instructions that we believe to be accurate. However, the examples, instructions, and other information are intended solely as illustrations and should be used in any particular application only by experienced personnel who are trained in the service, repair and modification of Volkswagen engine management systems and who have independently evaluated the repair, adjustment or modification. Implementation of a modification or attachment of an accessory to a Volkswagen engine management system may render the vehicle, attachment, or accessory unsafe for use in certain circumstances.

Do not perform the work described in this book unless you are familiar with basic automotive repair procedures. This book is not a substitute for full and up-to-date information from the vehicle manufacturer or for proper training as an automotive technician. Note that it is not possible for us to anticipate all of the ways or conditions under which vehicles may be serviced or to provide warnings and cautions as to all of the possible hazards that may result.

The vehicle manufacturer referred to in this book will continue to issue service information updates and parts retrofits after the editorial closing of this book. Some of these updates and retrofits may apply to procedures and specifications in this book. We regret that we cannot supply updates to purchasers of this book.

We have endeavored to ensure the accuracy of the information in this book. Please note, however, that considering the vast quantity and the complexity of the service information involved, we cannot warrant the accuracy or completeness of the information contained in this book.

FOR THESE REASONS, NEITHER THE AUTHOR NOR THE PUBLISHER MAKES ANY WARRANTIES, EXPRESS OR IMPLIED, THAT THE EXAMPLES, INSTRUCTIONS OR OTHER INFORMATION IN THIS BOOK ARE FREE OF ERROR, ARE CONSISTENT WITH INDUSTRY STANDARDS, OR THAT THEY WILL MEET THE REQUIREMENTS FOR A PARTICULAR APPLICATION. THE AUTHOR AND PUBLISHER EXPRESSLY DISCLAIM THE IMPLIED WARRANTIES OF MERCHANTABILITY AND OF FITNESS FOR A PARTICULAR PURPOSE, EVEN IF THE AUTHOR OR PUBLISHER HAVE BEEN ADVISED OF A PARTICULAR PURPOSE, AND EVEN IF A PARTICULAR PURPOSE IS INDICATED IN THE BOOK. THE AUTHOR AND PUBLISHER ALSO DISCLAIM ALL LIABILITY FOR DIRECT, INDIRECT, INCIDENTAL OR CONSEQUENTIAL DAMAGES THAT RESULT FROM ANY USE OF THE EXAMPLES, INSTRUCTIONS, OR OTHER INFORMATION IN THIS BOOK. IN NO EVENT SHALL OUR LIABILITY WHETHER IN TORT, CONTRACT OR OTHERWISE EXCEED THE COST OF THIS BOOK.

Your common sense and good judgment are crucial to safe and successful service work. Read procedures through before starting them. Think about how alert you are feeling, and whether the condition of your car, your level of mechanical skill, or your level of reading comprehension might result in or contribute in some way to an occurrence which might cause you injury, damage your car, or result in an unsafe repair. If you have doubts for these or other reasons about your ability to perform safe repair work on your car, have the work done at a qualified shop. **REPAIR OF AUTOMOBILES IS DANGEROUS UNLESS UNDERTAKEN WITH FULL KNOWLEDGE OF THE CONSEQUENCES.**

Before attempting any work on your vehicle, read the warnings and cautions on page viii and any warning or caution that accompanies a procedure in the service book. Review the warnings and cautions on page viii each time you prepare to work on your vehicle.

Copies of this manual may be purchased from authorized Volkswagen dealers, from selected booksellers and automotive accessories and parts dealers, or directly from the publisher by mail.

The publisher encourages comments from the reader of this manual. These communications have been and will be considered in the preparation of this and other manuals. Please write to Robert Bentley, Inc., Publishers at the address listed on the top of this page.

This manual was published by Robert Bentley, Inc., Publishers. Volkswagen has not reviewed and does not vouch for the accuracy of the technical specifications and procedures described in this manual.

Library of Congress Cataloging-in-Publication Data

Volkswagen scan tool companion, 1990-1995 : working with on-board diagnostics (OBD) data for engine management systems.
p. cm.
ISBN 0-8376-0393-5 (pbk. : alk. paper)
1. Volkswagen automobiles---Motors--Computer control systems--Handbooks, manuals, etc. 2. Volkswagen automobiles--Defects--Code numbers--Handbooks, manuals, etc. 3. Automotive sensors--Handbooks, manuals, etc.

TL215.V6 V633 2001
629.25'49--dc21

2001035427

VWoA Part No. LPV 800 902
Bentley Stock No. VD95

Editorial closing 03/01

03 02 01 10 9 8 7 6 5 4 3 2 1

The paper used in this publication is acid free and meets the requirements of the National Standard for Information Sciences-Permanence of Paper for Printed Library Materials. ♾

Manufactured in the United States of America

Volkswagen Scan Tool Companion 1990 ▸ 1995

Working with On Board Diagnostics (OBD) Data for Engine Management Systems

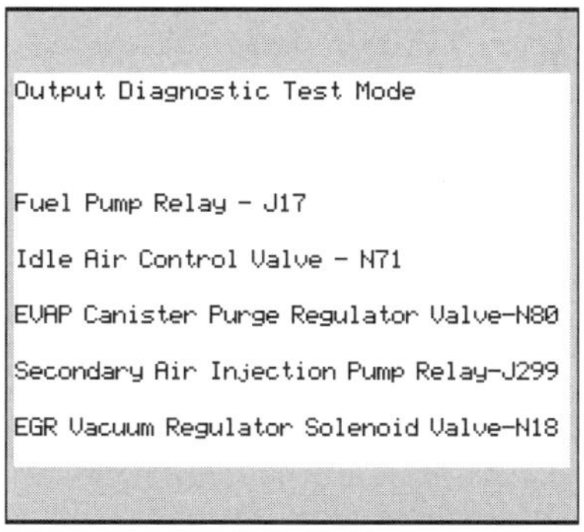

Complete descriptions of scan tool displays, including what the measuring values should be.

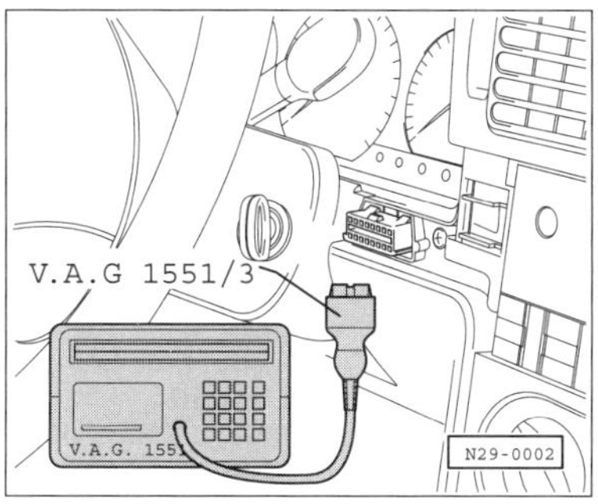

Model by model instructions for connecting the scan tool.

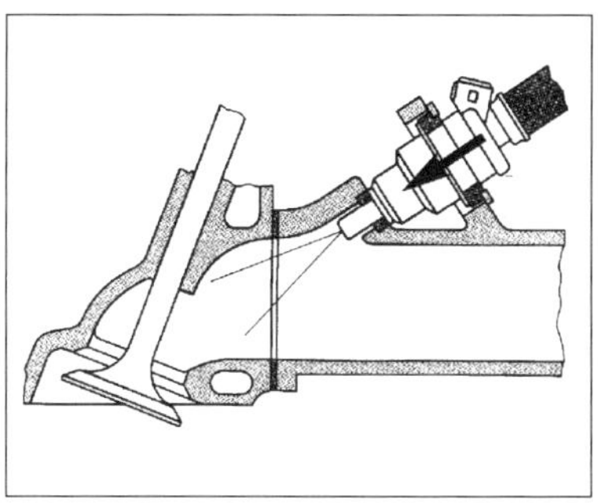

System overviews of Volkswagen fuel injection and emission control systems.

Table of Contents

Selected Books and Electronic Editions From Bentley Publishers

Volkswagen

Battle for the Beetle: The Story of the Battle for the Giant VW Factory and the Car that Became an Icon Around the Globe
Karl Ludvigsen ISBN 08376-0071-5

Volkswagen Model Documentation
Joachim Kuch ISBN 0-8376-0078-2

Volkswagen Sport Tuning for Street and Competition
Per Schroeder ISBN 0-8376-0161-4

Volkswagen Beetle: Portrait of a Legend
Edwin Baaske ISBN 0-8376-0162-2

Small Wonder: The Amazing Story of the Volkswagen Beetle
Walter Henry Nelson ISBN 0-8376-0147-9

Jetta, Golf, GTI Service Manual: 1999-2001 2.0L Gasoline, 1.9L TDI Diesel, 2.8L VR6, 1.8L Turbo
Bentley Publishers ISBN 0-8376-0388-9
Volkswagen Part No. LPV 800 118

Jetta, Golf, GTI Official Factory Repair Manual: 1999-2000 Electronic Edition
Bentley Publishers ISBN 0-8376-0765-5
VWoA Lit No.: W42 CD-ROM VW A4 00.05

Passat Official Factory Repair Manual 1998-2000 Electronic Edition
Bentley Publishers ISBN 0-8376-0763-9
VWoA Lit No.: W42 CD-ROM VW B5 00.01

New Beetle Official Factory Repair Manual 1998-2000 Electronic Edition
Bentley Publishers ISBN 0-8376-0760-4
VWoA Lit No.: W42 CD-ROM VW NB 99.10

New Beetle Service Manual: 1998-1999 2.0L Gasoline, 1.9L TDI Diesel, 1.8L Turbo
Bentley Publishers ISBN 0-8376-0385-4
Volkswagen Part No. LPV 800 401

Jetta, Golf, GTI, Cabrio Service Manual: 1993–1999, including Jetta$_{III}$ and Golf$_{III}$
Bentley Publishers ISBN 0-8376-0366-8
Volkswagen Part No. LPV 800 116

Passat Official Factory Repair Manual 1995-1997 Electronic Edition
Bentley Publishers ISBN 0-8376-0762-0
VWoA Lit No.: W42 CD-ROM VW B4 00.01

GTI/Golf/Jetta Service Manual 1985-1992 Electronic Edition
Bentley Publishers ISBN 0-8376-0759-0
VWoA Lit No.: W42 CD-ROM VW A2 92.03

GTI/Golf/Jetta Service Manual: 1985–1992 Gasoline, Diesel, and Turbo Diesel, including 16V
Bentley Publishers ISBN 0-8376-0342-0
Volkswagen Part No. LPV 800 112

Corrado Official Factory Repair Manual: 1990–1994 *Volkswagen of America*
ISBN 0-8376-0387-0
Volkswagen Part No. LPV 800 300

Passat Service Manual 1990-1993, including GL and Wagon
Bentley Publishers ISBN 0-8376-0378-1
Volkswagen Part No. LPV 800 205

Cabriolet and Scirocco Service Manual: 1985–1993, including 16V
Bentley Publishers ISBN 0-8376-0362-5
Volkswagen Part No. LPV 800 113

Fox Service Manual 1987-1993
Bentley Publishers ISBN 0-8376-0363-3
Volkswagen Part No. LPV 800 504

Vanagon Official Factory Repair Manual: 1980–1991 including Diesel, Syncro, and Camper *Volkswagen of America*
ISBN 0-8376-0336-6
Volkswagen Part No. LPV 800 148

Rabbit, Scirocco, Jetta Service Manual: 1980-1984 Gasoline Models, Including Pickup Truck, Convertible, and GTI
Bentley Publishers ISBN 0-8376-0183-5
Volkswagen Part No. LPV 800 104

Workshop Manual: Types 11, 14, and 15 (Beetle & Karmann Ghia): 1958-1960
Volkswagen of America ISBN 0-8376-0392-7
Volkswagen Part No. LPV 800 137

Super Beetle, Beetle and Karmann Ghia Official Service Manual Type 1: 1970–1979
Volkswagen of America ISBN 0-8376-0096-0
Volkswagen Part No. LPV 997 109

Station Wagon/Bus Official Service Manual Type 2: 1968–1979 *Volkswagen of America* ISBN 0-8376-0094-4
Volkswagen Part No. LPV 997 288

Fastback and Squareback Official Service Manual Type 3: 1968–1973
Volkswagen of America ISBN 0-8376-0057-X
Volkswagen Part No. LPV 997 383

Beetle and Karmann Ghia Official Service Manual Type 1: 1966–1969
Volkswagen of America ISBN 0-8376-0416-8
Volkswagen Part No. LPV 997 169

Transporter Workshop Manual: 1963-1967, Type 2, including Kombi, Micro Bus, Micro Bus Deluxe, Pickup, Delivery Van, and Ambulance
Bentley Publishers ISBN 0-8376-0391-9
Volkswagen Part No. LPV 800 135

1200 Workshop Manual: 1961-1965, Type 11, 14 and 15, Beetle, Beetle Convertible, Karmann Ghia Coupe, and Karmann Ghia Convertible
Bentley Publishers ISBN 0-8376-0390-0
Volkswagen Part No. LPV 800 121

Workshop Manual: Types 11, 14, and 15 (Beetle & Karmann Ghia): 1952-1957
Volkswagen of America ISBN 0-8376-0389-7
Volkswagen Part No. LPV 800 136

Audi

Audi: A History of Progress Chronicle of Audi AG
Audi AG ISBN 0-8376-0384-6

Audi A4/S4 Official Factory Repair Manual 1996-2000 Electronic Edition
Bentley Publishers ISBN 0-8376-0761-2
Audi of America Lit. No.: W42 CD-ROM AUB5 99.12

Audi TT Official Factory Repair Manual MY 2000 Electronic Edition
Audi of America ISBN 0-8376-0758-2
Audi of America Lit. No.: W42 AUDI TT CD-ROM 9.99

Audi 100, A6 Official Factory Repair Manual: 1992–1997, including S4, S6, Quattro and Wagon models *Audi of America*
ISBN 0-8376-0374-9
Audi Part No. LPV 800 702

Audi 80, 90, Coupe Quattro Official Factory Repair Manual: 1988–1992 Electronic Edition
Audi of America ISBN 0-8376-0367-6
Audi of America Lit. No.: W42 CD-ROM AU 80 96.12

Audi 100, 200 Official Factory Repair Manual: 1989-1991, including 100 Quattro, 200 Quattro, Wagon, Turbo and 20-valve
Audi of America ISBN 0-8376-0372-2
Audi Part No. LPV 800 701

Audi 5000S, 5000CS Official Factory Repair Manual: 1984-1988, Gasoline, Turbo, and Turbo Diesel, including Wagon and Quattro
Audi of America ISBN 0-8376-0370-6
Audi Part No. LPV 800 445

Audi 4000S, 4000CS, and Coupe GT Official Factory Repair Manual: 1984-1987, including Quattro and Quattro Turbo
Audi of America ISBN 0-8376-0373-0
Audi Part No. LPV 800 424

Engineering

Bosch Fuel Injection and Engine Management *Charles O. Probst, SAE*
ISBN 0-8376-0300-5

Maximum Boost: Designing, Testing, and Installing Turbocharger Systems
Corky Bell ISBN 0-8376-0160-6

Race Car Aerodynamics *Joseph Katz*
ISBN 0-8376-0142-8

The Scientific Design of Exhaust and Intake Systems
Philip H. Smith and John C. Morrison
ISBN 0-8376-0309-9

www.BentleyPublishers.com

BENTLEY PUBLISHERS | AUTOMOTIVE BOOKS & MANUALS

Bentley Publishers has published service manuals and automobile books since 1950. Please write Bentley Publishers at 1734 Massachusetts Avenue, Cambridge, MA 02138-1804, visit our web site at www.**BentleyPublishers**.com, or call 1-800-423-4595 for a free copy of our complete catalog.

Acknowledgments

The publisher wishes to acknowledge the assistance of the following individuals who graciously lent their vehicles, expertise, and experiences for research and testing.

Rex Ayers of Waldorf, MD
Rob Bellamy of Huntingtown, MD
Frank Connolly of Ann Arbor, MI
Howard S. Hinsdale Jr. of Glen Mills, PA
Amy L. LeBrun of Somerville, MA
Sharon L. LeBrun of Owings, MD
Steve McDonald of Chesapeake Beach, MD

Foreword

Volkswagen service is a top priority of the Volkswagen organization and has always included the continuing development and introduction of new and expanded services. In line with this purpose, Robert Bentley, Inc., has introduced the ***Volkswagen Scan Tool Companion: 1990–1995***.

This book covers Volkswagen models from 1990 through 1995. In addition, the 1996 Passat Turbo Diesel with the 1Z engine (OBD-D compliant) is also included. This book was created specifically to cover only models built for sale in the United States and Canada.

The objective of this book is to provide the Volkswagen service professional with an engine-specific field guide to OBD (on-board diagnostic) data. This book provides the technician with real world interpretation of the scan tool data. Where available, nominal value readings for a properly functioning engine management system have also been provided. Although this book has been written to support the Volkswagen diagnostic scan tool known as the VAG 1551, there are other 'aftermarket' scan tools that emulate the functions of the VAG 1551. The information contained in this book can also be used with aftermarket scan tools.

The information contained on the pages in this book has been gleaned from numerous sources, including official factory repair information, subject vehicle field testing, various scan tools (both original manufacturer's equipment and aftermarket equivalents), and Volkswagen service professionals recognized as engine management experts. Some of the information in this manual applies only to cars of a particular model year or range of years. For example, "1993 m.y." refers to the 1993 model year. The model year does not necessarily match the calendar year in which the car was manufactured or sold. To be sure of the model year of a particular car, check the vehicle identification number (VIN) on the car.

We have endeavored to insure the accuracy of the information in this book. When the vast array of data presented in the manual is taken into account, however, no claim to infallibility can be made. We therefore cannot be responsible for the result of any errors that may have crept into the text. The Publisher encourages comments from the readers of this manual with regard to errors, and also, suggestions for improvement in the presentation of the technical material. These communications have been and will be carefully considered in the preparation of this and other manuals. Please write contact Robert Bentley, Inc., at the address at the beginning of this manual.

Robert Bentley,
Publishers

Please read these warnings and cautions before proceeding with maintenance and repair work.

WARNING—

- Some repairs may be beyond your capability. If you lack the skills, tools and equipment, or a suitable workplace for any procedure described in this manual, we suggest you leave such repairs to an authorized Volkswagen dealer service department, or other qualified shop.

- Volkswagen is constantly improving its cars. Sometimes these changes, both in parts and specifications, are made applicable to earlier models. Therefore, before starting any major jobs or repairs to components on which passenger safety may depend, consult your authorized Volkswagen dealer about Technical Bulletins that may have been issued since the editorial closing of this manual.

- Do not re-use any fasteners that are worn or deformed in normal use. Many fasteners are designed to be used only once and become unreliable and may fail when used a second time. This includes, but is not limited to, nuts, bolts, washers, self-locking nuts or bolts, circlips and cotter pins. Always replace these fasteners with new parts.

- Never work under a lifted car unless it is solidly supported on stands designed for the purpose. Do not support a car on cinder blocks, hollow tiles or other props that may crumble under continuous load. Never work under a car that is supported solely by a jack. Never work under the car while the engine is running.

- If you are going to work under a car on the ground, make sure that the ground is level. Block the wheels to keep the car from rolling. Disconnect the battery negative (–) terminal (Ground strap) to prevent others from starting the car while you are under it.

- Never run the engine unless the work area is well ventilated. Carbon monoxide kills.

- Finger rings, bracelets and other jewelry should be removed so that they cannot cause electrical shorts, get caught in running machinery, or be crushed by heavy parts.

- Tie long hair behind your head. Do not wear a necktie, a scarf, loose clothing, or a necklace when you work near machine tools or running engines. If your hair, clothing, or jewelry were to get caught in the machinery, severe injury could result.

- Do not attempt to work on your car if you do not feel well. You increase the danger of injury to yourself and others if you are tired, upset or have taken medication or any other substance that may keep you from being fully alert.

- Illuminate your work area adequately but safely. Use a portable safety light for working inside or under the car. Make sure the bulb is enclosed by a wire cage. The hot filament of an accidentally broken bulb can ignite spilled fuel or oil.

- Catch draining fuel, oil, or brake fluid in suitable containers. Do not use food or beverage containers that might mislead someone into drinking from them. Store flammable fluids away from fire hazards. Wipe up spills at once, but do not store the oily rags, which can ignite and burn spontaneously.

- Always observe good workshop practices. Wear goggles when you operate machine tools or work with battery acid. Gloves or other protective clothing should be worn whenever the job requires working with harmful substances.

- Friction materials such as brake or clutch discs may contain asbestos fibers. Do not create dust by grinding, sanding, or by cleaning with compressed air. Avoid breathing asbestos fibers and asbestos dust. Breathing asbestos can cause serious diseases such as asbestosis or cancer, and may result in death.

- Disconnect the battery negative (–) terminal (ground strap) whenever you work on the fuel system or the electrical system. Do not smoke or work near heaters or other fire hazards. Keep an approved fire extinguisher handy.

- Batteries give off explosive hydrogen gas during charging. Keep sparks, lighted matches and open flame away from the top of the battery. If hydrogen gas escaping from the cap vents is ignited, it will ignite gas trapped in the cells and cause the battery to explode.

- Connect and disconnect battery cables, jumper cables or a battery charger only with the ignition switched off, to prevent sparks. Do not disconnect the battery while the engine is running.

- Do not quick-charge the battery (for boost starting) for longer than one minute. Wait at least one minute before boosting the battery a second time.

- Do not allow battery charging voltage to exceed 16.5 volts. If the battery begins producing gas or boiling violently, reduce the charging rate. Boosting a sulfated battery at a high charging rate can cause an explosion.

- The air-conditioning system is filled with chemical refrigerant, which is hazardous. The A/C system should be serviced only by trained technicians using approved refrigerant recovery/recycling equipment, trained in related safety precautions, and familiar with regulations governing the discharging and disposal of automotive chemical refrigerants.

- Do not expose any part of the A/C system to high temperatures such as open flame. Excessive heat will increase system pressure and may cause the system to burst.

- Some aerosol tire inflators are highly flammable. Be extremely cautious when repairing a tire that may have been inflated using an aerosol tire inflator. Keep sparks, open flame or other sources of ignition away from the tire repair area. Inflate and deflate the tire at least four times before breaking the bead from the rim. Completely remove the tire from the rim before attempting any repair.

- Most cars covered by this manual are equipped with a supplemental restraint system (SRS), that automatically deploys an airbag in the event of a frontal impact. The airbag is inflated by an explosive device. Handled improperly or without adequate safeguards, it can be accidently activated and cause serious injury.

- To prevent personal injury or airbag system failure, **only factory trained Volkswagen service technicians** should test, disassemble or service the airbag system.

- Disconnect the power supply before working on the airbag system, or when doing repairs that require removing airbag system components. Disconnect the battery negative (–) terminal and cover the battery.

continued on next page

Please read these warnings and cautions before proceeding with maintenance and repair work.

WARNING (continued) —

- On airbag-equipped cars, never apply stickers or any other type of covering on the steering wheel. Do not let chemical cleaners, oil or grease come into contact with vinyl covering of the airbag unit.

- Never open or otherwise attempt to repair airbag system parts. Always use new parts. Never leave airbag parts or the partially disassembled airbag system unattended.

- Never use a test light to conduct electrical tests on the airbag system. The system must only be tested by trained Volkswagen Service technicians using the Volkswagen VAG 1551/1552 Scan Tool (ST) or an approved equivalent. The airbag unit must never be electrically tested while it is not installed in the car.

- Do not expose the airbag unit to temperatures above 194°F (90°C), even for brief periods. Keep clear of heat sources such as hot plates, soldering irons, heat lamps and welding equipment.

- When driving or riding in an airbag-equipped vehicle, never hold test equipment in your hands or lap while the vehicle is in motion. Objects between you and the airbag can increase the risk of injury in an accident.

- Greases, lubricants and other automotive chemicals contain toxic substances, many of which are absorbed directly through the skin. Read manufacturer's instructions and warnings carefully. Use hand and eye protection. Avoid direct skin contact.

CAUTION—

- If you lack the skills, tools and equipment, or a suitable workshop for any procedure described in this manual, we suggest you leave such repairs to an authorized Volkswagen dealer or other qualified shop. We especially urge you to consult an authorized Volkswagen dealer before beginning repairs on any car that may still be covered wholly or in part by any of the extensive warranties issued by Volkswagen of America.

- Volkswagen offers extensive warranties, especially on components of fuel delivery and emission control systems. Therefore, before deciding to repair a Volkswagen that may still be covered wholly or in part by any warranties issued by Volkswagen of America, Inc., consult your authorized Volkswagen dealer. You may find that he can make the repair for free, or at minimal cost.

- Volkswagen part numbers listed in this manual are for identification purposes only, not for ordering. Always check with your authorized Volkswagen dealer to verify part numbers and availability before beginning service work that may require new parts.

- Before starting a job, make certain that you have all the necessary tools and parts on hand. Read all the instructions thoroughly, do not attempt shortcuts. Use tools appropriate to the work and use only replacement parts meeting Volkswagen specifications. Makeshift tools, parts and procedures will not make good repairs.

- Use pneumatic and electric tools only to loosen threaded parts and fasteners. Never use these tools to tighten fasteners, especially on light alloy parts. Always use a torque wrench to tighten fasteners to the tightening torque specification listed.

- Be mindful of the environment and ecology. Before you drain the crankcase, find out the proper way to dispose of the oil. Do not pour oil onto the ground, down a drain, or into a stream, pond or lake. Consult local ordinances that govern the disposal of wastes.

- On cars equipped with anti-theft radios, make sure you know the correct radio activation code before disconnecting the battery or removing the radio. If the wrong code is entered into the radio when power is restored, that radio may lock up and be rendered inoperable, even if the correct code is then entered.

- Connect and disconnect a battery charger only with the battery charger switched off.

- Do not quick-charge the battery (for boost starting) for longer than one minute. Wait at least one minute before boosting the battery a second time.

- Sealed or "maintenance free" batteries should be slow-charged only, at an amperage rate that is approximately 10% of the battery's ampere-hour (Ah) rating.

- Do not allow battery charging voltage to exceed 16.5 volts. If the battery begins producing gas or boiling violently, reduce the charging rate. Boosting a sulfated battery at a high charging rate can cause an explosion.

Engine Code

AAA

General

The vehicles listed below are equipped with engine code **AAA**. This 2.8 liter engine uses the Bosch® **Motronic M2.9** engine management system.

This engine is designated VR-6 as a result of the arrangement of the 6 cylinders in a narrow (15°), inline Vee.

Engine Code AAA Vehicles

Engine Code AAA	Model Years
Corrado / SLC	1992, 1993, 1994, 1995
Passat GLX	1993, 1994, 1995
Golf GTI VR6	1994, 1995
Jetta GLX	1994, 1995

Scan tool, connecting

The scan tool is connected through the DLC (Data Link Connector). The DLC location varies depending on model year.

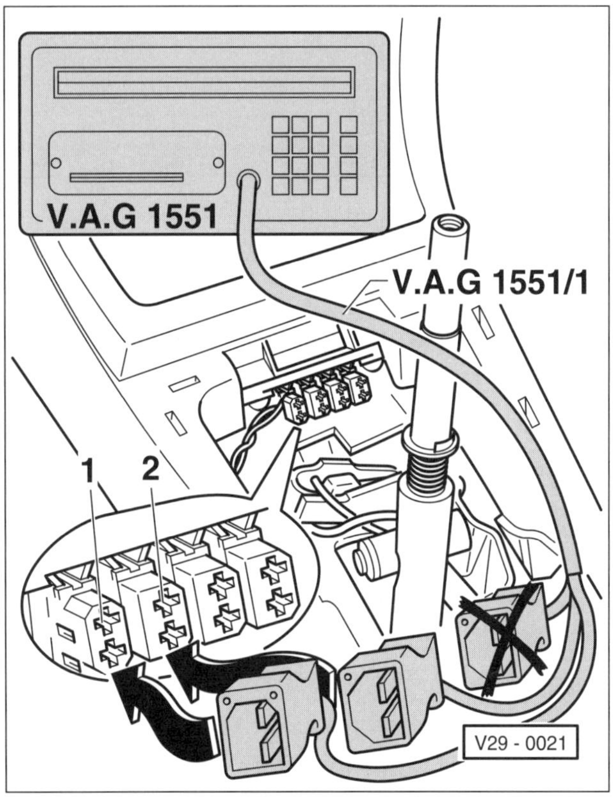

◄ **Corrado, all years,**
Passat, 1993-1994:
Manual transmission: center console under shift boot.
Automatic transmission: center console under selector indicator cover.

Black connector on scan tool is connected to black connector on vehicle (scan tool power). White connector is connected to white connector on vehicle (data transfer). Blue connector is not used.

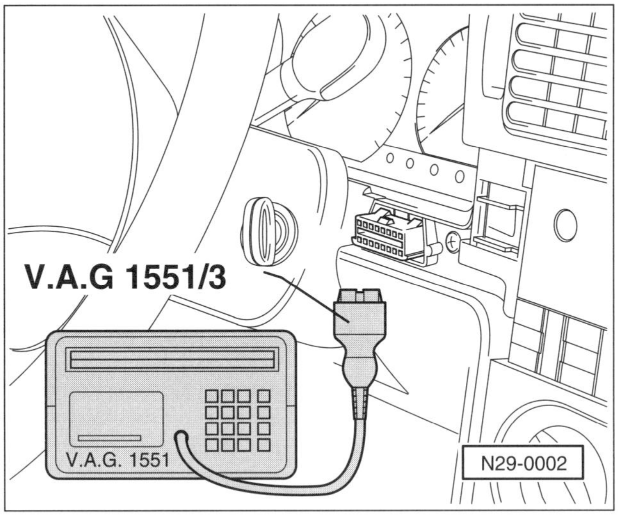

Passat, 1995:
Instrument panel, to right side of steering column, behind cover.

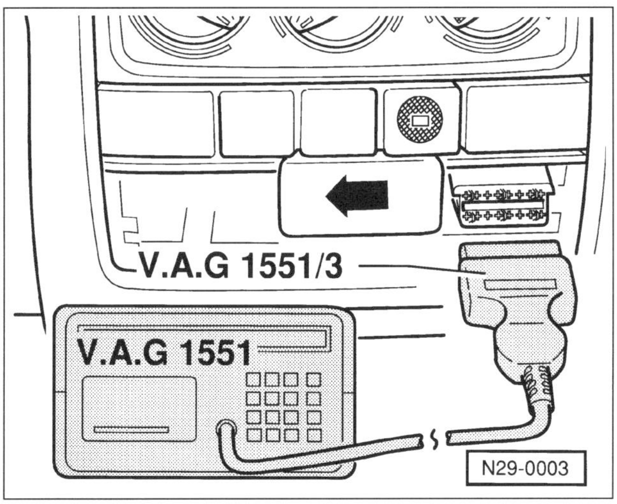

Golf GTI and Jetta GLX, 1994-1995:
Instrument panel center section, to right side of ashtray, behind cover.

Scan tool, functions available

Scan Tool Functions Available		Ignition on, not running	Engine at idle	Page
✔	Control unit version (01)	Yes	Yes	Appendix A
✔	Check DTC memory (02)	Yes	Yes	Appendix A
✔	Output diagnostic test mode (03)	Yes	No	11
✔	Basic settings (04)	No	Yes	9
✔	Erase DTC memory (05)	Yes	Yes	Appendix A
✔	End output (06)	Yes	Yes	Appendix A
✗	Code control module (07)	No	No	14
✔	Read measuring value blocks (08)	Yes	Yes	4
✗	Read indiv. measuring value blocks (09)	No	No	Appendix A

Read Measuring Value Blocks (Function 08)

Measuring value blocks are assembled and displayed in sets called display groups. For the AAA engine, display groups are numbered starting with 000 and continuing with 001 on up to 006.

```
Read Measuring Value Blocks        HELP
Input Display Group Number         XXX
```

◀ Scan tool display from VAG 1551 requesting Measuring Value Block Display Group information (XXX).

Display group overview, AAA engine

Function 08 Display Group Overview 000[OV-1]										
Display Field	**1**	**2**	**3**	**4**	**5**	**6**	**7**	**8**	**9**	**10**
	ECT	Load	RPM	HO2S	Idle load adaptation	Part load adaptation	Low load adaptation	Air correction adaptation	n/a	Ignition timing

OV-1) Some data is not relevant, or is unavailable. This data is identified as n/a.

Function 08 Display Group Overview 001 - 006				
Display Field	**1**	**2**	**3**	**4**
Display Group 001	RPM	ECT	Lambda	Ignition timing
Display Group 002	RPM	Injector duration	ECM Voltage	EGR temperature
Display Group 003	RPM	Load	TPS ∠	IAT
Display Group 004	RPM	Load	Vehicle speed	Input signals 1
Display Group 005	RPM	IAC adaptation	IAC duty cycle	Input signals 2
Display Group 006	HO2S	HO2S adaptation -idle	HO2S adaptation -medium/full	HO2S adaptation -part

Function 08
Display Group 000

Warm engine, running at idle speed, engine control module in **Read Measuring Value Block** (Function 08)

Display Field	Display Fields	Observed range: [000-1, 000-2]	Corresponds to:
10	**Ign. timing (varies)**	84-92	3.0 - 9.0 °BTDC
9	**Undefined data**	—	—
8	**Air correction value (adaptation)**	121-141	—
7	**Learning value for low load adaptation**	102-154	—
6	**Learning value for part load adaptation**	68-188	—
5	**Learning value for idle adaptation**	68-188 [000-3]	—
4	**Oxygen sensor factor (fast fluctuations over a wide range)**	102-154 [000-4]	—
3	**Engine speed (fluctuates slightly)**	64-72 [000-5]	640-720 rpm
2	**Engine load signal (fluctuates slightly)**	24–32 (MT) 24-46 (AT)	—
1	**Engine coolant temperature sensor (varies as radiator fan cycles on and off)**	181-224 [000-6]	80-110°C

000-1) Detailed information for this display group is not given. Data is averaged from scan tool observations of several "known good" vehicles.

000-2) Center of range for Fields 4,5,6,7, & 8 is 128.

000-3) Values greater than 188 indicate an air leak.

000-4) Values greater than 128 indicate a lean condition correcting towards rich, less than 128 indicate a rich condition correcting towards lean. No fluctuations indicate that control is not working. If value remains at 0, the engine is running excessively rich and the HO2S system cannot control it.

000-5) Multiply value by 10 to read actual engine rpm at idle.

000-6) Value of 181 equals 80°C.

Read Measuring Value Blocks (Function 08)

Function 08
Display Group 001

	1	2	3	4
Display	xxxx /min	xx.x °C	x.xx	xx.x ° v.OT
Indicated	Engine speed	Coolant temperature	Lambda factor	Ignition timing
Specification	650-750 idle rpm	none given[001-1]	none given[001-2]	none given[001-3]
		Open circuit shows a constant 77.7°		
Working range	650...6600 rpm	-46.5°C...141.0°C		

[001-1)] No specification given. Experience indicates that at idle, temperature will vary between approximately 92°C and 100°C depending on radiator fan operating cycle. Temperature must rise smoothly during engine warm-up. If display jumps up by 2°C to 5°C in display, ECM is raising temperature based on running time due to a faulty ECT Sensor.

[001-2)] No specification given. Experience indicates that at idle, lambda value will be between 0.80 and 1.20 with the center of the range at 1.00. Value will fluctuate slightly during warm idle.

[001-3)] No specification given. Experience indicates that ignition timing can vary widely but will generally be between 3° and 9° BTDC at idle. Variations are due to electronic Idle Speed Control (ISC). ISC varies timing in conjunction with the IAC to provide a smooth engine idle.

Function 08
Display Group 002

	1	2	3	4
Display	xxxx /min	xx.x ms	xx.x V	xx.x °C
Indicated	Engine speed	Fuel injector duration	ECM supply voltage	EGR temperature
Specification	650-750 idle rpm	none given[002-1]	none given[002-2]	none given[002-3]
			VAG 1551 Scan Tool operates 10V- 16V	If no EGR, shows a constant 217°C
Working range	650...6600 rpm		Maximum 14.5V	127.4°C...217°C

[002-1)] No specification given. Experience indicates that at idle, fuel injector duration will be approximately 3 to 5 mS.

[002-2)] No specification given. Experience indicates that ECM supply voltage should be approximate electrical system voltage.

[002-3)] No specification given. If no EGR, value will be a constant 217.0°C. Lowest value displayed is 127.4. When EGR is functioning, temperature will rise to a maximum indicated 217.0°C as exhaust gases pass EGR Temperature sensor.

Function 08 Display Group 003				
	1	2	3	4
Display	xxxx /min	xxx%	xx ∠°	xx.x °C
Indicated	Engine speed	Engine load	Throttle valve angle	Intake air temperature
Specification	650-750 idle rpm	none given[003-1]	9° to 19° at idle 90° to 101° at WOT[003-2]	none given[003-3]
				Open circuit shows a constant 19.6°
Working range	650...6600 rpm		9°...101°	

003-1) No specification given. Experience indicates that at idle, load value will vary between approximately 2% and 5%. Load value should increase by approximately 1% when electrical consumers and air conditioning are switched on while at idle.

003-2) Value must increase/decrease uniformly as throttle is opened and closed.

003-3) No specification given. Experience indicates that air temperature and coolant temperature will be approximately the same when a cold engine is first started. Intake air temperature is usually warmer than ambient air temperature and more closely approximates the temperature in the manifold temperature.

Function 08 Display Group 004				
	1	2	3	4
Display	xxxx /min	xxx%	xx	XXXXX
Indicated	Engine speed	Engine load	Vehicle speed	Operating mode 1, throttle positions
Specification	650-750 idle rpm	none given[004-1]	none given004-2	see Operating Mode 1 table below[004-3]
Working range	650...6600 rpm		0...210 km/h (governed top speed	

004-1) No specification given. Experience indicates that at idle, load value will vary between approximately 2% and 5%. Load value should increase by approximately 1% when electrical consumers and air conditioning are switched on at idle.

004-2) No specification given. Value is received from Vehicle Speed Sensor (VSS) and indicates approximate vehicle road speed.

004-3) Display will be either a 1 or a 0. For example, 00010 indicates idle position recognized. Multiple functions can occur simultaneously such as 00011 indicating idle position recognized but engine speed sufficient to enable deceleration fuel shut-off.

Operating Mode 1- Throttle Positions (see Display Group 004, Field 4)

Displayed: (1 = recognized/ enabled 0 = not)					Position recognized or function enabled
X					Acceleration enrichment
	X				Full load
		X			Part load
			X		Idle
				X	Overrun (deceleration fuel shut-off)

Read Measuring Value Blocks (Function 08)

Function 08 Display Group 005				
	1	**2**	**3**	**4**
Display	xxxx /min	x.xx	xx%	XX XX
Indicated	Engine speed	Idle stabilization adaptation	Idle stabilization duty cycle	Operating mode 2, input signals
Specification	650-750 idle rpm	none given[005-1]	none given[005-2]	see relevance below[005-3]
Working range	650...6600 rpm			

005-1) No specification given. Experience indicates that at idle, adaptation value will be approximately 1.00 ±0.20.

005-2) No specification given. Experience indicates that at idle, duty cycle value will be between 40% and 55%. Duty cycle value should increase slightly when electrical consumers and air conditioning are switched on at idle.

005-3) Display will be either a 1 or a 0. For example, 00 01 indicates the automatic transmission in gear signal is recognized. Multiple functions can occur simultaneously such as 11 01 indicating air conditioning compressor and system on and automatic transmission in gear.

Operating Mode 2 - Input Signals (see Display Group 005, Field 4)

Displayed (1 = recognized/ enabled, 0 = not)					**Signal recognized or function enabled**
X					Air conditioner compressor on
	X				Air conditioner system on
			X		Automatic transmission shift signal, TCM to ECM
				X	Manual transmission or Automatic transmission in Park or Neutral

Function 08 Display Group 006				
	1	**2**	**3**	**4**
Display	x.xx	x.xx	x.xx	x.xx
Indicated	Lambda factor	Lambda adaptation at idle	Lambda adaptation at medium/full load	Lambda adaptation at part load
Specification	none given [006-1]	none given[006-2]	none given[006-2]	none given[006-3]
Working range[006-4]				

006-1) No specification given. Experience indicates that at idle, lambda value will be between 0.75 and 1.25 with the center of the range at 1.00. Value will fluctuate slightly during warm idle. This information is the same as in Display Group 001, field 3.

006-2) No specification given. Experience indicates that lambda value will be between 0.53 and 1.47 with the center of the range at 1.00.

006-3) No specification given. Experience indicates that lambda value will be between 0.80 and 1.20 with the center of the range at 1.00.

006-4) Optimum air/fuel mixture is 14.7:1 and is referred as "lambda of 1 (λ=1)".
Values greater than 1.00 indicate excess air and a corresponding lean mixture. System response will be to richen the mixture.
Values less than 1.00 indicate insufficient air and a corresponding rich mixture. System response will be to lean out the mixture.

Basic Settings (Function 04)

AAA engines do not have provisions for adjustment of ignition timing, idle speed or mixture through **Basic Settings (Function 04)**. These operating parameters are pre-programmed into the ECM and adapted based on engine operating conditions. These adaptive settings are retained in the ECM's memory when the ignition is switched off and become the starting point for subsequent engine operation. These retained values are said to be "learned" values and can change or adapt as often as needed.

If the ECM is disconnected from the battery during repairs, the learned values are erased and the ECM will revert to the default values allowing the engine to run. The default values may not match the current needs of the engine, which can result in temporary poor performance and driveability. Also, when repairs have been made, such as repair of a vacuum leak, the default values will not match the current needs of the engine.

In both situations, the ECM will start from the default or baseline settings and re-learn and adapt to current operating conditions. This process can, however, take some time.

When a scan tool is properly connected to the Motronic M2.9 ECM on AAA coded engines and set to Basic Settings (Function 04), the ECM can be made to adapt to current operating conditions in several minutes rather than a longer period of time.

When Function 04 (basic settings) is selected, the scan tool does the following:

- Stabilize ignition timing.
- Stabilize idle speed.
- Disable the A/C compressor.
- Disable the EVAP system.

Initiating basic settings

Begin the basic settings procedure by observing the following requirements:

Preliminary requirements:

- Vehicle stationary, engine at idle, automatic transmission in P or N.
- Engine oil temperature at least 80°C (176°F)
- All electrical consumers switched off.
  (radiator cooling fan must not run during check)
  (daytime running lights (DRLs) can remain on)
- Air conditioning switched off.
- Exhaust system free from leaks.

Checking and adjusting Basic Settings:

- Connect scan tool
- From the initial Menu select:
  1 Rapid Data
- From the address word Menu select:
  01 Engine Electronics
- Advance to the Function Menu when the ECM responds with the version information
- From the Function Menu select:
  02 Check DTC memory
  Read DTCs and return to the Function Menu
- From the Function Menu select:
  04 Basic settings

```
Start Basic Setting                  HELP
Input Display Group Number           XXX
```

◄ From the Start Basic Settings display, input:
display group 001 (or 01 if applicable)

- Accelerate engine slightly over idle speed and allow to idle for at least 2 minutes
- Observe engine operating data after 2 minutes.
  Display field 1 . . . . .650 to 750 rpm
  Display field 2 . . . . .80°C or greater
  Display field 3 . . . . 1.00 ± 0.25 (fluctuating)
  Display field 4 . . . . 6° v.OT (slight fluctuation)

```
System in Basic Setting        01    -->
710 /min    85°C    1.02       6.2° v.OT
```

◄ Basic setting display as shown on a VAG 1551 showing values within specifications.

If operating data is within the listed specification and radiator coolant fan has not run for 2 minutes, exit basic settings and end output; basic settings are complete. If operating data is not within listed specification, determine malfunction and re-test.

> ***NOTE***
> *Information regarding other system components can be viewed via Function 08 (read measuring value blocks).*

Output Diagnostic Test Mode (Function 03)

Troubleshooting electrical faults in Motronic M2.9 equipped AAA engines is facilitated by the Output Diagnostic Test Mode or Function 03.

When this function is activated, the scan tool instructs the ECM to operate certain electrical components in a pre-determined sequence. The output diagnostic test mode can only be used when the ignition is switched on, but the engine is not running.

```
Rapid data transfer                Q
03 - Output Diagnostic Test Mode
```

◄ VAG 1551 Scan Tool display shown at beginning of Output Diagnostic Test Mode.

The following is a list of components checked in the order in which they are tested:

- Fuel injector, cylinder 1 (N30)[1]
- Fuel injector, cylinder 5
- Fuel injector, cylinder 3
- Fuel injector, cylinder 6
- Fuel injector, cylinder 2
- Fuel injector, cylinder 4
- Idle air control valve (IAC) (N71)
- Evaporative Emission (EVAP) Canister Purge Regulator Valve (N80)
- Heated Oxygen Sensor Relay (HO2S) relay
- Exhaust Gas Recirculation (EGR) Vacuum Regulator Solenoid Valve (N18)[2]
- Intake Manifold Change-Over Valve (N156)[3]
- Secondary Air Injection (AIR) Pump Relay (J299)[4]
- Secondary Air Injection (AIR) Solenoid Valve (N112)[4]

Notes:
1 Output diagnostic test mode always starts with the first cylinder in the firing order, cylinder 1 and continues with remaining cylinders in the firing order sequence: 1-5-3-6-2-4.
2 Where equipped.
3 USA and Canada specification engines are not equipped with this component, but it appears in the test procedure. Continue past it.
4 Where equipped.

Testing in Function 03

Before making the output test, review the following items:

- The Throttle Position (TP) Sensor must function properly because the Fuel injector test is advanced by partially opening the throttle.

Output Diagnostic Test Mode (Function 03)

- The engine must be at operating temperature for all of the tests to run. If this is not possible, the test can still be run on a cold engine, but usually only one or two of the injectors will operate. This facilitates later engine starts by minimizing spark plug fouling.
- The test can only be run once per engine start. After completion, the engine must be started before it can be repeated. Some ECM versions may allow a repeat after switching the ignition off and back on, but some components may be skipped.

```
Output Diagnostic Test Mode          →
Injector, Cyl. 1 - N30
```

< VAG 1551 Scan Tool display for first component checked in Output Diagnostic Test Mode.

After the scan tool has been connected and Function 03 selected, proceed with the test as indicated on the scan tool noting the following points:

1. **Fuel injector, cylinder 1 (N30)**
When Function 03 is selected, the first component checked is Fuel injector, Cylinder 1. To test this component, the throttle must be manually operated to the wide open position and then closed. The injector must be heard to click approximately 5 times. After operating the injector, the program will advance to the next injector in the firing order. All injectors operate in the same manner.

2. **Fuel injector, cylinder 5**

3. **Fuel injector, cylinder 3**

4. **Fuel injector, cylinder 6**

5. **Fuel injector, cylinder 2**

6. **Fuel injector, cylinder 4**

7. **Idle Air Control (IAC) Valve (N71)** – The IAC Valve will be operated from the fully closed position through the full open position and back resulting in a audible click. Advance the program with the right arrow button (-->).

8. **Evaporative Emission (EVAP) Canister Purge Regulator Valve (N80)** – The EVAP Canister Purge regulator Valve will be switched off and on (opened and closed). The resulting noise is faint and difficult to hear, but can also usually be felt. Advance the program with the right arrow button (-->).

NOTE
Do not confuse the EVAP Canister Purge Regulator Valve with the EGR Vacuum Regulator Solenoid Valve (N18), which is mounted next to it on some vehicles.

9. **Heated Oxygen Sensor (HO2S) Relay (J278)** – The HO2S Relay will be switched on and off. The relay is located inside the vehicle near the fuse/relay panel and the resulting noise can be heard in the passenger compartment near the pedals.

10. **Exhaust Gas Recirculation (EGR) Vacuum Regulator Solenoid Valve (N18)** – The EGR Vacuum Regulator Solenoid Valve will be switched on and off (opened and closed) resulting in an audible click. Advance the program with the right arrow button (-->).

11. **Intake Manifold Change-Over Valve (N156)** – Disregard. This component is not factory-installed on USA and Canadian vehicles. Advance the program with the right arrow button (-->).

12. **Secondary Air Injection (AIR) Solenoid Valve (N12)** – The AIR Solenoid Valve will be switched on and off (opened and closed) resulting in an audible click. Advance the program with the right arrow button (-->).

13. **Secondary Air Injection (AIR) Pump Relay (J299)** – The AIR Pump Relay will be switched on and off resulting in an audible click. Return the program to the Function Menu with the right arrow button (-->).

```
Output Diagnostic Test Mode

Injector, Cyl. 1-N30
Injector, Cyl. 2-N31
Injector, Cyl. 3-N32
Injector, Cyl. 4-N33
Injector, Cyl. 5-N83
Injector, Cyl. 6-N84
Idle Air Control Valve-N71
EVAP Canister Purge Regulator Valve-N80
Heated Oxygen Sensor Relay-J278
EGR Vacuum Regulator Solenoid Valve-N18
Intake Manifold Changeover Valve-N156
Secondary Air Injection Pump Relay-J299
Secondary Air Inject.Solenoid Valve-N112
```

When the VAG 1551 printer is switched on, the paper tape will be automatically printed with all of the tests in sequence.

The Output Diagnostic Test Mode is helpful in checking the electrical operation of a given component. It can also be helpful in diagnosing mechanical malfunctions as well. If, for example, an EGR Vacuum Regulator Solenoid was suspected of a malfunction, the hoses could be disconnected and the Output Diagnostic Test Mode run while blowing through the valve. This would help determine if it worked properly. Similar tests can be devised with many of the other components.

In the event of a component failing to operate, the component and the wiring should be checked for continuity, open circuits, and short circuits, including short circuits to ground. Always consult the appropriate wiring diagram.

NOTE

The Output Diagnostic Test Mode (ODTM) can be helpful in diagnosing mechanical malfunctions as well. If, for example, an EVAP Canister Purge Regulator Valve was suspected of a malfunction, the hoses could be disconnected and the ODTM run while blowing through the valve. Similar tests can be devised with other components.

Code Control Module (Function 07)

Control module coding by means of the scan tool is not a supported function with Motronic 2.9 ECMs in AAA coded engines. Coding information does appear, however, in Function 01 (control unit versions). ECM coding is generally accomplished through the use of special coding wires in the ECM wiring harness. Codes are used to identify the transmission type and if equipped with EGR.

Engine Control Module from 1995 Passat GLX shown with mounting bracket. Part number on ECM (**arrow**) matches Scan Tool display in Function 01 (021 906 258 BS). Coding information does not, however, appear externally.

ECM Coding (AAA)

Coding	Vehicle and Equipment
1	Manual transmission, without EGR
2	Automatic transmission, without EGR
3	Manual transmission, with EGR
4	Automatic transmission, with EGR

NOTE
Part numbers can change within the Volkswagen Parts system for several reasons and are not, therefore, listed here. Always consult with your Volkswagen Parts Department or aftermarket parts specialist for the latest parts information.

Component and Signal Overview, AAA Engine

AAA engines use the Bosch Motronic M2.9 engine management system. Signals from sensors and other input sources are processed by the ECM. Signals to control the engine are sent to actuators along with engine information needed by other systems or functions.

Component and Signal Overview, AAA Engine

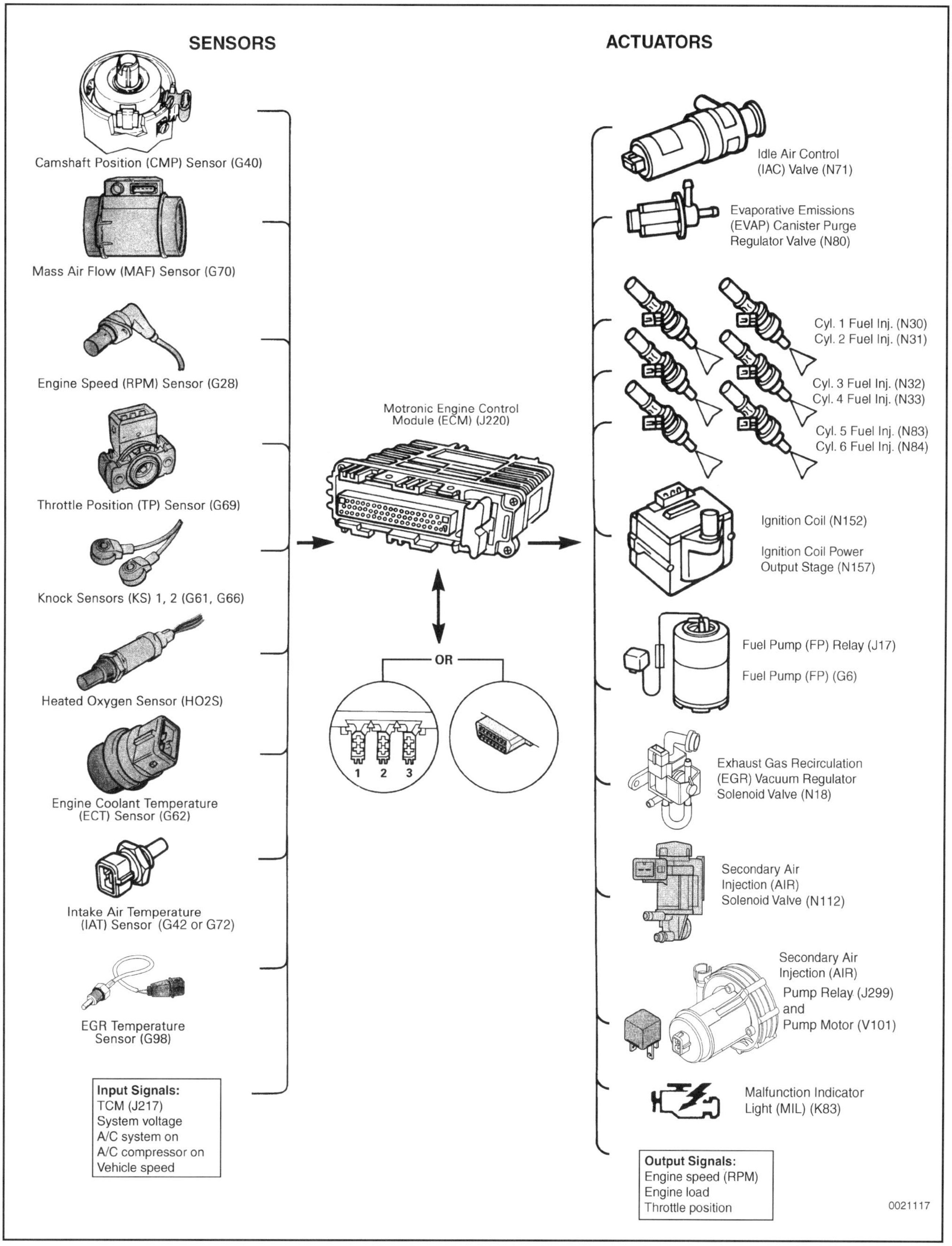

Component and Signal Overview, AAA Engine

Component and Signal Overview (AAA)

Bosch® Motronic M2.9, 6-cylinder	
Fuel injection	Sequential Multi-Point Fuel Injection with Lambda (Oxygen Sensor) Control, OBD-I
Fuel delivery	Tank-mounted 2-stage electric fuel pump, load-sensing mechanical pressure regulator
Ignition system	Distributor[1] / Distributor-less[2], Dual knock sensors, ECM controlled
Emission control	3-Way catalytic converter, evaporative emissions with carbon canister, positive crankcase ventilation, secondary air injection[3]
Diagnostics	On-Board Diagnostics via scan tool, Rapid data transfer[4], Non-volatile memory
Control Module	Single 68-pin Motronic Engine Control Module (ECM) (J220), supplied by Motronic ECM Power Supply Relay (J271)
Sensors	Camshaft Position (CMP) Sensor (G40)
	Mass Air Flow (MAF) Sensor (G71)[5]
	Engine Speed (RPM) Sensor (G28)[6]
	Throttle Position (TP) Sensor (G69)[7]
	Knock Sensors (KS) 1 (G61) and 2 (G66)
	Heated Oxygen Sensor (H2OS) (G39 or G79)
	Engine Coolant Temperature (ECT) Sensor (G62)
	Intake Air Temperature (IAT) Sensor (G42 or G72))
	Exhaust Gas Recirculation (EGR) Temperature Sensor (G98)[8]
Input signals	System voltage
	Air conditioner, system on
	Air conditioner, compressor on
	Vehicle speed
	Automatic Transmission Control Module (TCM) (J217)

Component and Signal Overview (AAA)

Actuators	Idle Air Control (IAC) Valve (N71)
	Evaporative Emission (EVAP) Canister Purge Regulator Valve (N80)
	Fuel Injectors: Cylinder 1 (N30), Cylinder 2 (N31), Cylinder 3 (N32), Cylinder 4 (N33), Cylinder 5 (N83), Cylinder 6 (N84)
	Ignition Coil Power Output Stage (N157), and Ignition Coil (N152)
	Fuel Pump (FP) Relay (J17), and Fuel Pump (FP) (G6)
	Heated Oxygen Sensor (HO2S) Relay (J278), and Heated Oxygen Sensor (HO2S) (G39)
	Exhaust Gas Recirculation (EGR) Vacuum Regulator Solenoid Valve (N18)[8]
	Secondary Air Injection (AIR) Solenoid Valve (N112)[3]
	Secondary Air Injection (AIR) Pump Relay (J299), and Pump Motor (V101)[3]
	Malfunction Indicator Light (MIL)[9] (K83)
Output signals	Engine speed (rpm)
	Engine load
	Throttle position[10]

[1] Corrado, MY 1992 and early MY 1993, and Passat, early MY 1993.
[2] Corrado and Passat, mid MY 1993 to 1995, Golf GTI and Jetta GLX MY 1994 and 1995.
[3] Except Corrado MY 1992 and early MY 1993, and Passat, early MY 1993.
[4] Also equipped with "blink code" diagnostics. The limited capabilities of this mode are outside the scope of this manual.
[5] Hot-wire MAF: Corrado and Passat to MY 1994, Hot-film MAF Corrado and Passat MY 1995, Golf GTI and Jetta GLX MY 1994 and 1995.
[6] Shutter wheel on crankshaft has 58 teeth plus 2 blank spaces to provide both engine speed and reference.
[7] Early vehicles with automatic transmissions use separate TP Sensors combined in a single housing. Later vehicles use a single TP Sensor and share data with the TCM.
[8] EGR only installed on vehicles for some market areas.
[9] MIL only functional on vehicles for some market areas.
[10] Automatic transmission vehicles only.

TECHNICAL DATA

Technical data is compiled from several Volkswagen publications. In some instances, the information from these sources differs slightly in the areas of horsepower and torque. In these cases, the most current specifications are listed.

> ***NOTE***
> *The AAA engine is also installed in some vehicles with OBD II capability. These versions are outside the scope of this manual.*

AAA (Corrado)	**Technical Data**
Type	6-cylinder in-line vee (15° VR-6), gasoline fuel
Construction	Cast iron block, aluminum 2V cylinder head, chain driven double overhead camshafts
Displacement	2.8 Liters (2792 cc), (170 cid)
Horsepower	178 hp (132 KW) @ 5800 rpm
Torque	173 lb-ft (235 Nm) @ 4200 rpm (177 lb-ft (240 Nm) with premium fuel)
Bore	81.0 mm
Stroke	90.3 mm
Compression ratio	10.0:1
Firing order	1-5-3-6-2-4
Management	Motronic M2.9

AAA (Passat/Golf/Jetta)	**Technical Data**
Type	6-cylinder in-line vee (15° VR-6), gasoline fuel
Construction	Cast iron block, aluminum 2V cylinder head, chain driven double overhead camshafts
Displacement	2.8 Liters (2792 cc), (170 cid)
Horsepower	172 hp (128 KW) @ 5800 rpm
Torque	173 lb-ft (235 Nm) @ 4200 rpm (177 lb-ft (240 Nm) with premium fuel)
Bore	81.0 mm
Stroke	90.3 mm
Compression ratio	10.0:1
Firing order	1-5-3-6-2-4
Management	Motronic M2.9

Engine Code
AAF

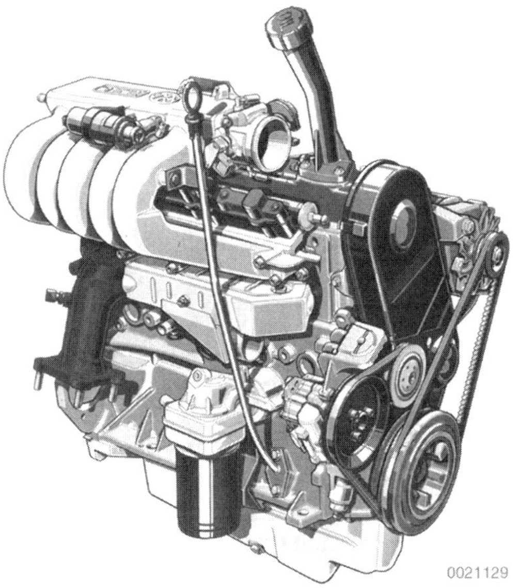
0021129

GENERAL

The vehicles listed below are equipped with engine code **AAF**. This engine uses Volkswagen's **Digifant** engine management system. The displacement of this inline 5-cylinder engine is 2.5 liters.

The AAF engine is the only available powerplant in USA-specification Eurovans. Most Canadian-specification Eurovans also use this engine.

Engine Code AAF Vehicles

Engine Code AAF	Model Years
Eurovan	1992 (Canada only)
Eurovan	1993

Scan tool, connecting

The scan tool is connected through the DLC (Data Link Connector). The location and type of DLC is the same for both 1992 and 1993 model years.

⊲ **Eurovan, 1992-1993**:
Scan tool DLC (Data Link Connector) can be accessed after removal of parcel shelf. Release catch button (**arrow**), pull shelf out from top and lift off.

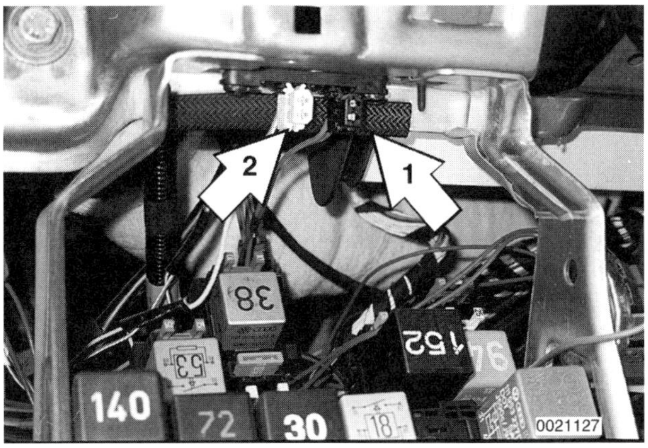

Eurovan, 1992-1993:
DLC is located at lower left side of steering column near fuse/relay panel. Black connector (**arrow 1**) on scan tool is connected to black connection on vehicle and provides scan tool power. White connector is connected to white connection on vehicle (**arrow 2**) for data transfer. Blue connector is not used.

Scan tool, functions available

Scan Tool Functions Available		Ignition on, not running	Engine at idle	Page
✔	Control unit version (01)	Yes	Yes	Appendix A
✔	Check DTC memory (02)	Yes	No	Appendix A
✔	Output diagnostic test mode (03)	Yes	No	36
✔	Basic settings (04)	No	Yes	33
✔	Erase DTC memory (05)	Yes	No	Appendix A
✔	End output (06)	Yes	Yes	Appendix A
✗	Code control module (07)	No	No	38
✔	Read measuring value blocks (08)	Yes	Yes	22
✗	Read indiv. measuring value blocks (09)	Yes	Yes	32

Read Measuring Value Blocks (Function 08)

Measuring value blocks are assembled and displayed in sets called display groups. For the AAF engine, display groups are numbered starting with 000 and continuing with 001 on up to 255. The information is repeated, however, over and over again in the same layout, so that the actual number of different display groups is approximately 9 and not 256.

The display format for information in the measuring value blocks differs slightly depending upon equipment. Vehicles up to chassis number 70P080000 are equipped with a Fuel Trim (FT) Potentiometer and are noted as "early", while vehicles from 70P080001 do not have an FT Potentiometer and are noted as "late". The information is basically the same in both cases.

Some early ECMs may also differ in the order of the displayed information. For example, in Display Group 001, Field 4, the information may be switched with Display Group 002, Field 4.

```
Read Measuring Value Blocks      HELP
Input Display Group Number        XXX
```

◄ Scan tool display from VAG 1551 requesting Measuring Value Block Display Group information (XXX).

Display group overview, AAF engine (early)

Function 08, (early) Display Group Overview 000[OV-1]										
Display Field	**1**	**2**	**3**	**4**	**5**	**6**	**7**	**8**	**9**	**10**
	n/a	CO fuel trim	ECT	n/a	HO2S	n/a	n/a	n/a	n/a	n/a

OV-1) Some data is not relevant, or is unavailable. This data is identified as n/a.

Function 08, (early) Display Group Overview 001 - 005[OV-2]				
Display Field	**1**	**2**	**3**	**4**
Display Group 001	RPM	Ignition timing	ECT	MAP (load)
Display Group 002	RPM	IAT	n/a	Injector duration
Display Group 003	RPM	ECT	n/a	Injector duration
Display Group 004	RPM	MAP (load)	n/a	Injector duration
Display Group 005	RPM	TPS ∠	n/a	Injector duration

OV-2) Some data is not relevant, or is unavailable. This data is identified as n/a. Data for display Groups above 005 is unavailable.

Display group overview, AAF engine (late)

Function 08, (late) Display Group Overview 000[OV-1]										
Display Field	**1**	**2**	**3**	**4**	**5**	**6**	**7**	**8**	**9**	**10**
	n/a	n/a	ECT	n/a	HO2S	n/a	n/a	n/a	n/a	n/a

OV-1) Some data is not relevant, or is unavailable. This data is identified as n/a.

Function 08, (late) Display Group Overview 001 - 008[OV-2]				
Display Field	**1**	**2**	**3**	**4**
Display Group 001	ECT	RPM	HO2S	Injector duration
Display Group 002	ECT	RPM	TPS ∠	MAP (load)
Display Group 003	ECT	RPM	IAT	ECM Voltage
Display Group 004	ECT	RPM	Ignition timing	MAP (load
Display Group 005	ECT	RPM	TPS ∠	ECM Voltage
Display Group 006	ECT	RPM	n/a	n/a
Display Group 007	ECT	RPM	Ignition timing	n/a
Display Group 008	ECT	RPM	Ignition timing	TPS position

OV-2) Some data is not relevant, or is unavailable. This data is identified as n/a. Data for Display Groups above 005 is taken from known-good vehicles.

Read Measuring Value Blocks (Function 08)

Function 08
Display Group 000 (early)

Warm engine, running at idle speed, engine control module in **Read Measuring Value Block** (Function 08)

Display Field	Display Fields	Specification range:[000-4]	Corresponds to:
10	**Undefined data**	—	—
9	**Undefined data**	—	—
8	**Undefined data**	—	—
7	**Undefined data**	—	—
6	**Undefined data**	—	—
5	**Heated Oxygen Sensor (HO2S) signal**	must vary by at least 14	—
4	**Undefined data**	—	—
3	**Engine Coolant Temperature (ECT)**[000-3]	less than 10	—
2	**Carbon Monoxide (CO) fuel trim**[000-2]	40–140	—
1	**Undefined data**[000-1]	—	—

000-1) Undefined data means that information is displayed on the scan tool but information to interpret or define it's meaning is unavailable.

000-2) Value only applicable up to chassis PH080001, early February 1993 production (vehicles with FT Potentiometer only).

000-3) Lower numbers are hotter.

000-4) Overall range of values is 0 - 255.

Function 08 Display Group 001 (early)				
	1	2	3	4
Display	xxxx /min	xx.x °v.OT	xx.x °C	xx%
Indicated	Engine speed	Ignition timing point	Coolant temperature	Engine load signal
Specification	775-825 idle rpm	none given[001-2]	none given[001-3]	20%-40%
			Open circuit shows a constant -40°	At idle
Working range	775...5500 rpm[001-1]		-40°C...141°C (approximately)	20%...100%[001-4]

001-1) Approximate maximum governed engine speed.

001-2) No specification given. This is a specified or calculated value only. It is not an actual timing value because the ECM has no way of referencing this value in relation to the crankshaft position. Moving the distributor to change the ignition timing will, in fact, change the timing, but will have little or no effect on this value. Ignition timing must be adjusted with a conventional timing light or engine tester. Display usually flashes at maximum advance levels.

001-3) No specification given. Experience indicates that at idle, temperature will vary between approximately 86°C and 105°C depending on radiator fan operating cycle. Temperature must rise smoothly during engine warm-up.

001-4) Signal from MAP sensor (G71) in ECM. Value must fluctuate slightly at idle. Values over 90% at idle indicate no vacuum at ECM. Values between 40% and 90% at idle indicate vacuum leaks or heavy engine load. With AC compressor running, value will increase by 10% to 15%. Maximum observed value 94%.

Function 08 Display Group 002 (early)				
	1	2	3	4
Display	xxxx /min	xx.x °C	xx	xx.x ms
Indicated	Engine speed	Intake air temperature	n/a[002-3]	Fuel injector duration
Specification	775-825 idle rpm	none given[002-2]		none given[002-4]
		Open circuit shows a constant -40°		
Working range	775...5500 rpm[002-1]	-40°C...141°C (approximately)		

002-1) As in Display Group 001, field 1.

002-2) No specification given. Experience indicates that air temperature and coolant temperature will be approximately the same when a cold engine is first started. Temperature will rise slightly during engine warm-up. Intake air temperature is usually warmer than ambient air temperature and more closely approximates intake manifold temperature.

002-3) The notation n/a means that information is displayed on the scan tool but Volkswagen does not supply information to interpret or define it's meaning.

002-4) No specification given. Experience indicates that at warm idle, fuel injector duration will be approximately 2 to 3 mS. Maximum observed value is 10.0 mS. Minimum observed value is 0.00 mS during deceleration fuel shut-off function.

Read Measuring Value Blocks (Function 08)

Function 08 Display Group 003 (early)				
	1	2	3	4
Display	xxxx /min	xx.x °C	xx	xx.x ms
Indicated	Engine speed	Coolant temperature	n/a[003-3]	Fuel injector duration
Specification	775-825 idle rpm	none given[003-2]		none given[003-4]
		Open circuit shows a constant -40°		
Working range	775...5500 rpm[003-1]	-40°C...141°C (approximately)		

003-1) As in Display Group 001, field 1.

003-2) As in Display Group 001, field 3.

003-3) As in Display Group 002, field 3.

003-4) As in Display Group 002, field 4.

Function 08 Display Group 004 (early)				
	1	2	3	4
Display	xxxx /min	xx%	xx	xx.x ms
Indicated	Engine speed	Engine load signal	n/a[004-3]	Fuel injector duration
Specification	775-825 idle rpm	20%-40%		none given[004-4]
		At idle		
Working range	775...5500 rpm[004-1]	20%...100%[004-2]		

004-1) As in Display Group 001, field 1.

004-2) As in Display Group 001, field 4.

004-3) As in Display Group 002, field 3.

004-4) As in Display Group 002, field 4.

Function 08 Display Group 005 (early)				
	1	**2**	**3**	**4**
Display	xxxx /min	x.x ∠°	xx	xx.x ms
Indicated	Engine speed	Throttle valve angle	n/a[005-3]	Fuel injector duration
Specification	775-825 idle rpm	0°		none given[005-4]
		At closed throttle position. Open circuit shows a constant 0°		
Working range	775...5500 rpm[005-1]	0°...to over 80° [005-3]		

[005-1] As in Display Group 001, field 1.

[005-2] Value must increase/decrease uniformly as throttle is opened and closed. Maximum observed value 87°.

[005-3] As in Display Group 002, field 3.

[005-4] As in Display Group 002, field 4.

Function 08
Display Group 000 (late)

Warm engine, running at idle speed, engine control module in **Read Measuring Value Block** (Function 08)

Field	Display Fields	Observed range: [000-3]	Corresponds to:
10	**Undefined data**	—	—
9	**Undefined data**	—	—
8	**Undefined data**	—	—
7	**Undefined data**	—	—
6	**Undefined data**	—	—
5	**Heated Oxygen Sensor (HO2S) signal**	must vary by at least 14	—
4	**Undefined data**	—	—
3	**Engine Coolant Temperature (ECT)**[000-2]	less than 10	—
2	**Undefined data**	—	—
1	**Undefined data**[000-1]	—	—

[000-1] Undefined data means that information is displayed on the scan tool but information to interpret or define it's meaning is unavailable.

[000-2] Lower numbers are hotter.

[000-3] Overall range of values is 0 - 255˙.

Read Measuring Value Blocks (Function 08)

Function 08 Display Group 001 (late)				
	1	2	3	4
Display	xx.x °C	xxxx /min	x.xx V	xx.x ms
Indicated	Coolant temperature	Engine speed	Oxygen sensor signal voltage	Fuel injector duration
Specification	none given[001-1]	775-825 idle rpm	0.0V -0.75V[001-3]	none given[001-4]
	Open circuit shows a constant -40°			
Working range	-40°C...141°C (approximately)	775...5500 rpm[001-2]		

001-1) No specification given. Experience indicates that at idle, temperature will vary between approximately 86°C and 105°C depending on radiator fan operating cycle. Temperature must rise smoothly during engine warm-up.

001-2) Approximate maximum governed engine speed.

001-3) Experience indicates that at idle, HO2S voltage must fluctuate rapidly. Low signal should be below 0.300 V and high signal should be above 0.700 V. If checked before a cold engine start, voltage must be 0.450 V and rise to approximately 0.750 V as the engine warms up. HO2S is considered on-line at this point due to plausible signal voltages and voltage must begin to fluctuate as noted above. The time from cold engine start to HO2S on-line is typically less than 1 minute and is not dependent on coolant temperature.

001-4) No specification given. Experience indicates that at warm idle, fuel injector duration will be approximately 2 to 3 mS. Maximum observed value is 10.0 mS. Minimum observed value is 0.00 mS during deceleration fuel shut-off function.

Function 08 Display Group 002 (late)				
	1	2	3	4
Display	xx.x °C	xxxx /min	x.x ∠°	xx%
Indicated	Coolant temperature	Engine speed	Throttle valve angle	Engine load signal
Specification	none given[002-1]	775-825 idle rpm	0°	20%-40%
	Open circuit shows a constant -40°		At closed throttle position. Open circuit shows a constant 0°	At idle
Working range	-40°C...141°C (approximately)	775...5500 rpm[002-2]	0°...to over 80°[002-3]	20%...100%[002-4]

002-1) As in Display Group 001, field 1.

002-2) As in Display Group 001, field 2.

002-3) Value must increase/decrease uniformly as throttle is opened and closed. Maximum observed value 87°.

002-4) Signal from MAP sensor (G71) in ECM. Value must fluctuate slightly at idle. Values over 90% at idle indicate no vacuum at ECM. Values between 40% and 90% at idle indicate vacuum leaks or heavy engine load. With AC compressor running, value will increase by 10% to 15%. Maximum observed value 94%.

Function 08 Display Group 003 (late)				
	1	**2**	**3**	**4**
Display	xx.x °C	xxxx /min	xx.x °C	xx.x V
Indicated	Coolant temperature	Engine speed	Intake air temperature	ECM supply voltage
Specification	none given[003-1]	775-825 idle rpm	none given[003-3]	none given[003-4]
	Open circuit shows a constant -40°		Open circuit shows a constant -40°	
Working range	-40°C...141°C (approximately)	775...5500 rpm[003-2]	-40°C...141°C (approximately)	Maximum 14.5 V

003-1) As in Display Group 001, field 1.

003-2) As in Display Group 001, field 2.

003-3) No specification given. Experience indicates that at idle, temperature will be approximately ambient air temperature. Intake air preheater will generally keep incoming air temperature to around 30°C, but may be substantially higher on a very hot day. Very high temperatures suggest a malfunctioning intake air pre-heater.

003-4) No specification given. Experience indicates that ECM supply voltage should be approximate electrical system voltage.

Function 08 Display Group 004 (late)				
	1	**2**	**3**	**4**
Display	xx.x °C	xxxx /min	xx.x °v.OT	xx%
Indicated	Coolant temperature	Engine speed	Ignition timing point	Engine load signal
Specification	none given[004-1]	775-825 idle rpm	none given[004-3]	20%-40%
	Open circuit shows a constant -40°			At idle
Working range	-40°C...141°C (approximately)	775...5500 rpm[004-2]		20%...100%[004-4]

004-1) As in Display Group 001, field 1.

004-2) As in Display Group 001, field 2.

004-3) No specification given. This is a specified or calculated value only. It is not an actual timing value because the ECM has no way of referencing this value in relation to the crankshaft position. Moving the distributor to change the ignition timing will, in fact, change the timing, but will have little or no effect on this value. Ignition timing must be adjusted with a conventional timing light or engine tester. Display usually flashes at maximum advance levels.

004-4) As in Display Group 002, field 4.

Read Measuring Value Blocks (Function 08)

Function 08
Display Group 005 (late)

	1	2	3	4
Display	xx.x °C	xxxx /min	x.x ∠°	xx.x V
Indicated	Coolant temperature	Engine speed	Throttle valve angle	ECM supply voltage
Specification	none given[005-1]	775-825 idle rpm	0°	none given[005-3]
	Open circuit shows a constant -40°		At closed throttle position. Open circuit shows a constant 0°	
Working range	-40°C...141°C (approximately)	775...5500 rpm[005-2]	0°...to over 80°[005-3]	Maximum 14.5 V

005-1) As in Display Group 001, field 1.

005-2) As in Display Group 001, field 2.

005-3) As in Display Group 002, field 3.

005-4) As in Display Group 003, field 4.

Function 08
Display Group 006 (late)

	1	2	3	4
Display	xx.x °C	xxxx /min	x	x
Indicated	Coolant temperature	Engine speed	0[006-3]	0[006-4]
Specification	none given[006-1]	775-825 idle rpm		
	Open circuit shows a constant -40°			
Working range	-40°C...141°C (approximately)	775...5500 rpm[006-2]		

006-1) As in Display Group 001, field 1.

006-2) As in Display Group 001, field 2.

006-3) Usually 0 at warm idle. Numbers change while driving, interpretation is unavailable.

006-4) Usually 0 at warm idle. Numbers change while driving, interpretation is unavailable.

Function 08 Display Group 007 (late)				
	1	2	3	4
Display	xx.x °C	xxxx /min	xx.x °v.OT	x
Indicated	Coolant temperature	Engine speed	Ignition timing point	0[007-4]
Specification	none given[007-1]	775-825 idle rpm	none given[007-3]	
	Open circuit shows a constant -40°			
Working range	-40°C...141°C (approximately)	775...5500 rpm[007-2]		

007-1) As in Display Group 001, field 1.

007-2) As in Display Group 001, field 2.

007-3) As in Display Group 004, field 3.

007-4) Range is 0 to 255. Centerpoint appears to be 0; values increase above (0 to 26 observed) and below (0 to 253 observed). Numbers change while driving, interpretation is unavailable.

Function 08 Display Group 008 (late)				
	1	2	3	4
Display	xx.x °C	xxxx /min	xx.x °v.OT	xxxxxxxx
Indicated	Coolant temperature	Engine speed	Ignition timing point	Recognized throttle position
Specification	none given[008-1]	775-825 idle rpm	none given[008-3]	none given
	Open circuit shows a constant -40°			
Working range	-40°C...141°C (approximately)	775...5500 rpm[008-2]		LEERLAUF TEILLAST VOLLAST 008-4

008-1) As in Display Group 001, field 1.

008-2) As in Display Group 001, field 2.

008-3) As in Display Group 004, field 3.

008-4) LEERLAUF = idle or closed throttle position (CTP).
TEILLAST = part throttle.
VOLLAST = full throttle or wide open throttle (WOT).

READ INDIVIDUAL MEASURING VALUES (FUNCTION 09)

Individual parts of the Display Groups can be separated and shown on the scan tool. Volkswagen has published almost no information on this function, preferring the Technician to look at the larger picture shown by the Display Groups instead.

Individual Measuring values are shown as separate channels ranging from 0 to 255. The data is given in the range format of 0 to 255. Interpretation of the displayed information is not readily apparent.

```
Read Individual Measuring Value
Input Display Channel Number      XXX
```

◄ Scan tool display from VAG 1551 requesting Individual Measuring Value Display Channel information (XXX).

Channels

For Eurovan Digifant, there is only one supported Individual Measuring Value channel and it is applicable only to those vehicles with a Fuel Trim Potentiometer.

Read Individual Measuring Values			
Channel	**Measuring value**	**Indicated**	**Specification range**
4	xxx	CO fuel trim potentiometer	40 - 140

```
Read Individual Measuring Value
Channel 4     Measuring value 68
```

◄ Scan tool display from VAG 1551 showing correct Channel 4 information (68).

BASIC SETTINGS (FUNCTION 04)

Baseline values for ignition timing and idle speed require manual adjustment and some AAF engines have provisions for adjustment of CO (carbon monoxide) content.

When Function 04 (basic settings) is selected, the scan tool instructs the ECM to:

- Stabilize ignition timing
- Stabilize idle speed
- Disable the EVAP system

Adjustment of basic settings requires the connection of several other pieces of test equipment in addition to a scan tool such as the VAG 1551.

An engine tester such as the VAG 1367 must be connected to the engine to measure ignition timing and engine speed, while an exhaust gas analyzer must be attached to the CO pick-up or sampling tube located ahead of the catalytic converter.

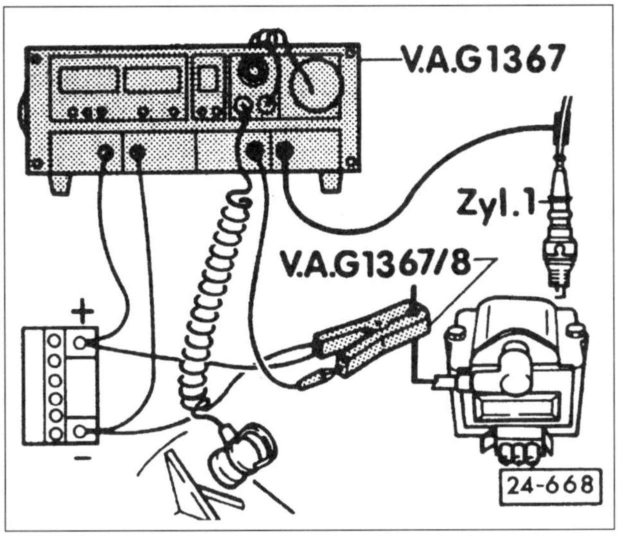

◄ Engine tester VAG 1367. must be used in conjunction with a scan tool and an exhaust gas analyzer to properly utilize Function 04.

0021108

◄ An exhaust gas analyzer, such as this 4-Gas unit manufactured by Sun, is required to check and/or adjust carbon monoxide (CO) content.

Basic Settings (Function 04)

Initiating basic settings

Begin the basic settings procedure by observing the following requirements:

Test conditions 1:

- Engine cold, ignition switched off.
- Connect engine tester VAG 1367 or equivalent.
- Connect CO tester to sampling tube insuring an airtight connect.

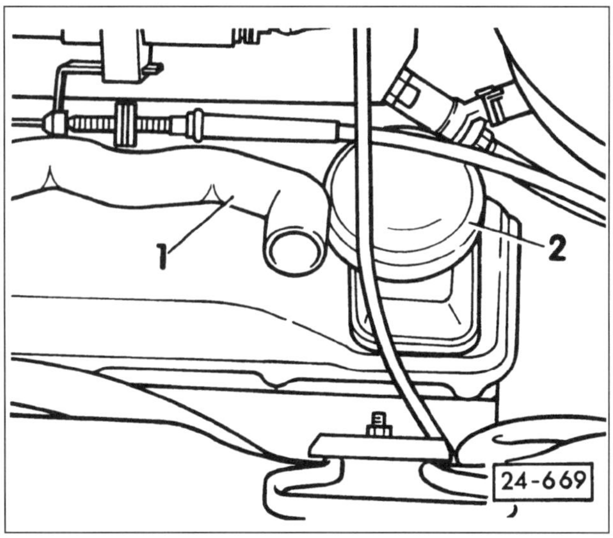

Disconnect crankcase breather hose (**1**) from PCV Valve (**2**) on cylinder head cover and position it so that only fresh air is drawn in.

- Connect scan tool.

Test conditions 2:

- Start engine.
- Vehicle stationary, engine at idle, automatic transmission in P or N.
- Engine oil temperature at least 80°C (176°F).
- All electrical consumers switched off (do not take measurements while radiator cooling fan is running).
- Air conditioning switched off.
- Throttle cable adjusted properly.
- TP sensor adjusted properly at closed throttle position.
- Exhaust system free from leaks.

Initiate Basic Settings:

- From the initial Menu select: 1 Rapid Data.
- From the address word Menu select: 01 Engine Electronics.
- Advance to the Function Menu when the ECM responds with the version information.
- From the Function Menu select: 02 Check DTC memory. Read DTCs and return to the Function Menu. (correct and erase any DTCs recorded)
- From the Function Menu select: 04 Basic Settings.

From the Start Basic Settings display, input: display group 000 (or 00 if applicable).

```
Start Basic Setting              HELP
Input Display Group Number        XXX
```

```
System in Basic Setting
XX XX XX XX XX XX XX XX XX XX
```

◄ Basic setting display on a VAG 1551. Disregard displayed values (shown as XX in this example).

- Disconnect blue harness connector from ECT sensor.
- Accelerate engine to between 2,000 and 2,500 rpm and read ignition timing on engine tester (not scan tool).

Ignition timing . . . . .4° - 8° BTDC (fluctuating)

- Adjust timing and re-test as required.
- Observe engine operating data on engine tester and exhaust gas analyzer (not scan tool) at idle (ECT sensor harness connector remains disconnected).

Idle speed .775 to 825 rpm
CO (with FT potentiometer) . . . . 0.5% to 0.9%
CO (without FT potentiometer) . . . . . 0.3% to 1.2%

- If operating data is within the listed specifications and radiator coolant fan is not running, exit basic settings and reconnect ECT sensor harness connector.
- If CO is not within specification:
  If equipped with FT potentiometer, adjust to center of range.
  If not equipped with FT potentiometer, determine the malfunction, correct and re-test.
- From the Function Menu select:
  02 Check DTC memory.
  Read DTCs and return to the Function Menu. (erase the ECT sensor (G62) DTC that may have been recorded)
- From the Function Menu select:
  06 End Output.
- Switch off ignition.
- Disconnect all test equipment, basic settings are complete.

If operating data does not fall within listed specification, determine the malfunction, correct and re-test.

Output Diagnostic Test Mode (Function 03)

Troubleshooting electrical faults in Eurovans with Digifant AAF engines is facilitated by the Output Diagnostic Test Mode (Function 03). When this function is activated, the scan tool instructs the ECM to operate certain electrical components in a pre-determined sequence. The output diagnostic test mode can only be used when the ignition is switched on, but the engine is not running.

Although fewer components are checked with this system as compared to some Motronic systems, even this relatively short list can be a substantial aid in troubleshooting. The following is a list of components checked during the output diagnostic test mode and the order in which they are tested:

- Fuel Pump (FP) Relay (J17)
- Idle Air Control Valve (IAC) (N71)
- Evaporative Emission (EVAP) Canister Purge Regulator Valve (N80)

```
Rapid data transfer                Q
03 - Output Diagnostic Test Mode
```

◄ Eurovan Digifant display for Function 03 as shown on a VAG 1551 showing first Output Diagnostic Mode test.

Testing in Function 03

Testing Digifant equipped engines with a scan tool in Function 03 is a relatively straight forward operation.

Some ECMs will only allow the output diagnostic tests to be run once per engine start. If this is the case, simply start the engine and allow it to run for a short time before re-testing.

```
Output Diagnostic Test Mode        -->
Fuel Pump Relay - J17
```

◄ Eurovan Digifant display for Function 03 as shown on a VAG 1551 showing first Output Diagnostic Mode test.

After the scan tool has been connected and Function 03 selected, proceed with the test as indicated on the scan tool noting the following points:

1. **Fuel Pump (FP) Relay (J17)** - The FP relay in the fuse/relay panel will be switched on and off with an audible clicking sound. The fuel pump should also be heard to run. Advance the program with the right arrow button (-->).

2. **Idle Air Control (IAC) Valve (N71)** – The IAC Valve will be operated through a range of positions with a buzzing or humming sound. The vibrations from operation can also be felt. Advance the program with the right arrow button (-->).

3. **Evaporative Emission (EVAP) Canister Purge Regulator Valve (N80)** – The EVAP Canister Purge regulator Valve will be switched off and on (opened and closed). The resulting noise is a deep thumping sound and can be difficult to hear, but it can usually be felt. Advance the program with the right arrow button (-->).


```
Output Diagnostic Test Mode

Fuel Pump Relay - J17
Idle Air Control Valve - N71
EVAP Canister Purge Regulator Valve-N80
```

When the VAG 1551 printer is switched on, the tape will be printed with all of the tests in sequence.

The Output Diagnostic Test Mode is helpful in checking the electrical operation of a given component. It can also be helpful in diagnosing mechanical malfunctions as well. If, for example, an (EVAP) Canister Purge Regulator Valve was suspected of a malfunction, the hoses could be disconnected and the Output Diagnostic Test Mode run while blowing through the valve. This would help determine if it worked properly. Similar tests can be devised with many of the other components.

In the event of a component failing to operate, the component and the wiring should be checked for continuity, open circuits, and short circuits, including short circuits to ground. Always consult the appropriate wiring diagram.

Code Control Module (Function 07)

Control module coding by means of the scan tool is not a supported function for AAF coded engines. Coding information does appear, however, in Function 01 (control unit versions), but has no apparent influence on engine operation.

Correct ECM operation is accomplished by different part number ECMs installed to match the equipment installed in the vehicle. Different ECMs are used for vehicles with the following equipment and market variations:

- USA/Canada with FT potentiometer and with manual transmission.
- USA/Canada without FT potentiometer and with manual transmission.
- USA/Canada with FT potentiometer and with automatic transmission.
- USA/Canada without FT potentiometer and with automatic transmission.
- California with FT potentiometer and with manual transmission.
- California without FT potentiometer and with manual transmission.
- California with FT potentiometer and with automatic transmission.
- California without FT potentiometer and with automatic transmission.

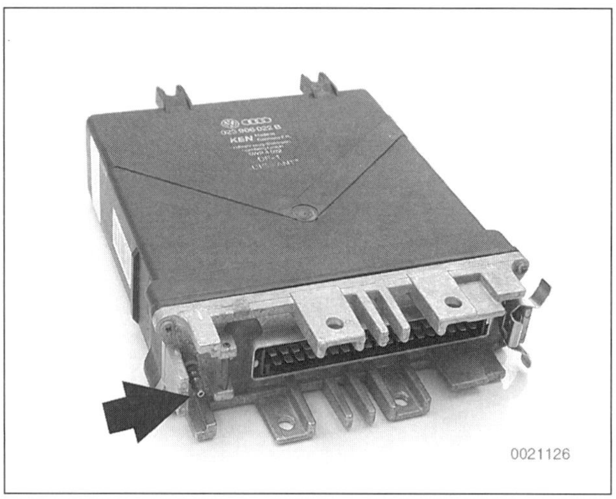

◄ Engine Control Module from an early 1993 Eurovan. Part number on ECM label matches Scan Tool display in Function 01. Note intake manifold vacuum connection (**arrow**).

NOTE
Always consult with your Volkswagen Parts Department or aftermarket parts specialist for the latest parts information.

Component and Signal Overview, AAF Engine

AAF engines use a version of the Volkswagen developed Digifant engine management system. Signals from sensors and other input sources are processed by the ECM. Signals to control the engine are sent to actuators along with engine information needed by other systems or functions.

Component and Signal Overview, AAF Engine

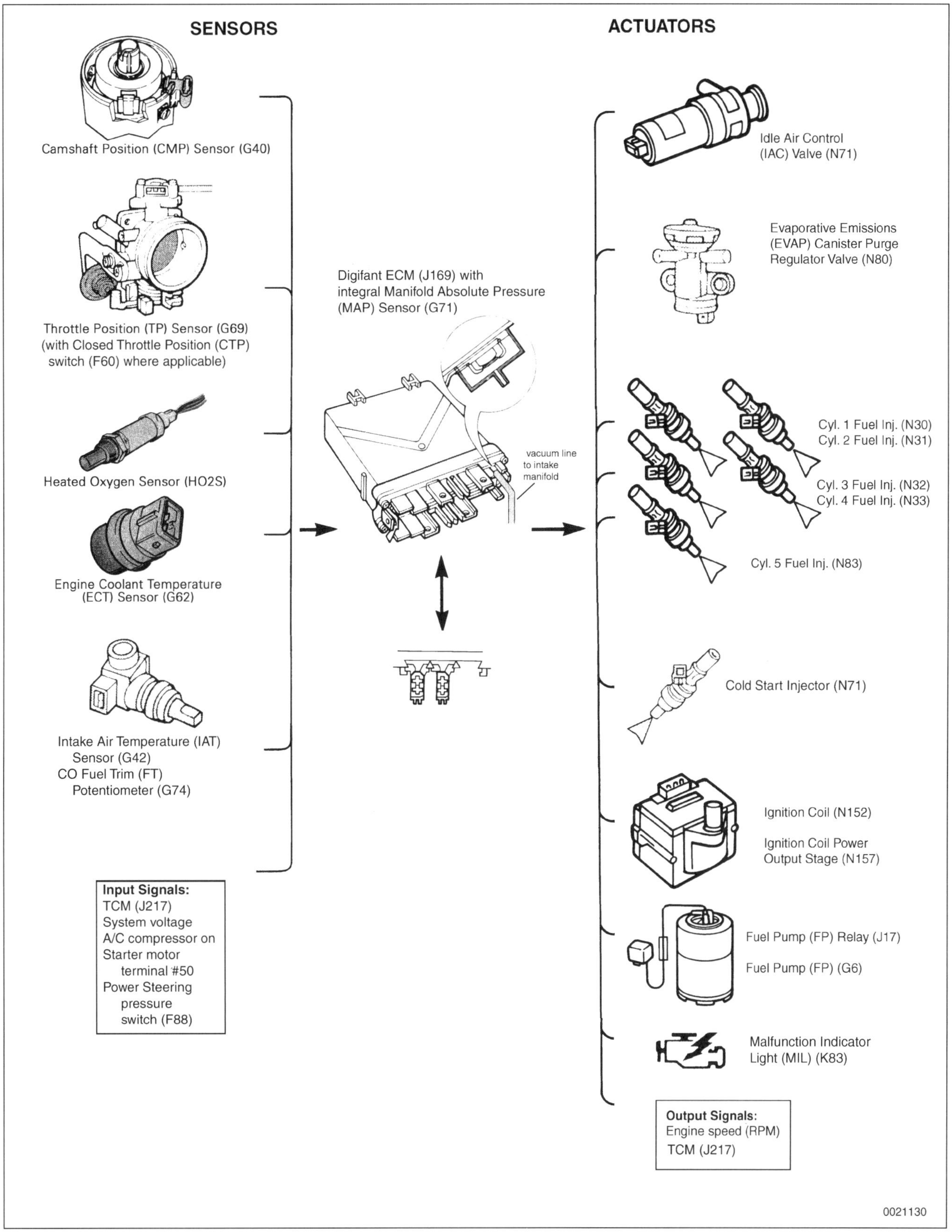

Component and Signal Overview, AAF Engine

Component and Signal Overview (AAF)

Volkswagen Digifant, 5-cylinder	
Fuel injection	Non-sequential (simultaneous) Multi-Point Fuel Injection with Lambda (Oxygen Sensor) Control, OBD-I
Fuel delivery	Tank-mounted 2-stage electric fuel pump, load-sensing mechanical pressure regulator
Ignition system	Distributor, power output stage and ignition coil, ECM controlled
Emission control	3-Way (TWC) catalytic converter, evaporative emissions with carbon canister, positive crankcase ventilation
Diagnostics	On-Board Diagnostics via scan tool, Rapid data transfer, Non-volatile memory
Control Module	Single 38-pin Digifant Engine Control Module (ECM) (J169) with integral Manifold Absolute Pressure (MAP) Sensor (G71), supplied by Digifant ECM Power Supply Relay (J176)
Sensors	Camshaft Position (CMP) Sensor (G40)
	Throttle Position (TP) Sensor (G69) with Closed Throttle Position (CTP) Switch (F60) (where applicable)[1]
	CO Fuel Trim (FT) Potentiometer (G74)[2]
	Heated Oxygen Sensor (H2OS) (G39)
	Engine Coolant Temperature (ECT) Sensor (G62)
	Intake Air Temperature (IAT) Sensor (G42)
Input signals	System voltage
	Air conditioner, compressor on
	Automatic Transmission Control Module (TCM) (J217)
	Pressure switch - power steering (F88)
	Starter motor- terminal 50
Actuators	Idle Air Control (IAC) Valve (N71)
	Evaporative Emission (EVAP) Canister Purge Regulator Valve (N80)
	Fuel Injectors: Cylinder 1 (N30), Cylinder 2 (N31), Cylinder 3 (N32), Cylinder 4 (N33), Cylinder 5 (N83)
	Ignition Coil Power Output Stage (N157), and Ignition Coil (N152)
	Fuel Pump (FP) Relay (J17), and Transfer Fuel Pump (FP) (G23)
	Cold Start Injector (N17)
	Malfunction Indicator Light (MIL)[3] (K83)
Output signals	Engine speed (rpm)
	Automatic Transmission Control Module (TCM) (J217)

[1] Vehicles with automatic transmissions use separate TP Sensors for each system.
[2] Built into IAT Sensor housing. CO Fuel Trim Potentiometer not used after chassis PH080001, (early February 1993 production).
[3] MIL only functional on vehicles intended for California market area.

TECHNICAL DATA

Technical data is compiled from several Volkswagen publications. In some instances, the information from these sources differed slightly. In these cases, the most current specifications are listed.

AAF (Eurovan)	Technical Data
Type	5-cylinder in-line (R5), gasoline fuel
Construction	Cast iron block, aluminum 2V cylinder head, belt driven single overhead camshaft
Displacement	2.5 Liters (2459 cc), (150 cid)
Horsepower	109 hp (81 Kw) @ 4500 rpm
Torque	140 lb-ft (190 Nm) @ 2200 rpm
Bore	81.0 mm
Stroke	95.5 mm
Compression ratio	8.5:1
Firing order	1-2-4-5-3
Management	Digifant

Notes

Engine Code
ABA

0021103

General

The vehicles listed below are equipped with engine code **ABA**. This 2.0 liter engine uses the Bosch® **Motronic M2.9** engine management system.

The ABA engine is installed as the standard powerplant in most USA-specification Golf and Jetta models and is the only engine available in the Cabrio.

Engine Code ABA Vehicles

Engine Code ABA	Model Years
Passat GLS	1995
Golf	1993, 1994, 1995
Jetta	1993, 1994, 1995
Cabrio	1995

Scan tool, connecting

The scan tool is connected through the DLC (Data Link Connector). The DLC location varies depending on model year.

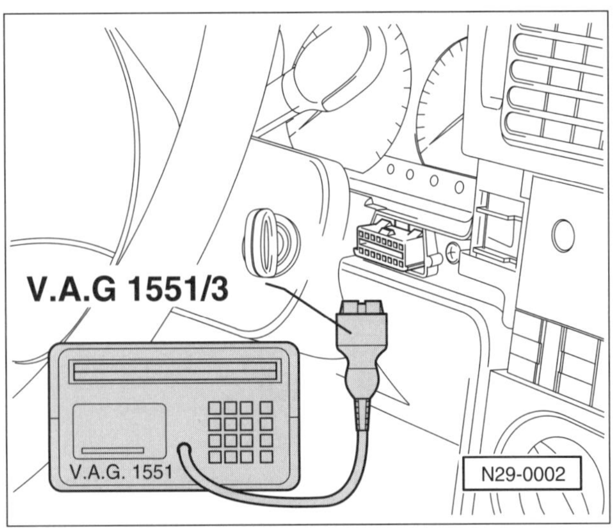

Passat, 1995:
Instrument panel, to the right side of the steering column, behind cover.

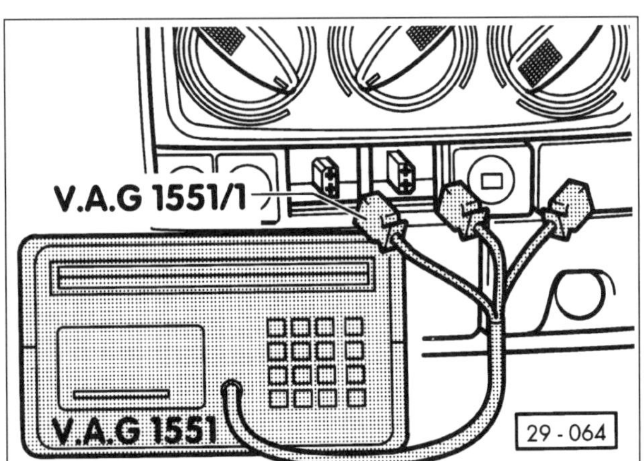

Golf and Jetta, 1993-1994 (early):
Instrument panel center section, below heater controls behind blank switch covers.
Black connector on scan tool is connected to black connector on vehicle (scan tool power). White connector is connected to white connector on vehicle (data transfer). Blue connector is not used.

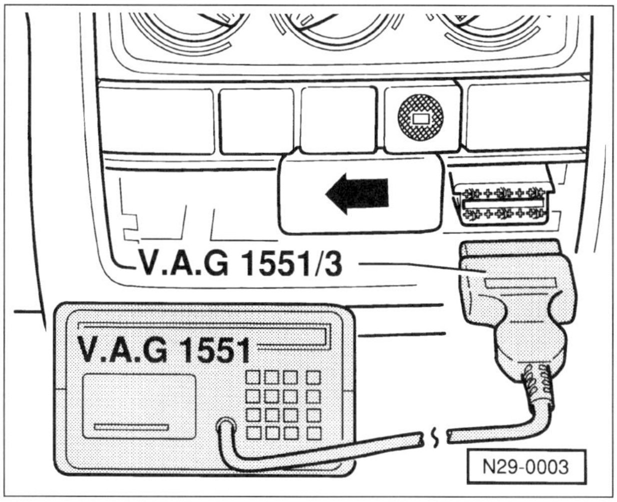

◄ **Golf, Jetta, Cabrio, 1994-1995**:
Instrument panel center section, to the right side of the ashtray, behind cover.

Scan tool, functions available

	Scan Tool Functions Available	Ignition on, not running	Engine at idle	Page
✔	Control unit version (01)	Yes	Yes	Appendix A
✔	Check DTC memory (02)	Yes	No	Appendix A
✔	Output diagnostic test mode (03)	Yes	No	58
✔	Basic settings (04)	No	Yes	56
✔	Erase DTC memory (05)	Yes	Yes	Appendix A
✔	End output (06)	Yes	Yes	Appendix A
✗	Code control module (07)	No	No	61
✔	Read measuring value blocks (08)	Yes	Yes	46
✗	Read indiv. measuring value blocks (09)	No	No	Appendix A

READ MEASURING VALUE BLOCKS (FUNCTION 08)

Measuring value blocks are assembled and displayed in sets called display groups. For the ABA engine, display groups are numbered starting with 000 and continuing with 001 on up to 006.

Read Measuring Value Blocks	HELP
Input Display Group Number	XXX

< Scan tool display from VAG 1551 requesting Measuring Value Block Display Group information (XXX).

Display group overview, ABA engine (Golf, Jetta, Cabrio)

Engine Code ABA, (Golf, Jetta, Cabrio) Display Group Overview 000										
Display Field	**1**	**2**	**3**	**4**	**5**	**6**	**7**	**8**	**9**	**10**
	ECT	Load	RPM	HO2S	Idle load adaptation	n/a[OV-1]	Low load adaptation	Air correction adaptation	n/a[OV-1]	Ignition timing

[OV-1] Some data is not relevant, or is unavailable. This data is identified as n/a.

Engine Code ABA (Golf, Jetta, Cabrio) Display Group Overview 001 - 006				
Display Field	**1**	**2**	**3**	**4**
Display Group 001	RPM	ECT	Lambda	Ignition timing
Display Group 002	RPM	Injector duration	ECM Voltage	EGR temperature
Display Group 003	RPM	Load	TPS ∠	IAT
Display Group 004	RPM	Load	Vehicle speed	Input signals 1
Display Group 005	RPM	IAC adaptation	IAC duty cycle	Input signals 2
Display Group 006	HO2S	HO2S adaptation -idle	**n/a**[OV-2]	HO2S adaptation -full

[OV-2] Some data is not relevant, or is unavailable. This data is identified as n/a.

Function 08
Display Group 000 (Golf, Jetta, Cabrio)

Warm engine, running at idle speed, engine control module in **Read Measuring Value Block** (Function 08)

Display Field	Display Fields	Observed range: [000-1]	Corresponds to:
10	Ign. timing (varies)	76-93	2.25 - 15.0° BTDC
9	Undefined data	—	—
8	Air correction value (adaptation)	114-154	—
7	Learning value for low load adaptation	92-164	—
6	Undefined data	—	—
5	Learning value for idle adaptation	83-241[000-2]	—
4	Oxygen sensor factor (fast fluctuations over a wide range)	92-164[000-3]	—
3	Engine speed (fluctuates slightly)	80-88[000-4]	800-880 rpm
2	Engine load signal (fluctuates slightly)	26–44	—
1	Engine coolant temperature sensor (varies as radiator fan cycles on and off)	181-224[000-5]	80-110°C

[000-1)] Center of range for Fields 4,5,7, & 8 is 128.

[000-2)] Values greater than 188 indicate an air leak.

[000-3)] Values greater than 128 indicate a lean condition correcting towards rich, less than 128 indicate a rich condition correcting towards lean. No fluctuations indicate that control is not working. If value remains at 0, the engine is running excessively rich and the HO2S system cannot control it.

[000-4)] Multiply value by 10 to read actual engine rpm at idle.

[000-5)] Value of 181 equals 80°C.

Read Measuring Value Blocks (Function 08)

Function 08
Display Group 001 (Golf, Jetta, Cabrio)

	1	2	3	4
Display	xxxx /min	xx.x °C	x.xx	xx.x ° v.OT
Indicated	Engine speed	Coolant temperature	Lambda factor	Ignition timing
Specification	800-880 idle rpm	none given[001-1]	none given[001-2]	none given[001-3]
		Open circuit shows a constant 77.7°		
Working range	800...6200 rpm	-46.5°C...141.0°C		

[001-1] No specification given. Experience indicates that at idle, temperature will vary between approximately 92°C and 100°C depending on radiator fan operating cycle. Temperature must rise smoothly during engine warm-up. If display jumps up by 2°C to 5°C in display, ECM is raising temperature based on running time due to a faulty ECT Sensor.

[001-2] No specification given. Experience indicates that at idle, lambda value will be between 0.70 and 1.30 with the center of the range at 1.00. Value will fluctuate slightly during warm idle.

[001-3] No specification given for Function 08. Experience indicates that ignition timing can vary widely but will generally be between 2.25° and 15° BTDC at idle. Variations are due to electronic Idle Speed Control (ISC). ISC varies timing in conjunction with the IAC to provide a smooth engine idle.

Function 08
Display Group 002 (Golf, Jetta, Cabrio)

	1	2	3	4
Display	xxxx /min	xx.x ms	xx.x V	xx.x °C
Indicated	Engine speed	Fuel injector duration	ECM supply voltage	EGR temperature
Specification	800-880 idle rpm	none given[002-1]	none given[002-2]	none given[002-3]
			VAG 1551 Scan Tool operates 10V- 16V	If no EGR, shows a constant 217°C
Working range	800...6200 rpm		Maximum 14.5V	127.4°C...217°C

[002-1] No specification given. Experience indicates that at idle, fuel injector duration will be approximately 3 to 5 mS.

[002-2] No specification given. Experience indicates that ECM supply voltage should be approximate electrical system voltage.

[002-3] No specification given. If no EGR, value will be a constant 217.0°C. Lowest value displayed is 127.4. When EGR is functioning, temperature will rise to a maximum indicated 217.0°C as exhaust gases pass EGR Temperature sensor.

Function 08 Display Group 003 (Golf, Jetta, Cabrio)				
	1	2	3	4
Display	xxxx /min	xxx%	xx ∠°	xx.x °C
Indicated	Engine speed	Engine load	Throttle valve angle	Intake air temperature
Specification	800-880 idle rpm	none given[003-1]	8° to 15° at idle 90° to 101° at WOT[003-2]	none given[003-3]
				Open circuit shows a constant 19.6°
Working range	800...6200 rpm		8°...101°	-46.5°C...141.0°C

[003-1)] No specification given. Experience indicates that at idle, load value will vary between approximately 2% and 5%. Load value should increase by approximately 1% when electrical consumers and air conditioning are switched on while at idle.

[003-2)] Value must increase/decrease uniformly as throttle is opened and closed.

[003-3)] No specification given. Experience indicates that air temperature and coolant temperature will be approximately the same when a cold engine is first started. Temperature will rise slightly during engine warm-up. Intake air temperature is usually warmer than ambient air temperature and more closely approximates intake manifold temperature.

Function 08 Display Group 004 (Golf, Jetta, Cabrio)				
	1	2	3	4
Display	xxxx /min	xxx%	xx	XXXXX
Indicated	Engine speed	Engine load	Vehicle speed	Operating mode 1, throttle positions
Specification	800-880 idle rpm	none given[004-1]	none given[004-2]	see Operating Mode 1 table below[004-3]
Working range	800...6200 rpm		0...210 km/h (governed top speed	

[004-1)] No specification given. Experience indicates that at idle, load value will vary between approximately 2% and 5%. Load value should increase by approximately 1% when electrical consumers and air conditioning are switched on at idle.

[004-2)] No specification given. Value is received from Vehicle Speed Sensor (VSS) and indicates approximate vehicle road speed.

[004-3)] Display will be either a 1 or a 0. For example, 00010 indicates idle position recognized. Multiple functions can occur simultaneously such as 00011 indicating idle position recognized but engine speed sufficient to enable deceleration fuel shut-off.

Operating Mode 1- Throttle Positions (see Display Group 004, Field 4)

Displayed: **(1 = recognized/ enabled** **0 = not)**					**Position recognized or function enabled**
X					Acceleration enrichment
	X				Full load
		X			Part load
			X		Idle
				X	Overrun (deceleration fuel shut-off)

Read Measuring Value Blocks (Function 08)

Function 08 **Display Group 005 (Golf, Jetta, Cabrio)**				
	1	**2**	**3**	**4**
Display	xxxx /min	x.xx	xx%	XX XX
Indicated	Engine speed	Idle stabilization adaptation	Idle stabilization duty cycle	Operating mode 2, input signals
Specification	800-880 idle rpm	none given[005-1]	none given[005-2]	see relevance below[005-3]
Working range	800...6200 rpm			

005-1) No specification given. Experience indicates that at idle, adaptation value will be approximately 1.00 ±0.20.

005-2) No specification given. Experience indicates that at idle, duty cycle value will be between 40% and 55%. Duty cycle value should increase slightly when electrical consumers and air conditioning are switched on at idle.

005-3) Display will be either a 1 or a 0. For example, 00 01 indicates the automatic transmission in gear signal is recognized. Multiple functions can occur simultaneously such as 11 01 indicating air conditioning compressor and system on and automatic transmission in gear.

Operating Mode 2 - Input Signals (see Display Group 005, Field 4)

Displayed (1 = recognized/enabled 0 = not)					**Signal recognized or function enabled**
X					A/C compressor on
	X				Air conditioner system on
			X		Automatic transmission shift signal, TCM to ECM
				X	Manual transmission or Automatic transmission in Park or Neutral

Function 08 Display Group 006 (Golf, Jetta, Cabrio)				
	1	**2**	**3**	**4**
Display	x.xx	x.xx	x.xx	x.xx
Indicated	Lambda factor	Lambda adaptation at idle	Not used, undefined data[006-3]	Lambda adaptation at part load
Specification	none given [006-1]	none given[006-2]		none given[006-4]
Working range[006-5]				

006-1) No specification given. Experience indicates that at idle, lambda value will be between 0.70 and 1.30 with the center of the range at 1.00. Value will fluctuate slightly during warm idle. This information is the same as in Display Group 001, field 3.

006-2) No specification given. Experience indicates that lambda value will be between 0.53 and 1.47 with the center of the range at 1.00.

006-3) Data is not relevant, or is unavailable.

006-4) No specification given. Experience indicates that lambda value will be between 0.80 and 1.20 with the center of the range at 1.00.

006-5) Optimum air/fuel mixture is 14.7:1 and is referred as "lambda of 1 (λ=1)".
Values greater than 1.00 indicate excess air and a corresponding lean mixture. System response will be to richen the mixture.
Values less than 1.00 indicate insufficient air and a corresponding rich mixture. System response will be to lean out the mixture.

Display group overview, ABA engine (Passat)

Engine Code ABA, (Passat) Display Group Overview 000										
Display Field	1	2	3	4	5	6	7	8	9	10
	ECT	Load	RPM	HO2S	Idle load adaptation	Part load adaptation	Full load adaptation	Air correction adaptation	n/a[OV-1]	Ignition timing

OV-1) Some data is not relevant, or is unavailable. This data is identified as n/a.

Engine Code ABA (Passat) Display Group Overview 001 - 006				
Display Field	**1**	**2**	**3**	**4**
Display Group 001	RPM	ECT	Lambda	Ignition timing
Display Group 002	RPM	Injector duration	ECM Voltage	EGR temperature
Display Group 003	RPM	Load	TPS ∠	IAT
Display Group 004	RPM	Load	Vehicle speed	Input signals 1
Display Group 005	RPM	IAC adaptation	IAC duty cycle	Input signals 2
Display Group 006	HO2S	HO2S adaptation -idle	HO2S adaptation -part	HO2S adaptation -full

ABA

Read Measuring Value Blocks (Function 08)

Function 08
Display Group 000 (Passat)

Warm engine, running at idle speed, engine control module in **Read Measuring Value Block** (Function 08)

Field	Display Fields	Observed range: 000-1	Corresponds to:
10	Ign. timing (varies)	76-93	2.25 - 15.0° BTDC
9	Undefined data	—	—
8	Air correction value (adaptation)	114-154	2.8-5.2 kg/h
7	Learning value for low load adaptation	92-164	0.7-1.3
6	Learning value for part load adaptation	__ 000-2	__ 000-2
5	Learning value for idle adaptation	83-241	0.87-1.22
4	Oxygen sensor factor (fast fluctuations over a wide range)	92-164 000-3	0.7-1.3
3	Engine speed (fluctuates slightly)	80-88 000-4	800-880 rpm
2	Engine load signal (fluctuates slightly)	26-44	1.3-2.2 ms
1	Engine coolant temperature sensor (varies as radiator fan cycles on and off)	181-224 000-5	80-110°C

000-1) Center of range for Fields 4,5,7, & 8 is 128.

000-2) Specification range not determined.

000-3) Values greater than 128 indicate a lean condition correcting towards rich, less than 128 indicate a rich condition correcting towards lean. No fluctuations indicate that control is not working. If value remains at 0, the engine is running excessively rich and the HO2S system cannot control it.

000-4) Multiply value by 10 to read actual engine rpm at idle.

000-5) Value of 181 equals 80°C.

Function 08
Display Group 001 (Passat)

	1	2	3	4
Display	xxxx /min	xx.x °C	x.xx	xx.x ° v.OT
Indicated	Engine speed	Coolant temperature	Lambda factor	Ignition timing
Specification	800-880 idle rpm[001-1]	80-110°C[001-2]	0.7-1.30[001-3]	2.25-15°BTDC[001-4]
		Open circuit shows a constant 77.7°		
Working range	800...6200 rpm	-46.5°C...141.0°C		

001-1) At warm idle.

001-2) Temperature varies as radiator fan cycles on and off.

001-3) Center of range at 1.00. Value will fluctuate slightly during warm idle.

001-4) Variations are due to electronic Idle Speed Control (ISC). ISC varies timing in conjunction with the IAC to provide a smooth engine idle.

Function 08
Display Group 002 (Passat)

	1	2	3	4
Display	xxxx /min	xx.x ms	xx.x V	xx.x °C
Indicated	Engine speed	Fuel injector duration	ECM supply voltage	EGR temperature
Specification	800-880 idle rpm[002-1]	2.8-5.2 ms[002-2]	12.5-15.0 V[002-3]	127.4°C[002-4]
			VAG 1551 Scan Tool operates 10V- 16V	If no EGR, shows a constant 217°C
Working range	800...6200 rpm		Maximum 14.5V	127.4°C...217°C

002-1) At warm idle.

002-2) Fuel injector duration (opening period) at idle.

002-3) ECM supply voltage should be approximate electrical system voltage. Maximum specified charging system voltage 14.5.

002-4) EGR valve temperature. Lowest value displayed is 127.4. When EGR is functioning, temperature will rise to a maximum indicated 217.0°C as exhaust gases pass EGR Temperature sensor.

Read Measuring Value Blocks (Function 08)

Function 08 Display Group 003 (Passat)				
	1	**2**	**3**	**4**
Display	xxxx /min	xxx%	xx ∠°	xx.x °C
Indicated	Engine speed	Engine load	Throttle valve angle	Intake air temperature
Specification	800-880 idle rpm[003-1]	0-5%[003-2]	5° to 19°[003-3]	ambient[003-4]
				Open circuit shows a constant 19.6°
Working range	800...6200 rpm	0-100%	8°...101°	-46.5°C...141.0°C

003-1) At warm idle.

003-2) Calculated data from Mass Air Flow Sensor at warm idle. Value will fluctuate slightly and should change as engine speed is increased.

003-3) Data from Throttle Position Sensor.

003-4) Signal from Intake Air Temperature Sensor. Intake air temperature is usually warmer than ambient air temperature and more closely approximates intake manifold temperature.

Function 08 Display Group 004 (Passat)				
	1	**2**	**3**	**4**
Display	xxxx /min	xxx%	xx	XXXXX
Indicated	Engine speed	Engine load	Vehicle speed	Operating mode 1, throttle positions
Specification	800-880 idle rpm[004-1]	0-5%[004-2]	0 Km/h[004-3]	see Operating Mode 1 table below[004-4]
Working range	800...6200 rpm		0...210 km/h (governed top speed	

004-1) At warm idle.

004-2) Same as Display Group 003, Field 2.

004-3) Value is received from Vehicle Speed Sensor (VSS) and indicates approximate vehicle road speed.

004-4) Display will be either a 1 or a 0. For example, 00010 indicates idle position recognized. Multiple functions can occur simultaneously such as 00011 indicating idle position recognized but engine speed sufficient to enable deceleration fuel shut-off.

Operating Mode 1- Throttle Positions (see Display Group 004, Field 4)

Displayed: (1 = recognized/ enabled 0 = not)					**Position recognized or function enabled**
X					**Acceleration enrichment**
	X				**Full load**
		X			**Part load**
			X		**Idle**
				X	**Overrun (deceleration fuel shut-off)**

Function 08
Display Group 005 (Passat)

	1	2	3	4
Display	xxxx /min	xxx kg/h	xx%	XX XX
Indicated	Engine speed	Idle stabilization adaptation	Idle stabilization duty cycle	Operating mode 2, Input Signals
Specification	800-880 idle rpm[005-1]	2.8-5.2 kg/h[005-1]	50-60%[005-2]	see Operating Mode 2 table below[005-3]
Working range	800...6200 rpm			

005-1) At warm idle.

005-2) Duty cycle value should increase slightly when electrical consumers and air conditioning are switched on at idle.

005-3) Display will be either a 1 or a 0. For example, 00 01 indicates the automatic transmission in gear signal is recognized. Multiple functions can occur simultaneously such as 11 01 indicating air conditioning compressor and system on and automatic transmission in gear.

Operating Mode 2 - Input Signals
(see Display Group 005, Field 4)

Displayed (1 = recognized/ enabled, 0 = not)					**Signal recognized or function enabled**
X					Air conditioner compressor on
	X				Air conditioner system on
			X		Automatic transmission shift signal, TCM to ECM
				X	Undefined and/or not relevant

Function 08
Display Group 006 (Passat)

	1	2	3	4
Display	x.xx	x.xx	x.xx	x.xx
Indicated	Lambda factor	Lambda adaptation at idle	Not used, undefined data[006-3]	Lambda adaptation at part load
Specification	0.7-1.3[006-1]	0.87-1.22[006-2]		0.7-1.3[006-4]
Working range[006-5]				

006-1) Same as in Display Group 001, field 3. Center of the range at 1.00. Value will fluctuate slightly during warm idle.

006-2) Center of the range is 1.00. Value may fluctuate slightly during warm idle.

006-3) Specification range not determined.

006-4) Center of the range is 1.00.

Basic Settings (Function 04)

ABA engines do not have provisions for adjustment of ignition timing, idle speed, or mixture. These operating parameters are pre-programmed into the ECM as default or baseline values. During engine operation, data is received from the various sensors and corrections are made as required. These corrections are retained in the ECM's memory when the ignition is switched off and become the starting point for subsequent engine operation. These retained values are said to be "learned" values and can change or adapt as often as needed.

> ***NOTE***
> *If the ECM is disconnected from the battery during repairs, the learned values are erased and the ECM will revert to the default values allowing the engine to run. The default values may not match the current needs of the engine, which can result in temporary poor performance and driveability. Also, when repairs have been made, such as repair of a vacuum leak, the default values will not match the current needs of the engine.*

In both situations, the ECM will start from the default or baseline settings and re-learn and adapt to current operating conditions. This process can, however, take some time.

When an appropriate scan tool is properly connected to the Motronic M2.9 ECM on ABA coded engines and set to Function 04 (basic settings), the ECM can be made to adapt to current operating conditions in several minutes rather than a longer period of time.

When Function 04 (basic settings) is selected, the scan tool instructs the ECM to:

- Stabilize ignition timing
- Stabilize idle speed
- Disable the A/C compressor
- Disable the EVAP system

When these influences have been removed, the engine management system is able to accurately adjust to current operating parameters.

```
Start Basic Setting                HELP
Input Display Group Number          XXX
```

```
System in Basic Setting      01     -->
710/min   85°C   1.02   6.2°v.OT
```

Initiating basic settings

Preliminary requirements:

- Vehicle stationary, engine at idle, automatic transmission in P or N.
- Engine oil temperature at least 80°C (176°F)
- All electrical consumers switched off.
  (radiator cooling fan must not run during check)
  (daytime running lights (DRLs) can remain on)
- Air conditioning switched off.
- Exhaust system free from leaks.

Checking and adjusting Basic Settings:

- Connect scan tool
- From the initial Menu select:
  1 Rapid Data
- From the address word Menu select:
  01 Engine Electronics
- Advance to the Function Menu when the ECM responds with the version information
- From the Function Menu select:
  02 Check DTC memory
  Read DTCs and return to the Function Menu
- From the Function Menu select:
  04 Basic settings

From the Start Basic Settings display, input:
display group 001 (or 01 if applicable)

- Accelerate engine slightly over idle speed and allow to idle for at least 2 minutes

Observe engine operating data after 2 minutes.
Display field 1: . . . . .650 to 750 rpm
Display field 2: . . . . .80°C or greater
Display field 3: . . . . 1.00 ± 0.25 (fluctuating)
Display field 4: . . . . 6° v.OT (slight fluctuation)

If operating data **is** within the listed specification and radiator coolant fan has not run for 2 minutes, exit basic settings and end output; basic settings are complete.

If operating data is **not** within listed specification, determine malfunction and re-test.

Other display groups can be shown in the scan tool window, however only group 001 is required for basic settings. It is the only group that will show the desired information in the same scan tool window.

NOTE
Information regarding other system components can be viewed via Function 08 (read measuring value blocks).

```
Rapid data transfer                Q
03 - Output Diagnostic Test Mode
```

OUTPUT DIAGNOSTIC TEST MODE (FUNCTION 03)

When Output Diagnostic Test Mode or Function 03 is activated, the scan tool instructs the ECM to operate certain electrical components in a pre-determined sequence. The output diagnostic test mode can only be used when the ignition is switched on, but the engine is not running.

The following is a list of components checked during the output diagnostic test mode and the order in which they are tested:

- Fuel injector, cylinder 1 (N30)[1]
- Fuel injector, cylinder 3
- Fuel injector, cylinder 4
- Fuel injector, cylinder 2
- Idle air control valve (IAC) (N71)
- Evaporative Emission (EVAP) Canister Purge Regulator Valve (N80)
- Heated Oxygen Sensor Relay (HO2S) relay
- Exhaust Gas Recirculation (EGR) Vacuum Regulator Solenoid Valve (N18)[2]
- Intake Manifold Change-Over Valve (N156)[3]
- Secondary Air Injection (AIR) Pump Relay (J299)[4]

Notes:

1 Output diagnostic test mode always starts with the first cylinder in the firing order (cylinder 1), and continues in the firing order sequence. 1-3-4-2.

2 Where equipped.

3 USA and Canada specification engines are not equipped with this component, but it appears in the test procedure. Continue past it. Does not appear on Passat ABA systems.

4 Where equipped.

Testing in Function 03

Testing Motronic-equipped VR-6 engines with a scan tool in Function 03 is a relatively straight forward operation. There are, however several items to consider before beginning:

- The Throttle Position (TP) Sensor must function properly because the Fuel injector test is advanced by opening the throttle partially.
- The engine must be at operating temperature for all of the tests to run. If this is not possible, the test can still be run on a cold engine, but usually only one or two of the injectors will operate. This facilitates later engine starts.
- The test can only be run once per start. After completion, the engine must be started before it can be repeated. Some ECM versions may allow a repeat after switching the ignition off and back on, but some components may be skipped.

⊲ VAG 1551 Scan Tool display for first component checked in the Output Diagnostic Test Mode.

```
Output Diagnostic Test Mode          →
Injector, Cyl. 1 - N30
```

After the scan tool has been connected and Function 03 selected, proceed with the test as indicated on the scan tool noting the following points: After the scan tool has been connected and Component Checking (Function 03) selected, proceed with the test as indicated on the scan tool noting the following points:

1. **Fuel injector, cylinder 1 (N30)**
The first component checked is Fuel injector, Cylinder 1. To test this component, the throttle must be manually operated to the wide open position and then closed. The injector must be heard to click approximately 5 times. After operating the injector, the program will advance to the next injector in the firing order.

2. **Fuel injector, cylinder 2 (N31**)

3. **Fuel injector, cylinder 3 (N32)**

4. **Fuel injector, cylinder 4 (N33)**

5. **Idle Air Control (IAC) Valve (N71)** – The IAC Valve will be operated from the fully closed position through the full open position and back resulting in an audible click. Advance the program with the right arrow button (-->).

Output Diagnostic Test Mode (Function 03)

6. **Evaporative Emission (EVAP) Canister Purge Regulator Valve (N80)** – The EVAP Canister Purge regulator Valve will be switched off and on (opened and closed). The resulting noise is faint and difficult to hear, but can also usually be felt. Do not confuse the EVAP Canister Purge Regulator Valve with the EGR Vacuum Regulator Solenoid Valve (N18), which is mounted next to it on some vehicles. Advance the program with the right arrow button (-->).

7. **Heated Oxygen Sensor (HO2S) Relay (J278)** – The HO2S Relay will be switched on and off. The relay is located inside the vehicle near the fuse/relay panel and the resulting noise can be heard in the passenger compartment near the pedals.

8. **Exhaust Gas Recirculation (EGR) Vacuum Regulator Solenoid Valve (N18)** (where equipped) – The EGR Vacuum Regulator Solenoid Valve will be switched on and off (opened and closed) resulting in an audible click. Do not confuse the EGR Vacuum Regulator Solenoid Valve with the EVAP Canister Purge Regulator Valve (N80), which is mounted next to it on some vehicles. Advance the program with the right arrow button (-->).

9. **Intake Manifold Change-Over Valve (N156)** – (Disregard if displayed). This component is not factory installed on USA and Canadian vehicles. Advance the program with the right arrow button (-->).

10. **Secondary Air Injection (AIR) Pump Relay (J299)** (where equipped)– The AIR Pump Relay will be switched on and off resulting in an audible click. Return the program to the Function Menu with the right arrow button (-->).

```
Output Diagnostic Test Mode

Injector, Cyl. 1-N30
Injector, Cyl. 2-N31
Injector, Cyl. 3-N32
Injector, Cyl. 4-N33
Idle Air Control Valve-N71
EVAP Canister Purge Regulator Valve-N80
Heated Oxygen Sensor Relay-J278
EGR Vacuum Regulator Solenoid Valve-N18
Intake Manifold Changeover Valve-N156
Secondary Air Injection Pump Relay-J299
```

When the VAG 1551 printer is switched on, the tape will be printed with all of the tests.

The Output Diagnostic Test Mode is helpful in checking the electrical operation of a given component. It can also be helpful in diagnosing mechanical malfunctions as well. If, for example, an EGR Vacuum Regulator Solenoid was suspected of a malfunction, the hoses could be disconnected and the Output Diagnostic Test Mode run while blowing through the valve. This would help determine if it worked properly. Similar tests can be devised with many of the other components.

In the event of a component failing to operate, the component and the wiring should be checked for continuity, open circuits, and short circuits, including short circuits to ground. Always consult the appropriate wiring diagram.

Code Control Module (Function 07)

Control module coding by the scan tool is not a supported function with Motronic M2.9 ECMs in ABA coded engines. Coding information does appear, however, in Function 01 (control unit versions). ECM coding is generally accomplished through the use of special coding wires in the ECM wiring harness. Codes are used to identify the transmission type and to indicate if equipped with EGR.

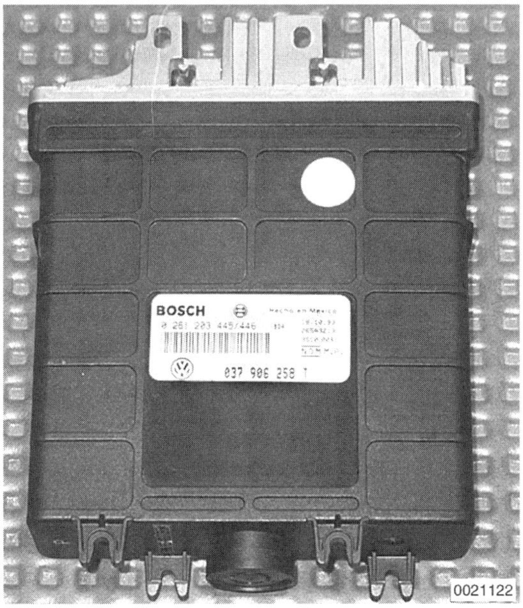

0021122

◄ Part number on ECM label matches Scan Tool display in Function 01. Coding information does not, however, appear externally.

ECM Coding (ABA)

Coding	Vehicle and Equipment
1HS	Manual transmission, with EGR and Secondary Air Injection System (Passat)
2AG	Automatic transmission, with EGR and Secondary Air Injection System (Passat)
1	Manual transmission (Golf, Jetta)
2	Automatic transmission (Golf, Jetta)
3	Manual transmission, with EGR
4	Automatic transmission, with EGR

NOTE
Some vehicles with automatic transmissions may have been intentionally mis-coded as manual transmission vehicles to improve idle quality and to eliminate hesitation when accelerating from idle.

Component and Signal Overview, ABA Engine

COMPONENT AND SIGNAL OVERVIEW, ABA ENGINE

ABA engines use the Bosch Motronic M2.9 engine management system. Signals from sensors and other input sources are processed by the ECM. Signals to control the engine are sent to actuators along with engine information needed by other systems or functions.

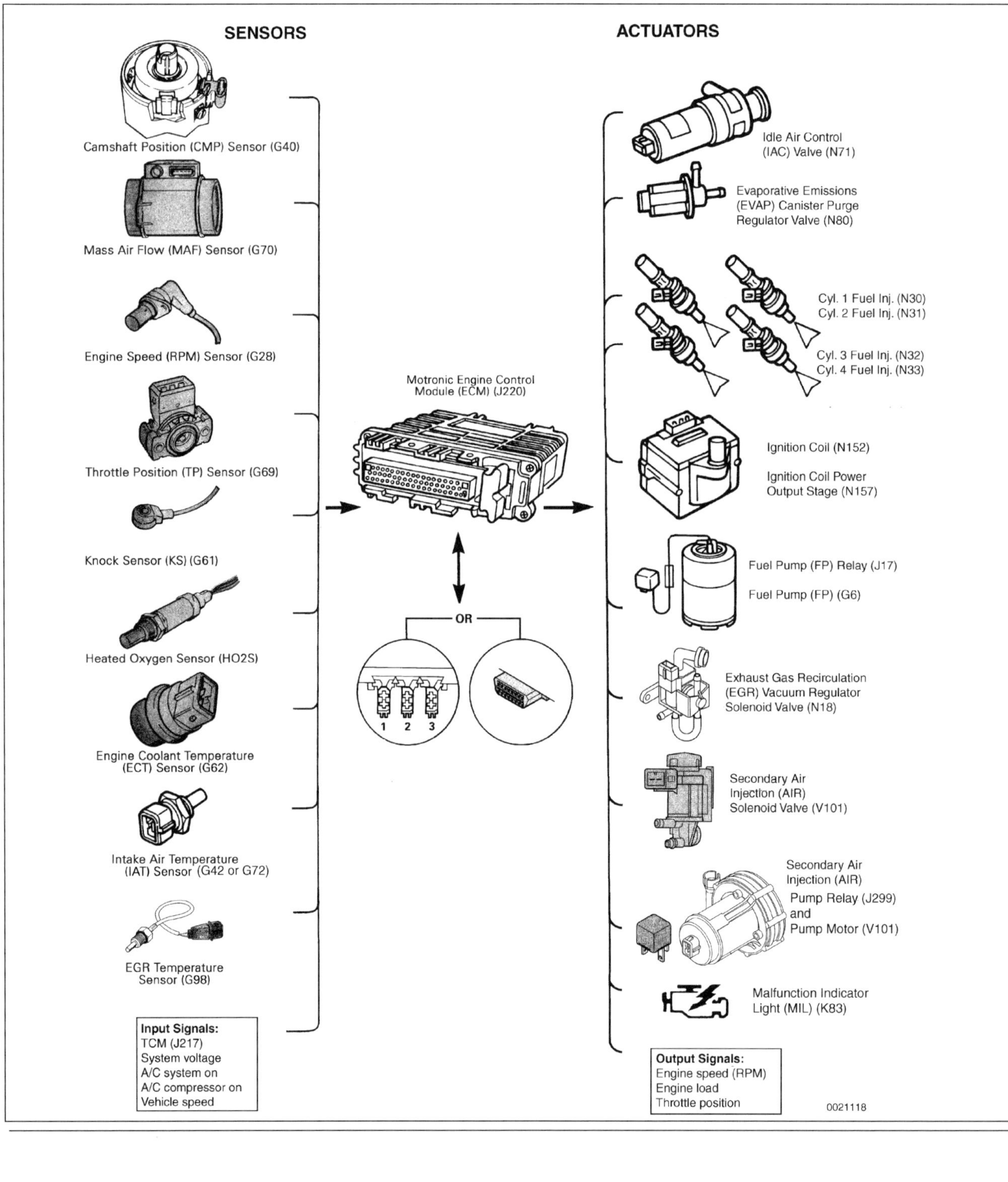

Component and Signal Overview (ABA)

Bosch® Motronic M2.9, 4-cylinder	
Fuel injection	Sequential Multi-Point Fuel Injection with Lambda (Oxygen Sensor) Control, OBD-I
Fuel delivery	Tank-mounted 2-stage electric fuel pump, load-sensing mechanical pressure regulator
Ignition system	Distributor, power output stage and ignition coil, single knock sensors, ECM controlled
Emission control	3-Way catalytic converter, evaporative emissions with carbon canister, positive crankcase ventilation, secondary air injection[1]
Diagnostics	On-Board Diagnostics via scan tool, Rapid data transfer[2], Non-volatile memory
Control Module	Single 68-pin Motronic Engine Control Module (ECM) (J220), supplied by Motronic ECM Power Supply Relay (J271)
Sensors	Camshaft Position (CMP) Sensor (G40)
	Mass Air Flow (MAF) Sensor (G71)
	Engine Speed (RPM) Sensor (G28)[3]
	Throttle Position (TP) Sensor (G69)[4]
	Knock Sensor (KS) (G61)
	Heated Oxygen Sensor (H2OS) (G39)
	Engine Coolant Temperature (ECT) Sensor (G62)
	Intake Air Temperature (IAT) Sensor (G42 or G72))
	Exhaust Gas Recirculation (EGR) Temperature Sensor (G98)[5]
Input signals	System voltage
	Air conditioner, system on
	Air conditioner, compressor on
	Vehicle speed
	Automatic Transmission Control Module (TCM) (J217)

Component and Signal Overview, ABA Engine

Actuators	Idle Air Control (IAC) Valve (N71)
	Evaporative Emission (EVAP) Canister Purge Regulator Valve (N80)
	Fuel Injectors: Cylinder 1 (N30), Cylinder 2 (N31), Cylinder 3 (N32), Cylinder 4 (N33)
	Ignition Coil (N152) and Ignition Coil Power Output Stage (N157)
	Fuel Pump (FP) Relay (J17), and Fuel Pump (FP) (G6)
	Heated Oxygen Sensor (HO2S) Relay (J278), and Heated Oxygen Sensor (HO2S) (G39)
	Exhaust Gas Recirculation (EGR) Vacuum Regulator Solenoid Valve (N18)[5]
	Secondary Air Injection (AIR) Solenoid Valve (N112)[1]
	Secondary Air Injection (AIR) Pump Relay (J299), and Pump Motor (V101)[1]
	Malfunction Indicator Light (MIL)[6] (K83)
Output signals	Engine speed (rpm)
	Engine load
	Throttle position[7]

1 Passat, MY 1995.
2 Also equipped with "blink code" diagnostics. The limited capabilities of this mode are outside the scope of this manual.
3 Shutter wheel on crankshaft has 58 teeth plus 2 blank spaces to provide both engine speed and reference signals.
4 Early vehicles with automatic transmissions use separate TP Sensors combined in a single housing. Later vehicles use a single TP Sensor and share data with the TCM.
5 EGR only installed on vehicles for some market areas.
6 MIL only functional on vehicles for some market areas.
7 Automatic transmission vehicles only.

ABA

TECHNICAL DATA

Technical data is compiled from several Volkswagen publications. In some instances, the information from these sources differed slightly in the areas of horsepower, torque and compression ratio. In the cases, the most current specifications are listed.

> ***NOTE***
> *The ABA engine is also installed in some vehicles with OBD II capability. This version is outside the scope of this manual.*

ABA (Passat, Golf, Jetta, Cabrio)	**Technical Data**
Type	4-cylinder in-line (R4), gasoline fuel
Construction	Cast iron block, aluminum 2V cylinder head, belt driven single overhead camshaft
Displacement	2.0 Liters (1984 cc), (121 cid)
Horsepower	115 hp (85 Kw) @ 5400 rpm
Torque	122 lb-ft (165 Nm) @ 3200 rpm
Bore	82.5 mm
Stroke	92.8 mm
Compression ratio	9.6:1 (Golf, Jetta), 9.4:1 (Cabrio, Passat)
Firing order	1-3-4-2
Management	Motronic M2.9

Notes

Engine Code
ABG

GENERAL

The vehicles listed below are equipped with engine code **ABG**. This engine uses a version of Volkswagen's **Digifant** engine management system. The displacement of this inline 4-cylinder engine is 1.8 liters.

The **ABG** engine is installed in the Volkswagen Fox for all 50 States and Canada for model years 1987 through 1993. Only engines originally certified for sale in California for model years 1991 through 1993 are equipped with the scan tool capability detailed in this section.

Engine Code ABG Vehicles

Engine Code ABG	Model Years
Fox	1991, 1992, 1993 (California certified only)

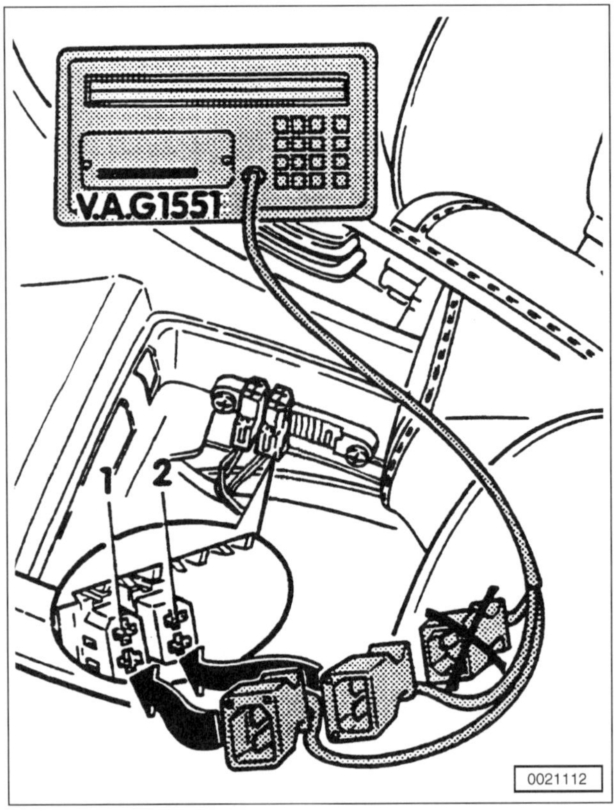

Scan tool, connecting

The scan tool is connected through the DLC (Data Link Connector).

◄ **Fox, 1991-1993 (California only)**:
Center console under shifter boot.
Black connector on scan tool harness is connected to black connection on vehicle (**1**) and provides scan tool power. White connector is connected to the white connection on the vehicle (**2**) for data transfer. Blue connector (**3**) is not used.

Scan tool, functions available

	Scan Tool Functions Available	Ignition on, not running	Engine at idle	Page
✔	Control unit version (01)	Yes	Yes	Appendix A
✔	Check DTC memory (02)	Yes	Yes	Appendix A
✔	Output diagnostic test mode (03)	No	No	75
✔	Basic settings (04)	No	No	74
✔	Erase DTC memory (05)	Yes	Yes	Appendix A
✔	End output (06)	Yes	Yes	Appendix A
✗	Code control module (07)	No	No	76
✔	Read measuring value blocks (08)	Yes	Yes	69

Read Measuring Value Blocks (Function 08)

Measuring value blocks are assembled and displayed in sets called display groups. For the ABG engine, display groups are numbered starting with 000 and continuing with 001 on up to 005.

Read Measuring Value Blocks HELP
Input Display Group Number XXX

◄ Scan tool display from VAG 1551 requesting Measuring Value Block Display Group information (XXX).

Display group overview, ABG engine (Fox - California only)

Function 08, (Fox - California only)
Display Group Overview 000[OV-1]

Display Field	1	2	3	4	5	6	7	8	9	10
	n/a	n/a	ECT	n/a	HO2S	n/a	n/a	n/a	n/a	n/a

OV-1) Some data is not relevant, or is unavailable. This data is identified as n/a.

Function 08 (Fox - California only)
Display Group Overview 001 - 005[OV-2]

Display Field	1	2	3	4
Display Group 001	RPM	VAF	ECT	Injector duration
Display Group 002	RPM	IAT	n/a	Injector duration
Display Group 003	RPM	ECT	n/a	Injector duration
Display Group 004	RPM	VAF	n/a	Injector duration
Display Group 005	RPM	TPS	n/a	Injector duration

OV-2) Some data is not relevant, is or is unavailable. This data is identified as n/a.

Read Measuring Value Blocks (Function 08)

Function 08
Display Group 000

Engine running at idle speed, coolant temperature above 80°C (176°F), ECM in **Read Measuring Value Block** (Function 08)

Display Field	Display Fields	Observed range:[000-1]	Corresponds to:
10	Undefined data[000-2]	—	—
9	Undefined data	—	—
8	Undefined data	—	—
7	Undefined data	—	—
6	Undefined data	—	—
5	Heated Oxygen Sensor (HO2S) signal	must vary by at least 14[000-3]	operation OK
4	Undefined data	—	—
3	Engine Coolant Temperature (ECT) Sensor	less than 11[000-4]	80°C (176°F)
2	Undefined data	—	—
1	Undefined data	—	—

000-1) Overall range of values is 0 - 255.

000-2) Undefined data means that information is displayed on the scan tool but information for interpretation unavailable.

000-3) Values between 0 - 5 indicate short circuit to positive in HO2S wiring to ECM
Values between 164 - 168 indicate open circuit in HO2S wiring to ECM.
Values between 230 and 255 indicate short circuit to ground in HO2S wiring to ECM.

000-4) Lower numbers are hotter. Temperature must rise (value will decrease) smoothly during engine warm-up.

Function 08 Display Group 001				
	1	**2**	**3**	**4**
Display	xxxx /min	xx%	xx.x °C	xx.x ms
Indicated	Engine speed	VAF signal	Coolant temperature	Fuel injector duration
Specification	800-1000 idle rpm[001-1]	16%-26%	none given[001-4]	none given[001-5]
		At idle with coolant temperature at least 80°C (176°F)	Open circuit shows a constant -40° Short circuit shows a constant 80°C	
Working range	800...6300 rpm[001-2]	0%...100%[001-3]	-40°C...141°C (approximately)	

001-1) Valid with coolant temperature of at least 80° (176°F).

001-2) Approximate maximum governed rpm.

001-3) Values in this display field are valid only at idle with a coolant temperature of at least 80°C (176°F).
Values between 16 - 26% indicate VAF Sensor and ECM control OK.
Values between 5 - 15% indicate intake air leaks.
Values between 0 - 2% indicate open circuit in VAF Sensor wiring to ECM.

001-4) No specification given. Experience indicates that at idle, temperature will vary between approximately 86°C and 105°C depending on radiator fan operating cycle. Temperature must rise smoothly during engine warm-up. If value displayed does not increase jumps up by 2°C to 5°C in display, ECM is raising temperature based on running time due to a faulty ECT Sensor.

001-5) No idle specification given. Increase engine speed above 3000 rpm at least 3 times and let speed return to idle for at least 2 minutes. Note value. Again increase engine speed above 3000 rpm; fuel injector duration display must increase. Allow engine speed to return to idle. Value must drop to 0.00 mS to indicate deceleration fuel shut-off as speed decreases. Previously displayed idle value should again be shown.

Read Measuring Value Blocks (Function 08)

Function 08 Display Group 002				
	1	2	3	4
Display	xxxx /min	xx.x °C	xxx	xx.x ms
Indicated	Engine speed	Intake air temperature	n/a[002-3]	Fuel injector duration
Specification	800-1000 idle rpm[002-1]	none given[002-2]		none given[002-4]
		Open circuit shows a constant 19.6°		
Working range	800...6300 rpm[002-1]	-46.5°C...141.0°C		

002-1) As in Display Group 001, Field 1.

002-2) No specification given. Experience indicates that at idle, temperature will be approximately ambient air temperature. Intake air pre-heater will generally keep incoming air temperature to around 30°C, but may be substantially higher on a very hot day. Very high temperatures suggest a malfunctioning intake air pre-heater.

002-3) Data is not relevant, is undefined, or is unsupported by the factory.

002-4) As in Display Group 001, Field 4.

Function 08 Display Group 003				
	1	2	3	4
Display	xxxx /min	xx.x °C	xxx	xx.x ms
Indicated	Engine speed	Coolant temperature	n/a[003-3]	Fuel injector duration
Specification	800-1000 idle rpm[003-1]	none given[003-2]		none given[003-4]
		Open circuit shows a constant -40° Short circuit shows a constant 80°C		
Working range	800...6300 rpm[003-1]	-40°C...141°C (approximately)		

003-1) As in Display Group 001, Field 1.

003-2) As in Display Group 001, Field 3.

003-3) As in Display Group 002, Field 3.

003-4) As in Display Group 001, Field 4.

Function 08 Display Group 004				
	1	2	3	4
Display	xxxx /min	xx%	xxx	xx.x ms
Indicated	Engine speed	VAF signal	n/a[004-3]	Fuel injector duration
Specification	800-1000 idle rpm[004-1]	16%-26%		none given[004-4]
		At idle with coolant temperature at least 80°C (176°F)		
Working range	800...6300 rpm[004-1]	0%...100%[004-2]		

004-1) As in Display Group 001, Field 1.

004-2) As in Display Group 001, Field 2.

004-3) As in Display Group 002, Field 3.

004-4) As in Display Group 001, Field 4.

Function 08 Display Group 005				
	1	2	3	4
Display	xxxx /min	xx.x ∠°	xxx	xx.x ms
Indicated	Engine speed	TPS angle	n/a[005-3]	Fuel injector duration
Specification	800-1000 idle rpm[005-1]	5-50°		none given[005-4]
		At CTP		
Working range	800...6300 rpm[005-1]	0°...to over 90°[005-2]		

005-1) As in Display Group 001, Field 1.

005-2) Momentarily operate throttle to WOT. Value displayed should be 90.0 ∠° or greater.
0.0 ∠° indicates open circuit in TPS wiring to ECM.
90.0 ∠° or greater at idle indicates short circuit to positive in TPS wiring to ECM.
Value must increase uniformly and without interruption when throttle is opened.

005-3) As in Display Group 002, Field 3.

005-4) As in Display Group 001, Field 4.

Basic Settings (Function 04)

Adjustment of engine settings through the use of Function 04 (basic settings) is not a supported function in this version of Digifant. Baseline values for ignition timing, idle speed, and CO (carbon monoxide) content require manual adjustment.

Adjustment of engine settings does not require use of a scan tool, but does requires the connection of several other pieces of test equipment. After adjustment of engine settings, it will, however, be necessary to connect a scan tool and erase DTCs that are recorded during the normal adjusting procedures.

Test equipment required to adjust engine settings includes the following:

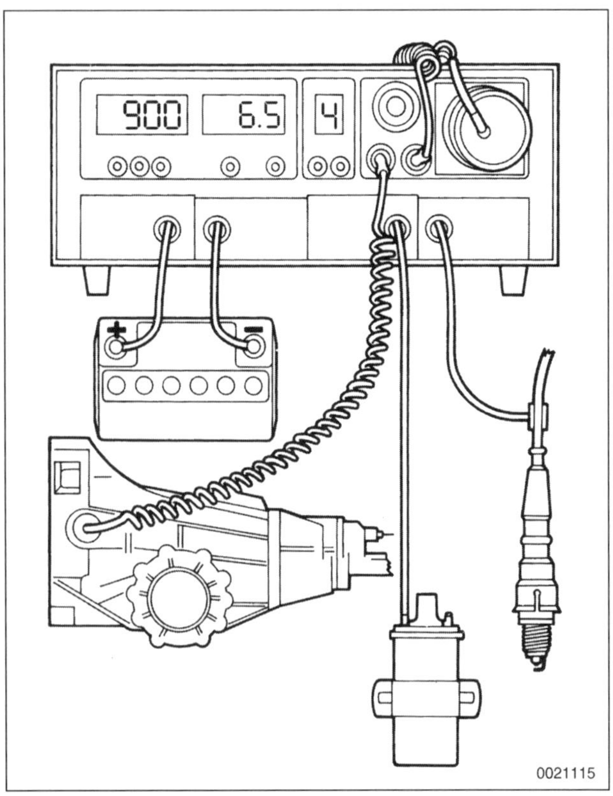

- ◄ An engine tester such as the VAG 1367 must be connected to the engine to measure ignition timing and engine speed.

- An exhaust gas analyzer must be attached to the CO pick-up or sampling tube located ahead of the catalytic converter to measure CO (carbon monoxide) content.

OUTPUT DIAGNOSTIC TEST MODE (FUNCTION 03)

Troubleshooting electrical faults in the Fox with ABG Digifant I engines must be done with a test harness such as the Volkswagen supplied VAG 1598. The ability of the scan tool to instruct the ECM to operate certain electrical components is not a supported function in this version of Digifant.

Use of a test harness on Digifant I systems requires that the ECM be disconnected during continuity and resistance checks and re-connected to test voltages.

In the event of a suspected component malfunction, the component and the wiring should be checked for continuity, open circuits, and short circuits, including short circuits to ground. Always consult the appropriate wiring diagram.

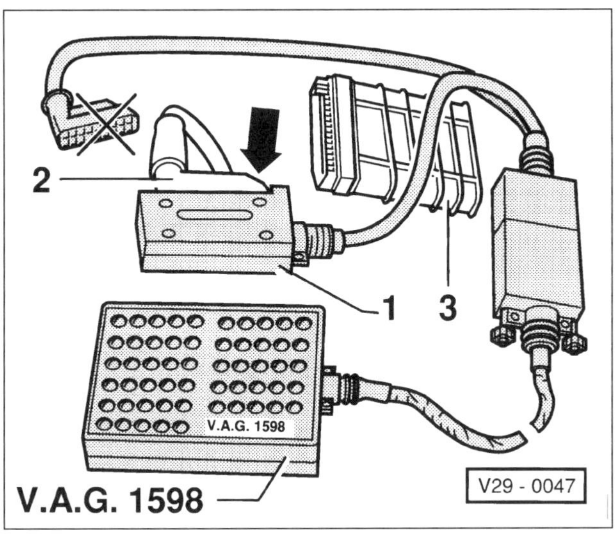

◄ Test box VAG 1598 shown attached to Digifant I vehicle wiring harness (arrow) with appropriate adapter (**1**). ECM harness connector (**2**) must remain disconnected from the ECM (**3**) during resistance checks to insure accuracy.

CODE CONTROL MODULE (FUNCTION 07)

Control module coding by means of the scan tool is not a supported function with California Digifant I ECMs. Coding information does appear, however, in Function 01 (control unit versions). ECM coding is generally accomplished through the use of specific part number ECMs.

```
037 906 023 S       DIGIFANT     0883
CODING        00000
```

< VAG 1551 scan tool display for Engine Control Module from a 1991 California Fox. Part number on ECM label will match Scan Tool display in Function 01.

NOTE
Always consult with your Volkswagen Parts Department or aftermarket parts specialist for the latest parts information.

COMPONENT AND SIGNAL OVERVIEW, ABG ENGINE

ABG engines use a version of the Volkswagen-developed **Digifant** engine management system. This version of Digifant is generally known as Digifant II except in California where it is designated Digifant I due to legal requirements.

Signals from sensors and other input sources are processed by the ECM. Signals to control the engine are sent to the actuators.

Component and Signal Overview, ABG Engine

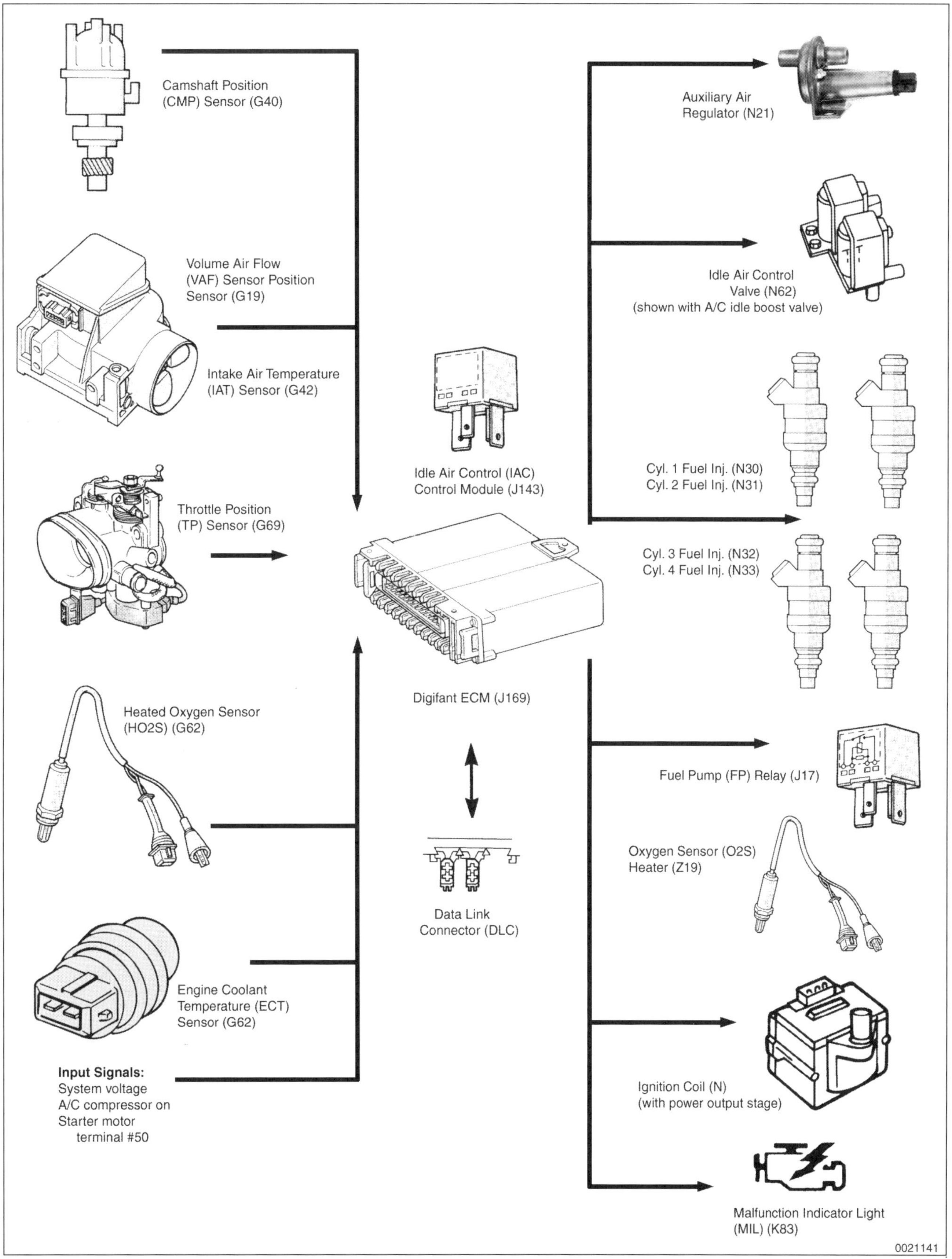

Component and Signal Overview, ABG Engine

Component and Signal Overview (ABG)

Volkswagen California Digifant 1, 4-cylinder	
Fuel injection	Non-sequential (simultaneous) Multi-Point Fuel Injection with Lambda (Oxygen Sensor) Control, OBD-I
Fuel delivery	Tank-mounted electric transfer fuel pump, externally-mounted electric fuel pump, load-sensing mechanical pressure regulator
Ignition system	Distributor, power output stage and ignition coil, ECM controlled
Emission control	3-Way catalytic converter, carbon canister with mechanical (vacuum) control valve, positive crankcase ventilation
Diagnostics	On-Board Diagnostics via scan tool, Rapid data transfer, Non-volatile memory
Control Modules	Single 38-pin Digifant Engine Control Module (ECM) (J169) supplied by Digifant ECM Power Supply Relay (J176), Idle Air Control (IAC) Control Module (J143)
Sensors	Camshaft Position (CMP) Sensor (G40)
	Volume Air Flow (VAF) Sensor Position Sensor (G19)
	Intake Air Temperature (IAT) Sensor (G42)[1]
	Throttle Position (TP) Sensor (G69)
	Heated Oxygen Sensor (H2OS) (G39)
	Engine Coolant Temperature (ECT) Sensor (G62)
Input signals	System voltage
	Starter motor (terminal 50)
	Air conditioner, compressor on
Actuators	Idle Air Control (IAC) Valve (N62)[2]
	Fuel Injectors: Cylinder 1 (N30), Cylinder 2 (N31), Cylinder 3 (N32), Cylinder 4 (N33)
	Ignition Coil (N), (includes power output stage)
	Fuel Pump (FP) Relay (J17), Transfer Fuel Pump (FP) (G23), Fuel Pump (FP) (G6)
	Malfunction Indicator Light (MIL) (K83)
Output signals	No additional output signals

[1] Built into VAF Sensor Position Sensor housing.
[2] Vehicles with air conditioning use an idle speed boost valve activated with the compressor in addition to the IAC Valve.

TECHNICAL DATA

Technical data is compiled from several Volkswagen publications. In some instances, the information from these sources differed slightly. In these cases, the most current specifications are listed.

ABG (Fox, California)	**Technical Data**
Type	4-cylinder in-line (R4), gasoline fuel
Construction	Cast iron block, aluminum 2V cylinder head, belt driven single overhead camshaft
Displacement	1.8 Liters (1781 cc), (109 cid)
Horsepower	81 hp (60 Kw) @ 5500 rpm
Torque	93 lb-ft (126 Nm) @ 3250 rpm
Bore	81.0 mm
Stroke	86.4 mm
Compression ratio	9.0:1
Firing order	1-3-4-2
Management	Digifant I

Notes

Engine Code
ACC

GENERAL

The ACC engine is equipped with a Bosch Mono-Motronic engine management system.

Engine Code ACC Vehicles

Engine Code ACC	Model Years
Golf (Canada)	1993, 1994, 1995, 1996, 1997

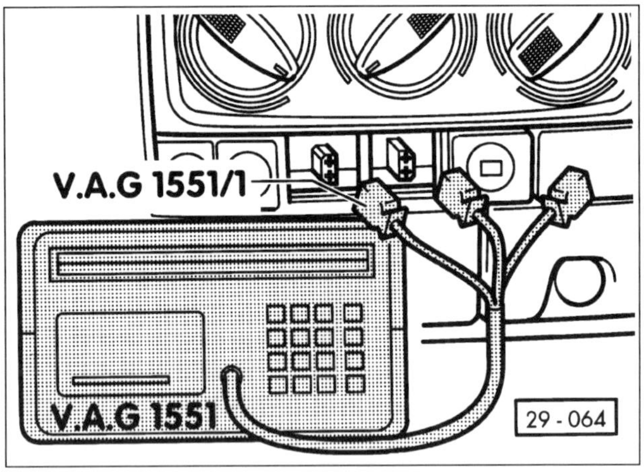

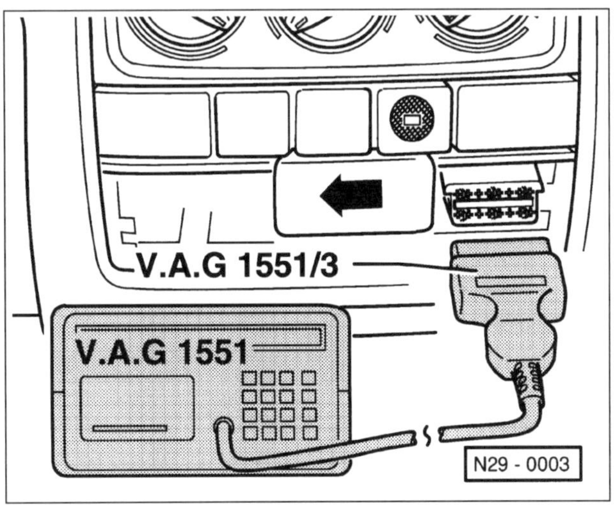

Scan tool, connecting

The scan tool is connected through the DLC (Data Link Connector). The DLC location varies depending on model year.

◄ **Golf CL, 1993-1994 (early):**
Instrument panel center section, below heater controls behind blank switch covers. Black connector on scan tool is connected to black connector on vehicle (scan tool power). White connector is connected to white connector on vehicle (data transfer). Blue connector is not used.

◄ **Golf CL, 1994-1997**:
Instrument panel center section, to right side of the ashtray behind cover.

Scan tool, functions available

	Scan Tool Functions Available	Ignition on, not running	Engine at idle	Page
✔	Control unit version (01)	Yes	Yes	Appendix A
✔	Check DTC memory (02)	Yes	No	Appendix A
✔	Output diagnostic test mode (03)	Yes	No	91
✔	Basic settings (04)	No	Yes	89
✔	Erase DTC memory (05)	Yes	Yes	Appendix A
✔	End output (06)	Yes	Yes	Appendix A
✗	Code control module (07)	No	No	92
✔	Read measuring value blocks (08)	Yes	Yes	83
✗	Read indiv. measuring value blocks (09)	No	No	Appendix A

READ MEASURING VALUE BLOCKS (FUNCTION 08)

Measuring value blocks are assembled and displayed in sets called display groups. For the ACC engine, display groups are numbered starting with 000 and continuing with 001 on up to 005.

> ***NOTE***
> *Early Mono-Motronic ECMs support display group 000 only. Later versions support display groups 000 through 005.*

Display group overview, ACC engine

Function 08 Display Group Overview 000 (early vehicles, ignition on only) [OV-1]										
Display Field	**1**	**2**	**3**	**4**	**5**	**6**	**7**	**8**	**9**	**10**
	ECT	TP actuator path 1	TP actuator path 1 & 2	CTP	Injector adaptation	Mixture control adaptation	Basic air adaptation	Idle control adaptation	ECM voltage	EVAP adaptation

OV-1) Some data is not relevant, or is unavailable.

Function 08 Display Group Overview 000 (early and later vehicles engine idling)										
Display Field	**1**	**2**	**3**	**4**	**5**	**6**	**7**	**8**	**9**	**10**
	ECT	TP actuator path 1	RPM	IAT	HO2S control	Mixture control adaptation	Basic air adaptation	Idle control adaptation	ECM voltage	EVAP adaptation

OV-1) Some data is not relevant, or is unavailable.

Function 08 Display Group Overview 001 - 005				
Display Field	**1**	**2**	**3**	**4**
Display Group 001	RPM	ECT	Lambda	Input signals 1
Display Group 002	RPM	Injector duration	ECM Voltage	IAT
Display Group 003	RPM	Load	TPS ∠	Ignition timing
Display Group 004	RPM	Load	n/a[OV-2]	Input signals 2
Display Group 005	RPM	EVAP	Lambda	Mixture correction

OV-2) Some data is not relevant, or is unavailable.

Read Measuring Value Blocks (Function 08)

Function 08
Display Group 000 (ignition on, engine on, early and later ECM versions)

Ignition switched on, engine running at idle, engine control module in “read measuring value blocks” **Function 08**

Field	Display Fields	Observed range:	Corresponds to:
10	**Adaptation value for EVAP Canister Purge Regulator Valve**	__[000-1]	—
9	**Battery Positive (ECM Supply) Voltage**	150 - 180	—
8	**Adaptation value for idle speed control**	0 - 25	—
7	**Adaptation value for basic air requirement**	250 - 255 or 0 - 10	—
6	**Adaptation value for mixture control**	162 - 255 or 0 - 30	Altitude corrected[000-2]
5	**Oxygen Sensor control factor**	90 - 170[000-3]	—
4	**Intake air temperature**	88 - 45[000-4]	—
3	**Engine speed (rpm)**	30 - 34[000-5]	750 to 1000 rpm
2	**Throttle Position Actuator (path 1)**	10 - 70[000-6]	—
1	**Engine coolant temperature (varies as radiator fan cycles on and off)**	22 - 11[000-7]	22 = 185°F (85°C)

000-1) No specification given.

000-2) Identify workshop altitude and consult **Altitude Correction Factor** table for specification.

000-3) Should fluctuate at idle. The specification of 106 -150 has also been listed by VW in some publications.

000-4) Lower numbers are hotter. Theoretical range is 255 - 0.

000-5) Maximum value is 255.

000-6) Value in field must increase steadily until throttle is approx. ¼ open. It should not change if throttle is opened further.

000-7) Lower numbers are hotter. Temperature must rise (value will decrease) smoothly during engine warm-up. If display jumps in consistent 2°C to 5°C values, ECM is using substitute values. Theoretical range is 255 - 0.

Altitude Correction Factor (see Display Field 6)

Altitude of workshop		Specification	Altitude of workshop		Specification
0 (sea level)	0 (sea level)	241 - 255 **or** 3 - 30	5740 ft.	1750 m	195 - 240
820 ft.	250 m	235 - 255 **or** 0 - 24	6560 ft.	2000 m	188 - 233
1640 ft.	500 m	228 - 255 **or** 0 - 17	7380 ft.	2250 m	182 - 227
2460 ft.	750 m	222 - 255 **or** 0 - 11	8200 ft.	2500 m	175 - 220
3280 ft.	1000 m	215 - 255 **or** 0 - 4	9020 ft.	2750 m	168 - 213
4100 ft.	1250 m	209 - 254	9840 ft.	3000 m	162 - 207
4920 ft.	1500 m	202 - 247			

Function 08 Display Group 001				
	1	**2**	**3**	**4**
Display	xxxx /min	xx.x °C	x.xx	XXXXXXXX
Indicated	Engine speed	Coolant temperature	Lambda factor	Input signals
Specification	750-1000 idle rpm	none given[001-1]	none given[001-2]	see Operating Mode 1 table below[001-3]
Working range	750...6300 rpm	-46.5°C...141.0°C		

[001-1)] No specification given. Experience indicates that at idle, temperature will vary between approximately 92°C and 100°C depending on radiator fan operating cycle. Temperature must rise smoothly during engine warm-up. If display jumps up by 2°C to 5°C in display, ECM is raising temperature based on running time due to a faulty ECT Sensor.

[001-2)] No specification given. Experience indicates that at idle, lambda value will be between 0.70 and 1.30 with the center of the range at 1.00. Value will fluctuate slightly during warm idle.

[001-3)] Display will be either a 1 or a 0. For example, 01000000 indicates the CTP Switch is recognized. Multiple functions can occur simultaneously such as 01011000 indicating air conditioning compressor and system on and CTP Switch recognized.

Operating Mode 1 - Input Signals (see Display Group 001, Field 4)

Displayed (1 = recognized/enabled, 0 = not)								**Signal recognized or function enabled**
X								Not relevant/unavailable data
	X							Closed throttle position
		X						Not relevant/unavailable data
			X					A/C compressor on
				X				Air conditioner system on
					X			Not relevant/unavailable data
						X		Manual trans. or Automatic trans. in P or N
							X	Automatic trans. in gear

Read Measuring Value Blocks (Function 08)

Function 08 Display Group 002				
	1	2	3	4
Display	xxxx /min	xx.x ms	xx.x V	xx.x °C
Indicated	Engine speed	Fuel injector duration	ECM supply voltage	Intake air temperature
Specification	750-1000 idle rpm	none given[002-1]	none given[002-2]	none given[002-3]
Working range	750...6300 rpm		Maximum 14.5V	-46.5°C...141.0°C

[002-1] No specification given.

[002-2] No specification given. Experience indicates that ECM supply voltage should be approximate electrical system voltage. Note that VAG 1551 scan tool operating range is 10 -16VDC

[002-3] No specification given. Experience indicates that air temperature and coolant temperature will be approximately the same when a cold engine is first started. Temperature will rise slightly during engine warm-up. Intake air temperature is usually warmer than ambient air temperature.

Function 08 Display Group 003				
	1	2	3	4
Display	xxxx /min	xxx%	xx ∠°	xx.x °v.OT
Indicated	Engine speed	Engine load	Throttle valve angle	Ignition timing point
Specification	750-1000 idle rpm	none given[003-1]	none given[003-2]	none given[003-3]
Working range	750...6300 rpm			

[003-1] No specification given. Experience indicates that load value should increase when electrical consumers and air conditioning are switched on at idle.

[003-2] Value must increase/decrease uniformly as throttle is opened and closed.

[003-3] No specification given. This is a specified or calculated value only. It is not an actual timing value because the ECM has no way of referencing this value in relation to the crankshaft position. Moving the distributor to change the ignition timing will, in fact, change the timing, but will have little or no effect on this value. Ignition timing must be adjusted with a conventional timing light or engine tester with Basic Settings (Function 04).

Function 08 Display Group 004				
	1	2	3	4
Display	xxxx /min	xxx%	xx	XXXXX
Indicated	Engine speed	Engine load	Not used, undefined data	Operating mode 2, throttle positions
Specification	750-1000 idle rpm	none given[004-1]		see Operating Mode 2 table below[004-2]
Working range	750...6300 rpm			

004-1) No specification given. Experience indicates that load value should increase when electrical consumers and air conditioning are switched on at idle.

004-2) Display will be either a 1 or a 0. For example, 00000010 indicates closed throttle position recognized. Multiple functions can occur simultaneously such as 00000011 indicating closed throttle position recognized but engine speed sufficient to enable deceleration fuel shut-off.

Operating Mode 2 - Throttle Positions (see Display Group 004, Field 4)

Displayed (1 = recognized/ enabled, 0 = not)								Signal recognized or function enabled
X								Not relevant/unavailable data
	X							Not relevant/unavailable data
		X						Not relevant/unavailable data
			X					Acceleration enrichment
				X				Full throttle (WOT)
					X			Part load
						X		Closed throttle position
							X	Overrun (decel. fuel shut-off)

Function 08 Display Group 003				
	1	2	3	4
Display	xxxx /min	xxx%	xx ∠°	xx.x °v.OT
Indicated	Engine speed	Engine load	Throttle valve angle	Ignition timing point
Specification	750-1000 idle rpm	none given[003-1]	none given[003-2]	none given[003-3]
Working range	750...6300 rpm			

003-1) No specification given. Experience indicates that load value should increase when electrical consumers and air conditioning are switched on at idle.

003-2) Value must increase/decrease uniformly as throttle is opened and closed.

003-3) No specification given. This is a specified value only. It is not an actual timing value because the ECM has no way of referencing this value in relation to the crankshaft position. Moving the distributor to change the ignition timing will, in fact, change the timing, but will usually have little or no effect on this value. Ignition timing must be adjusted with a conventional timing light or engine tester with Basic Settings (Function 04).

Read Measuring Value Blocks (Function 08)

Function 08 Display Group 004				
	1	2	3	4
Display	xxxx /min	xxx%	xx	XXXXX
Indicated	Engine speed	Engine load	Not used, undefined data	Operating mode 2, throttle positions
Specification	750-1000 idle rpm	none given[004-1]		see Operating Mode 2 table below[004-2]
Working range	750...6300 rpm			

004-1) No specification given. Experience indicates that load value should increase when electrical consumers and air conditioning are switched on at idle.

004-2) Display will be either a 1 or a 0. For example, 00000010 indicates closed throttle position recognized. Multiple functions can occur simultaneously such as 00000011 indicating closed throttle position recognized but engine speed sufficient to enable deceleration fuel shut-off.

Operating Mode 2 - Throttle Positions (see Display Group 004, Field 4)

Displayed (1 = recognized/ enabled, 0 = not)								Signal recognized or function enabled
X								Not relevant/Undefined data
	X							Not relevant/Undefined data
		X						Not relevant/Undefined data
			X					Acceleration enrichment
				X				Full throttle (WOT)
					X			Part load
						X		Closed throttle position
							X	Overrun (decel. fuel shut-off)

Function 08 Display Group 005				
	1	2	3	4
Display	xxxx /min	xx%	x.xx	xx%
Indicated	Engine speed	EVAP Solenoid 1 duty cycle	Lambda factor	Mixture correction factor
Specification	750-1000 idle rpm	none given[005-1]	none given[005-2]	none given[005-3]
Working range	750...6300 rpm			

005-1) No specification given.

005-2) No specification given. Experience indicates that at idle, lambda value will be between 0.70 and 1.30 with the center of the range at 1.00. Value will fluctuate slightly during warm idle.

005-3) No specification given.

Basic Settings (Function 04)

ACC engines do not have provisions for adjustment of idle speed or mixture through **Basic Settings (Function 04)**. Idle speed and mixture are pre-programmed into the ECM and adapted based on engine operating conditions. These adaptive settings are retained in the ECM's memory when the ignition is switched off and become the starting point for subsequent engine operation.

Ignition timing, however, still requires manual adjustment. **Basic Settings (Function 04)** is required to accomplish this operation on the ACC engine.

NOTE
If the ECM is disconnected from the battery during repairs, the learned values are erased and the ECM will revert to the default values allowing the engine to run. The default values may not match the current needs of the engine, which can result in temporary poor performance and driveability. Also, when repairs have been made, such as repair of a vacuum leak, the default values may not match the current needs of the engine.

When an appropriate scan tool is properly connected to the Mono-Motronic ECM on ACC coded engines and set to Function 04 (basic settings), ignition timing will be stabilized for ignition timing checking and/or adjusting purposes.

Basic Settings (Function 04)

Initiating basic settings

Begin the basic settings/ignition timing procedure by observing the following requirements:

Test conditions:

- Engine cold, ignition switched off.
- Connect engine tester VAG 1367 or equivalent.
- Connect scan tool.
- Start engine:
  Vehicle stationary, engine at idle, automatic transmission in P or N, handbrake on.
- Engine oil temperature at least 80°C (176°F).
- All electrical consumers switched off
  (daytime running lights (DRLs) can remain on).
- Air conditioning switched off.

Initiate Basic Settings:

- From the Function Menu select:
  04 Basic Settings
- From the Start Basic Settings display, input or select: display group 000 (or 00 if applicable)
- Disregard information appearing on scan tool display.
- Observe ignition timing on engine tester:
  Specification:
  checking. . . . . 4° - 8°BTDC
  adjusting . . . . 5° - 7°BTDC
- Adjust timing and re-test as required.

```
Output Diagnostic Test Mode          →
Throttle Position Actuator - V60
MONO 11
CODING 01
```

OUTPUT DIAGNOSTIC TEST MODE (FUNCTION 03)

When Function 03 is selected, the scan tool signals the ECM to operate certain electrical components in a pre-determined sequence. The output diagnostic test mode can only be used when the ignition is switched on, and the engine is **not** running.

The following is a list of components checked during the output diagnostic test mode and the order in which they are tested:

- Throttle Position (TP) Actuator (V60)
- Early Fuel Evaporation (EFE) Relay (J81)
- Evaporative Emission (EVAP) Canister Purge Regulator Valve (N80)

Be sure the Throttle Position (TP) Sensor is functioning properly. Also note that engine temperature is not a critical factor for this function.

After the scan tool has been connected and Component Checking (Function 03) selected, proceed with the test as indicated on the scan tool noting the following points:

1. **Throttle Position (TP) Actuator (V60)** – The TP Actuator plunger will move to the rest position (fully pulled in) and remain there when the test is first initiated. Advancing the test will cause the actuator to move the plunger in and out continuously until the program is advanced further.

2. **Early Fuel Evaporation (EFE) Relay (J81)** – The EFE Relay will be switched on and off. The relay is located inside the vehicle near the fuse/relay panel and the resulting noise can be heard in the passenger compartment near the pedals.

3. **Evaporative Emission (EVAP) Canister Purge Regulator Valve (N80)** – The EVAP Canister Purge regulator Valve will be switched off and on (opened and closed). The resulting noise is faint and difficult to hear, but can also usually be felt. Advance the program with the right arrow button (-->).

NOTE
The Output Diagnostic Test Mode can also be helpful in diagnosing mechanical malfunctions as well. If, for example, an EVAP Canister Purge Regulator Valve was suspected of a malfunction, the hoses could be disconnected and the ODTM run while blowing through the valve. Similar tests can be devised with other components.

Code Control Module (Function 07)

Control module coding by means of the scan tool is not a supported function with Mono-Motronic ECMs in ACC coded engines. Coding information does appear, however, in Function 01 (control unit versions). ECM coding is generally accomplished through the use of special coding wires in the ECM wiring harness. Codes are used to identify the transmission type only. Correct ECM is determined by the Vehicle Identification Number (VIN).

NOTE
Part numbers can change within the Volkswagen Parts system for several reasons and are not, therefore, listed here. Always consult with your Volkswagen Parts Department or aftermarket parts specialist for the latest parts information.

Component and Signal Overview, ACC Engine

ACC engines use the Bosch Mono-Motronic engine management system. Signals from sensors and other input sources are processed by the ECM. Signals to control the engine are sent to actuators along with engine information needed by other systems or functions. **Table a** lists the Mono-Motronic system component and signal overview.

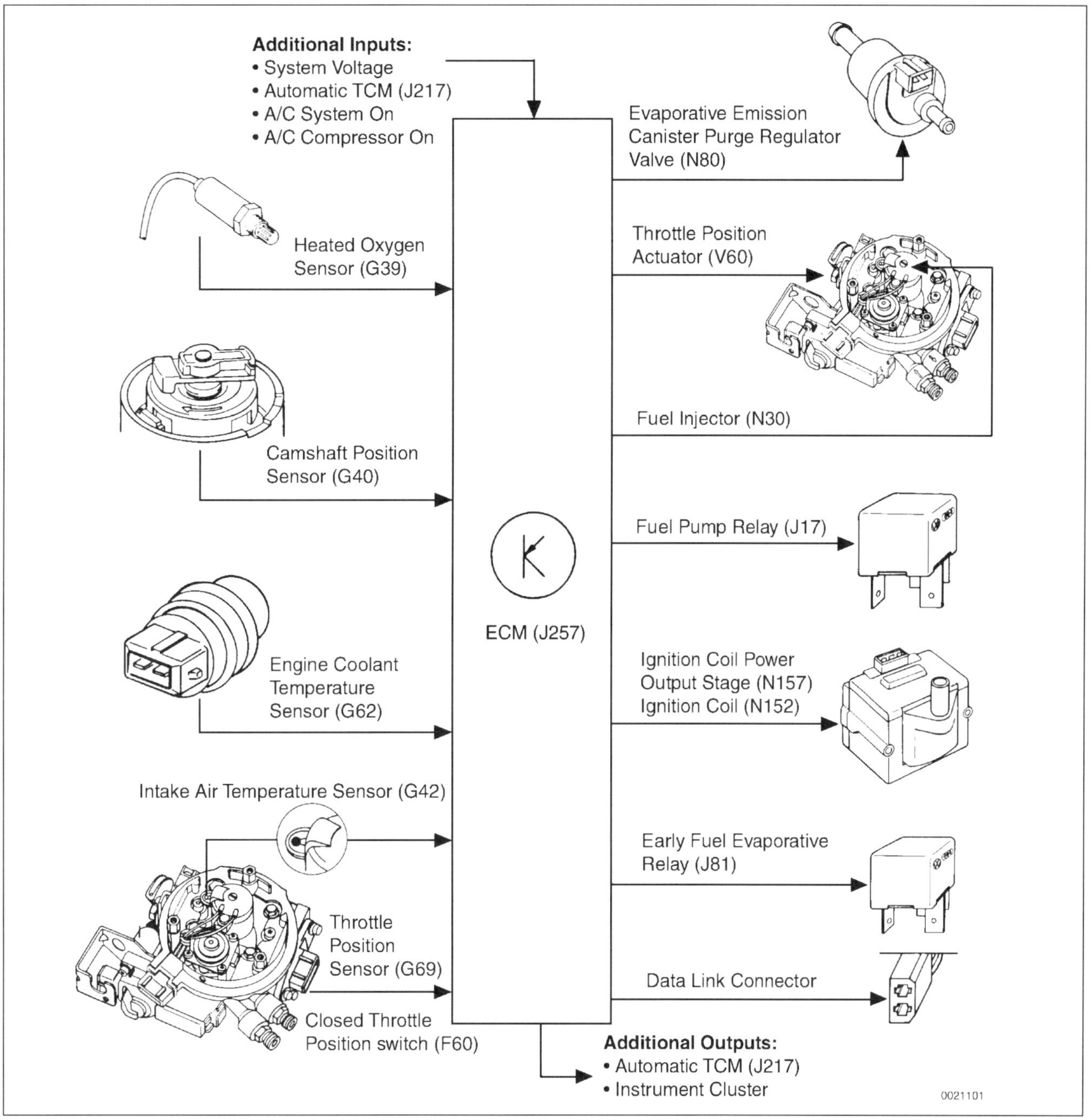

Component and Signal Overview, ACC Engine

Component and Signal Overview (ACC)

Bosch® Mono-Motronic	
Fuel injection	Throttle Body Fuel Injection (TBI) with Lambda (Oxygen Sensor) Control, OBD-I
Fuel delivery	Tank-mounted 2-stage electric fuel pump, load-sensing mechanical pressure regulator
Ignition system	Distributor, with power output stage and ignition coil, ECM controlled
Emission control	3-Way catalytic converter, evaporative emissions with carbon canister, positive crankcase ventilation,
Diagnostics	On-Board Diagnostics via scan tool, Rapid data transfer, Non-volatile memory
Control Module	Mono-Motronic Engine Control Module (ECM) (J257), 45-pin
Sensors	Camshaft Position (CMP) Sensor (G40)
	Throttle Position (TP) Sensor (G69)[1]
	Closed Throttle Position (CTP) Switch (F60)
	Heated Oxygen Sensor (H2OS) (G39)
	Engine Coolant Temperature (ECT) Sensor (G62)
	Intake Air Temperature (IAT) Sensor (G42)
Input signals	Battery voltage
	Air conditioner, system on
	Air conditioner, compressor on
	Automatic Transmission Control Module (TCM) (J217)
Actuators	Throttle Position (TP) Actuator (V60)
	Evaporative Emission (EVAP) Canister Purge Regulator Valve (N80)
	Fuel Injector (N30)
	Ignition Coil Power Output Stage (N157), and Ignition Coil (N152)
	Fuel Pump (FP) Relay (J17), and Fuel Pump (FP) (G6)
	Early Fuel Evaporation (EFE) Relay (J81), Early Fuel Evaporation (EFE) Heating Element (N51)
Output signals	Engine speed (rpm)
	Automatic Transmission Control Module (TCM) (J217)

[1] Vehicles with automatic transmissions use separate TP Sensors combined in a single housing.

TECHNICAL DATA

Technical data is compiled from several Volkswagen publications. In some instances, the information from these sources differed slightly. In these cases, the most current specifications are listed.

ACC (Golf 1993-97)	
Type	4-cylinder in-line, gasoline fuel
Construction	Cast iron block, aluminum 2V cylinder head, belt driven single overhead camshaft
Displacement	1.8 Liters (1781 cc), (109 cid)
Horsepower	90 hp (66 Kw) @ 5,500 rpm
Torque	107 lb-ft (145 Nm) @ 2,500 rpm
Bore	81.0 mm
Stroke	86.4 mm
Compression ratio	9.0:1
Firing order	1-3-4-2
Management	Mono-Motronic

Notes

Engine Code ACU

General

The vehicles listed below are equipped with engine code **ACU**. This engine uses Volkswagen's **Digifant** engine management system. The displacement of this inline 5-cylinder engine is 2.5 liters.

The ACU engine is the only available powerplant in USA-specification Eurovans. Most Canadian-specification Eurovans also use this engine.

Engine Code ACU Vehicles

Engine Code ACU	Model Years
Eurovan Winnebago Camper	1995
Eurovan Winnebago Rialta	1995

◄ Winnebago Rialta motorhome is built on a Eurovan chassis in Forest City, Iowa, USA. This version uses the 5-cylinder ACU engine. Later model years use a version of the VR-6 engine.

Scan tool, connecting

The scan tool is connected through the DLC (Data Link Connector). The location and type of DLC is the same for both model years.

◄ **Eurovan Winnebago Camper and Rialta, 1995**: Scan tool DLC (Data Link Connector) can be accessed after removal of parcel shelf. Release catch button (**arrow**), pull shelf out from top and lift out.

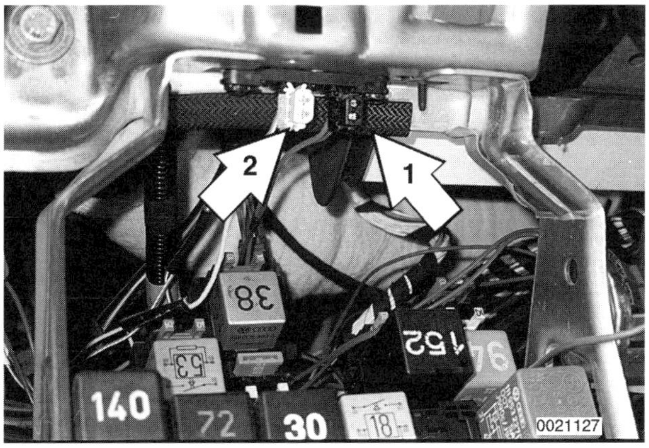

◀ **Eurovan Winnebago Camper and Rialta, 1995**: DLC is located at lower left side of steering column near fuse/relay panel. Black connector (**arrow 1**) on scan tool is connected to black connection on vehicle and provides scan tool power. White connector is connected to white connection on the vehicle (**arrow 2**) for data transfer. Blue connector is not used.

Scan tool, functions available

	Scan Tool Functions Available	Ignition on, not running	Engine at idle	Page
✔	Control unit version (01)	Yes	Yes	Appendix A
✔	Check DTC memory (02)	Yes	No	Appendix A
✔	Output diagnostic test mode (03)	Yes	No	109
✔	Basic settings (04)	No	Yes	106
✔	Erase DTC memory (05)	Yes	No	Appendix A
✔	End output (06)	Yes	Yes	Appendix A
✗	Code control module (07)	No	No	111
✔	Read measuring value blocks (08)	Yes	Yes	100
✗	Read indiv. measuring value blocks (09)	No	No	Appendix A

Read Measuring Value Blocks (Function 08)

READ MEASURING VALUE BLOCKS (FUNCTION 08)

Measuring value blocks are assembled and displayed in sets called display groups. For the ACU engine, display groups are numbered starting with 000 and continuing on up to the ECM's maximum capacity. ACU engine display groups continue past 006, although the information is undefined or unavailable.

```
Read Measuring Value Blocks        HELP
Input Display Group Number          XXX
```

◀ Scan tool display from VAG 1551 requesting Measuring Value Block Display Group information (XXX).

Display group overview, ACU engine

Function 08 Display Group Overview 000[OV-1]										
Display Field	1	2	3	4	5	6	7	8	9	10
	IAT	ECM voltage	ECT	Air quantity	HO2S	HO2S control time counter	HO2S status counter	TPS	injector duration	RPM

OV-1) Some data is not relevant, or is unavailable. This data is identified as n/a.

Function 08 Display Group Overview 001 - 006[OV-2]				
Display Field	1	2	3	4
Display Group 001	RPM	ECT	HO2S	Input signals 1
Display Group 002	RPM	Injector duration	ECM voltage	IAC
Display Group 003	RPM	MAP (load)	TPS ∠	Injector duration
Display Group 004	RPM	MAP (load)	n/a	Input signals 2
Display Group 005	RPM	EVAP	n/a	n/a
Display Group 006	Mixture adaptation	Mixture adaptation	IAC	TPS

OV-2) Some data is not relevant, or is unavailable. This data is identified as n/a. Display Groups above 006 contain data but interpretation is unavailable.

Function 08
Display Group 000

Warm engine, running at idle speed, engine control module in **Read Measuring Value Block** (Function 08)[000-4]

Display Field	Display Fields	Observed range:[000-3]	Corresponds to:
10	RPM	212—186	775 to 1200 rpm
9	Fuel injector duration	4 — 12	2 to 6 mS
8	Throttle Position Sensor	10 — 130	0.2 to 2.5 Volts
7	Heated Oxygen Sensor status counter	0 — 5[000-2]	actual value
6	Heated Oxygen Sensor control time counter	0	actual value
5	Heated Oxygen Sensor signal	230 — 120	0.0 to 0.8 Volts
4	Air quantity	15 — 150	5 to 60%
3	Engine Coolant Temperature[000-1]	2 — 9	80 to 110°C
2	Engine Control Module supply voltage	115 — 155	10.8 to 14.4 Volts
1	Intake air temperature	70 — 15	12 to 65°C

000-1) Lower numbers are hotter.

000-2) The display will show high values when there is no HO2S signal (such as a after a cold engine start). The display value can increase to 255 for certain malfunctions such as an inoperative heater element or defective wiring.

000-3) Overall range of values is 0 - 255.

000-4) Specifications are valid only when Function 04 is displayed. Values will be different for Function 08.

Read Measuring Value Blocks (Function 08)

Function 08 Display Group 001				
	1	2	3	4
Display	xxxx /min	xx.x °C	x.xx V	xxxxxxxx
Indicated	Engine speed	Coolant temperature	HO2S signal voltage	Operating mode 1 Input signals 1
Specification	775-825 idle rpm	none given[001-2]	0.0V -0.80V[001-3]	00000000[001-4]
		Open circuit shows a constant -40°	Coolant temperature over 85°C and after minimum 2 minute idle	See Operating Mode 1 table below
Working range	775...5500 rpm[001-1]	-40°C...141°C (approximately)		

001-1) Approximate maximum governed engine speed.

001-2) No specification given. Experience indicates that at idle, temperature will vary between approximately 86°C and 105°C depending on radiator fan operating cycle. Temperature must rise smoothly during engine warm-up.

001-3) Voltage must fluctuate up and down at idle.

001-4) Display will be either a 1 or a 0. For example, 00010000 indicates CTP switch recognized as open. Multiple functions can occur simultaneously such as 00110001, indicating CTP switch recognized as open, A/C compressor on, and coolant temperature below 80°C.

Operating Mode 1 - Input Signals (see Display Group 001, Field 4)

Displayed: (1 = recognized/enabled 0 = not								Signal recognized or function enabled
X								Not relevant/Undefined data
	X							Automatic transmission signal, TCM to ECM
		X						A/C compressor on
			X					CTP switch open
				X				HO2S control malfunction
					X			Throttle open
						X		Engine speed over 2300 rpm
							X	Engine coolant temperature below 80°C

Function 08 Display Group 002				
	1	2	3	4
Display	xxxx /min	xx.x ms	xx.x V	xx.x °C
Indicated	Engine speed	Fuel injector duration	ECM supply voltage	Intake air temperature
Specification	775-825 idle rpm	none given[002-2]	none given[002-3]	none given[002-4]
				Open circuit shows a constant -40°
Working range	775...5500 rpm[002-1]		6.1...15.5V	-40°C...141°C (approximately)

002-1) As in Display Group 001, field 1.

002-2) No specification given. Experience indicates that at warm idle, fuel injector duration will be approximately 2 to 3 mS.

002-3) No specification given. Maximum Volkswagen system voltage is generally 14.5 V. Experience indicates that ECM supply voltage should be approximate electrical system voltage. Voltages above or below the working range will cause a DTC to be stored although engine will not run at low voltages. Charging system over-voltage malfunctions can be noted here.

002-4) No specification given. Experience indicates that air temperature and coolant temperature will be approximately the same when a cold engine is first started. Temperature will rise slightly during engine warm-up. Intake air temperature is usually warmer than ambient air temperature and more closely approximates intake manifold temperature.

Function 08 Display Group 003				
	1	2	3	4
Display	xxxx /min	xx%	x.x ∠°	xx%
Indicated	Engine speed	Engine load signal	Throttle valve angle	IAC valve opening
Specification	775-825 idle rpm	20%-40%[003-2]	0-5 ∠° CTP 80-90 ∠° WOT[003-3]	0-35%[003-4]
		At idle		
Working range	775...5500 rpm[003-1]		0...90∠°	

003-1) As in Display Group 001, field 1.

003-2) Signal from MAP sensor (G71) in ECM. Value must fluctuate slightly at idle. Experience indicates values over 90% at idle indicate no vacuum at ECM. Values between 40% and 90% at idle indicate vacuum leaks or heavy engine load. With AC compressor running, value will increase by 10% to 15%

003-3) Signal from TPS (G69). Displayed value must increase/decrease uniformly over the full operating range.

003-4) Specification is at idle with coolant temperature greater than 85°C. Value may fluctuate slightly. Should change substantially under the following conditions: cold engine, A/C switched on, electrical consumers switched on, heavy power steering load, incorrect ignition timing.

Read Measuring Value Blocks (Function 08)

Function 08 Display Group 004				
	1	2	3	4
Display	xxxx /min	xx%	xxx	xxxxxxxx
Indicated	Engine speed	Engine load signal	n/a[004-3]	Operating mode 2 Throttle positions
Specification	775-825 idle rpm	20%-40%[004-2]		00000000[004-4]
		At idle		See Operating Mode 2 table below
Working range	775...5500 rpm[004-1]			

004-1) As in Display Group 001, field 1.

004-2) As in Display Group 003, field 2.

004-3) Data is not relevant, is undefined, or is unsupported by the Factory.

004-4) Display will be either a 1 or a 0. For example, 01000000 indicates idle position recognized. Multiple functions can occur simultaneously such as 11000000 indicating idle position recognized but engine speed sufficient to enable deceleration fuel shut-off.

Operating Mode 2 - Throttle Positions (see Display Group 004, Field 4)

Displayed: (1=recognized/enabled 0=not)								Position recognized or function enabled
X								Overrun
	X							Idle position
		X						Partially open throttle
			X					Full load (WOT)
				X				Not relevant/undefined data
					X			Not relevant/undefined data
						X		Not relevant/undefined data
							X	Not relevant/undefined data

Function 08 Display Group 005				
	1	**2**	**3**	**4**
Display	xxxx /min	xxx%	xxx	xxxxxxxx
Indicated	Engine speed	EVAP canister purge regulator valve duty cycle	n/a[005-3]	n/a[005-3]
Specification	775-825 idle rpm	none given[005-2]		
Working range	775...5500 rpm[005-1]			

005-1) As in Display Group 001, field 1.

005-2) No specification given, value will vary with engine speed and load changes.

005-3) Data is not relevant, is undefined, or is unsupported by the Factory.

Function 08 Display Group 006				
	1	**2**	**3**	**4**
Display	xxx	xxx	x	x
Indicated	Mixture adaptation value - learned	Mixture adaptation value - constant	Idle speed control value - learned[006-3]	TPS memory value (from basic settings Function 04)[006-4]
Specification	88-168[006-1]	88-168[006-2]	8-30	Value varies
Working range	0...255	0...255		

006-1) For values greater than 168, check the following: crankcase for oil dilution, leaking fuel injector(s), fuel return line kinked or blocked, fuel pressure too high.
For values less than 88, check the following: fuel pressure too low, blocked or restricted fuel injector nozzle(s), O2 sensor heater malfunction, unmeasured air (air leaks) in intake system, exhaust leaks, particularly between cylinder head and HO2S.

006-2) Same as above. Initiate basic settings procedure (Function 04) after repairs.

006-3) For values greater than 30, check the following: IAC valve, IAC valve wiring for open circuit.
For values less than 8, check the following: unmeasured air (air leaks) in intake system

006-3) Value is “learned” during basic settings, Function 04.

Basic Settings (Function 04)

ACU engines do not have provisions for adjustment of idle speed or mixture. These operating parameters are pre-programmed into the ECM as default or baseline values. During engine operation, data is received from the various sensors and corrections are made as required. These corrections are retained in the ECM's memory when the ignition is switched off and become the starting point for subsequent engine operation.

These retained values are said to be "learned" values and can change or adapt as often as needed. Ignition timing, however, still requires manual adjustment.

In both situations, the ECM will start from the default or baseline settings and re-learn and adapt to current operating conditions. This process can, however, take some time.

When an appropriate scan tool is properly connected to the ECM on ACU coded engines and set to Function 04 (basic settings), the ECM can be made to adapt to current operating conditions in several minutes rather than a longer period of time.

Adjustment of engine settings through the use of Function 04 (basic settings) is similar to Eurovans with AAF engines.

When Function 04 (basic settings) is selected, the scan tool instructs the ECM to:

- Stabilize ignition timing
- Stabilize idle speed
- Disable the EVAP system
- Match the ECM to the engine components

Adjustment of basic settings requires the connection of several other pieces of test equipment in addition to a scan tool such as the VAG 1551.

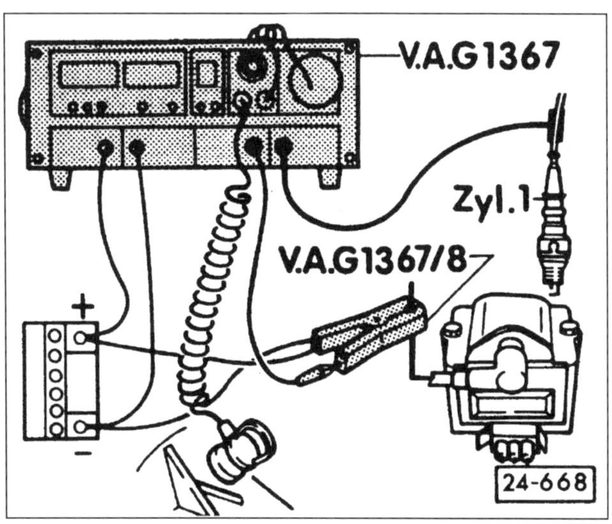

An engine tester such as the VAG 1367 must be connected to the engine to measure ignition timing and engine speed, while an exhaust gas analyzer must be attached to the CO pick-up or sampling tube located ahead of the catalytic converter.

0021108

◄ An exhaust gas analyzer, such as this 4-Gas unit manufactured by Sun, is required to check and/or adjust carbon monoxide (CO) content.

Initiating basic settings

Begin the basic settings procedure by observing the following requirements:

Test conditions 1:

- Engine cold, ignition switched off.
- Connect engine tester VAG 1367 or equivalent.
- Connect CO tester to sampling tube insuring an airtight connect.

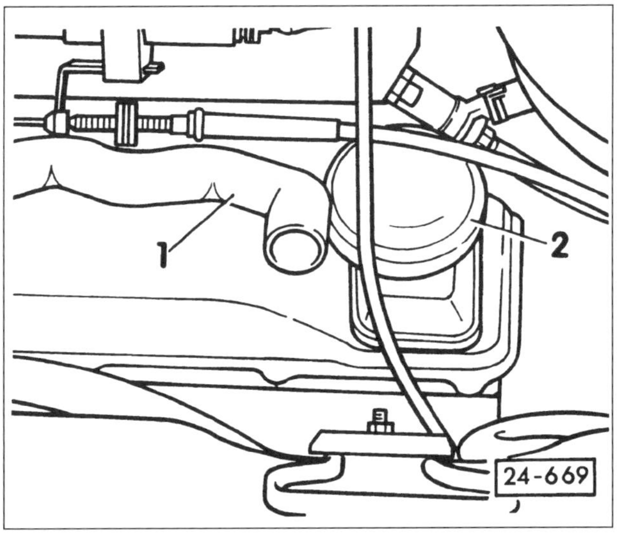

◄ Disconnect crankcase breather hose (**1**) from PCV Valve (**2**) on cylinder head cover and position it so that only fresh air is drawn in.

- Connect scan tool.

Test conditions 2:

- Start engine.
- Vehicle stationary, engine at idle, automatic transmission in P or N.
- Engine oil temperature at least 80°C (176°F).
- All electrical consumers switched off (do not take measurements while radiator cooling fan is running).
- Air conditioning switched off.
- Throttle cable adjusted properly.
- TP sensor adjusted properly at closed throttle position.
- Exhaust system free from leaks.

Basic Settings (Function 04)

Initiate Basic Settings:

- From the initial Menu select: 1 Rapid Data.
- From the address word Menu select: 01 Engine Electronics.
- Advance to the Function Menu when the ECM responds with the version information.
- From the Function Menu select:
  02 Check DTC memory.
  Read DTCs and return to the Function Menu.
  (correct and erase any DTCs recorded)
- From the Function Menu select: 04 Basic Settings

Start Basic Setting	HELP
Input Display Group Number	XXX

◄ From the Start Basic Settings display, input: display group 001 (or 01 if applicable).

System in Basic Setting			001
800/min	86°C	0.325V	00000000

◄ Observe values in display fields:
Field 1 . . . . N/A
Field 2 . . . . 85°C (minimum)
Field 3 . . . . N/A
Field 4 00000000

- When above values are reached, accelerate engine to between 2,000 and 2,500 rpm and read ignition timing on engine tester (not scan tool).

Ignition timing
Checking . . . . .3° - 8° BTDC (fluctuating)
Adjusting . . . . 5° - 7° BTDC

- Adjust timing and re-test as required.
- Continue with Basic Settings.
- Observe values in scan tool display fields:
  Field 1 . . . . .775 /min to 825 /min
  Field 2 . . . . 85°C (minimum)
  Field 3 . . . . N/A
  Field 4 00000000
- Observe engine operating data on engine tester and exhaust gas analyzer (not scan tool) at idle:

Idle speed . . . . .775 to 825 rpm
CO . . . . 0.3% to 1.2%

- If operating data is within the listed specifications and radiator coolant fan is not running, exit basic settings.
- From the Function Menu select:
  06 End Output.
- Switch off ignition.
- Disconnect all test equipment, basic settings are complete.

If operating data on exhaust gas analyzer and/or engine tester does not fall within listed specification, determine the malfunction and re-test. Idle speed and CO content are not adjustable.

OUTPUT DIAGNOSTIC TEST MODE (FUNCTION 03)

Troubleshooting electrical faults in Eurovans with Digifant ACU engines is facilitated by the Output Diagnostic Test Mode (Function 03). When this function is activated, the scan tool instructs the ECM to operate certain electrical components in a pre-determined sequence. The output diagnostic test mode can only be used when the ignition is switched on, but the engine is not running.

The following is a list of components checked during the output diagnostic test mode and the order in which they are tested:

- Fuel Pump (FP) Relay (J17)
- Idle Air Control Valve (IAC) (N71)
- Evaporative Emission (EVAP) Canister Purge Regulator Valve (N80)
- Secondary AIr Injection (AIR) Pump Relay (J299)[1]
- Exhaust Gas Recirculation (EGR) Vacuum Regulator Solenoid Valve (N18)[1]

Note:

[1] Only applicable on some vehicles with 6-pin fuel rail wiring harness connector.

```
Rapid data transfer                Q
03 - Output Diagnostic Test Mode
```

◀ Eurovan Digifant display for Function 03 as shown on a VAG 1551 showing first Output Diagnostic Mode test.

Testing with Function 03

Testing Digifant equipped engines with a scan tool in Function 03 is a relatively straight forward operation.

Some ECMs will only allow the output diagnostic tests to be run once per engine start. If this is the case, simply start the engine and allow it to run for a short time before re-testing.

```
Output Diagnostic Test Mode       -->
Fuel Pump Relay - J17
```

◀ After the scan tool has been connected and Function 03 selected, proceed with the test as indicated on the scan tool noting the following points:

1. **Fuel Pump (FP) Relay (J17)** - The FP relay in the fuse/relay panel will be switched on and off with an audible clicking sound. The fuel pump should also be heard to run. Advance the program with the right arrow button (-->).

Output Diagnostic Test Mode (Function 03)

```
Output Diagnostic Test Mode

Fuel Pump Relay-J17
Idle Air Control Valve-N71
EVAP Canister Purge Regulator Valve-N80
Secondary Air Injection Pump Relay-J299
EGR Vacuum Regulator Solenoid Valve-N18
```

2. **Idle Air Control (IAC) Valve (N71)** – The IAC Valve will be operated through a range of positions with a buzzing or humming sound. The vibrations from operation can also be felt. Advance the program with the right arrow button (-->).

3. **Evaporative Emission (EVAP) Canister Purge Regulator Valve (N80)** – The EVAP Canister Purge regulator Valve will be switched off and on (opened and closed). The resulting noise is a deep thumping sound that can be difficult to hear, but can be felt. Advance the program with the right arrow button (-->).

4. **Secondary Air Injection (AIR) Pump Relay (J299)** – The AIR Pump Relay in the fuse/relay panel will be switched on and off with an audible clicking sound. The AIR Solenoid Valve (N112) will be switched off and on (opened and closed), also with an audible clicking sound. The AIR Pump Motor (V101) should also be heard to run in short pulses. Advance the program with the right arrow button (-->).

5. **Exhaust Gas Recirculation (EGR) Vacuum Regulator Solenoid Valve (N80)** – The EGR Vacuum Regulator Solenoid Valve will be switched on and off with an audible clicking sound. Advance the program with the right arrow button (-->).

◄ When the VAG 1551 printer is switched on, the tape will be printed with all of the tests in sequence.

The Output Diagnostic Test Mode is helpful in checking the electrical operation of a given component. It can also be helpful in diagnosing mechanical malfunctions as well. If, for example, an (EVAP) Canister Purge Regulator Valve was suspected of a malfunction, the hoses could be disconnected and the Output Diagnostic Test Mode run while blowing through the valve. This would help determine if it worked properly. Similar tests can be devised with many of the other components.

In the event of a component failing to operate, the component and the wiring should be checked for continuity, open circuits, and short circuits, including short circuits to ground. Always consult the appropriate wiring diagram.

Code Control Module (Function 07)

Control module coding by means of the scan tool is not a supported function with Eurovan Camper and Rialta Digifant ECMs in ACU coded engines. Coding information may appear, however, in Function 01 (control unit versions), but has no apparent influence on engine operation. Correct ECM operation is accomplished by different part number ECMs installed to match the equipment installed in the vehicle. Different ECMs are used for vehicles with the following equipment and market variations

- USA/Canada with manual transmission up to chassis SH071871 (January 1995 production).
- USA/Canada with manual transmission from chassis SH071872 (January 1995 production).
- USA/Canada with automatic transmission up to chassis SH071871 (January 1995 production)
- USA/Canada with automatic transmission from chassis SH071872 (January 1995 production)

Part numbers can change within the Volkswagen Parts system for several reasons and are not, therefore, listed here.

NOTE
Always consult with your Volkswagen Parts Department or aftermarket parts specialist for the latest parts information.

Component and Signal Overview, ACU Engine

ACU engines use a version of the Volkswagen developed Digifant engine management system that is slightly different from the version found in 1992 and 1993 Eurovans. The compression ratio has been increased from 8.5:1 to 10:1, but output remains the same.

Several new components have been added to reduced emissions resulting in the designation of Tier 1 for emissions purposes.

Signals from sensors and other input sources are processed by the ECM. Signals to control the engine are sent to actuators along with engine information needed by other systems or functions.

Component and Signal Overview, ACU Engine

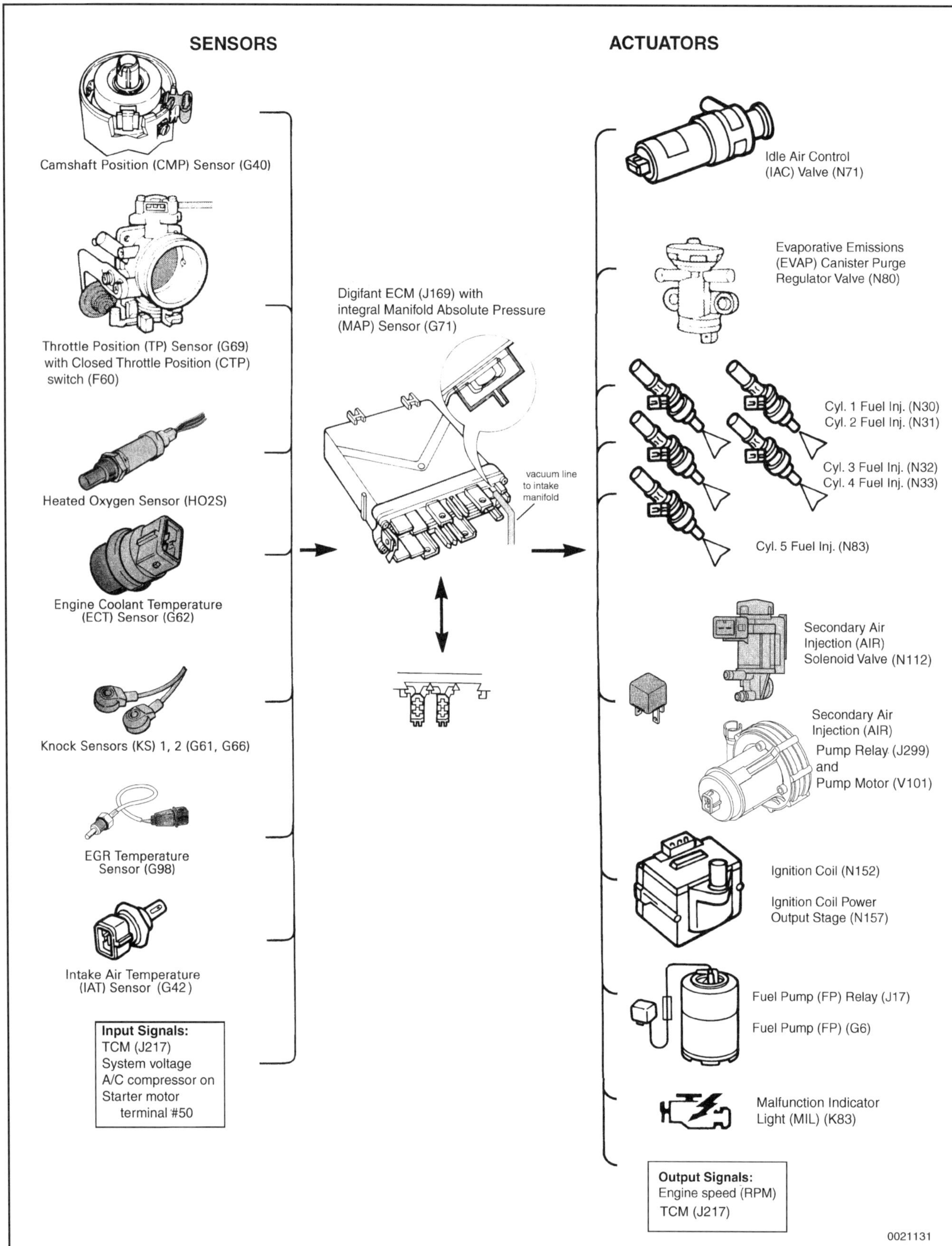

Component and Signal Overview (ACU)

Volkswagen Digifant, 5-cylinder	
Fuel injection	Non-sequential (simultaneous) Multi-Point Fuel Injection with Lambda (Oxygen Sensor) Control, OBD-I, Tier-1
Fuel delivery	Tank-mounted 2-stage electric fuel pump, load-sensing mechanical pressure regulator
Ignition system	Distributor, power output stage and ignition coil, dual knock sensors, ECM controlled
Emission control	3-Way (TWC) catalytic converter, evaporative emissions with carbon canister, positive crankcase ventilation
Diagnostics	On-Board Diagnostics via scan tool, Rapid data transfer, Non-volatile memory
Control Module	Single 68-pin Digifant Engine Control Module (ECM) (J169) with integral Manifold Absolute Pressure (MAP) Sensor (G71), supplied by Digifant ECM Power Supply Relay (J176)
Sensors	Camshaft Position (CMP) Sensor (G40)
	Throttle Position (TP) Sensor (G69)[1]
	Closed Throttle Position (CTP) Switch (F60)
	Heated Oxygen Sensor (H2OS) (G39)
	Engine Coolant Temperature (ECT) Sensor (G62)
	Intake Air Temperature (IAT) Sensor (G42)
	Exhaust Gas Recirculation (EGR) Temperature Sensor (G98)
	Knock Sensor (KS) I (G61)
	Knock Sensor (KS) II (G66)
Input signals	System voltage
	Air conditioner, compressor on
	Automatic Transmission Control Module (TCM) (J217)
	Starter motor- terminal 50
Actuators	Idle Air Control (IAC) Valve (N71)
	Evaporative Emission (EVAP) Canister Purge Regulator Valve (N80)
	Fuel Injectors: Cylinder 1 (N30), Cylinder 2 (N31), Cylinder 3 (N32), Cylinder 4 (N33), Cylinder 5 (N83)
	Ignition Coil Power Output Stage (N157), and Ignition Coil (N152)
	Fuel Pump (FP) Relay (J17), and Transfer Fuel Pump (FP) (G23)
	Secondary Air Injection (AIR) Pump Relay (J299), Secondary Air Injection (AIR) Solenoid Valve (N112), and Secondary Air Injection (AIR) Pump Motor (V101)
	Malfunction Indicator Light (MIL)[2] (K83)
Output signals	Engine speed (rpm)
	Automatic Transmission Control Module (TCM) (J217)

[1] Vehicles with automatic transmissions use separate TP Sensors for each system.
[2] MIL only functional on vehicles intended for California market area.

Notes

TECHNICAL DATA

Technical data is compiled from several Volkswagen publications. In some instances, the information from these sources differed slightly. In these cases, the most current specifications are listed.

ACU (Eurovan Winnebago)	**Technical Data**
Type	5-cylinder in-line (R5), gasoline fuel
Construction	Cast iron block, aluminum 2V cylinder head, belt driven single overhead camshaft
Displacement	2.5 Liters (2459 cc), (150 cid)
Horsepower	109 hp (81 Kw) @ 4500 rpm
Torque	140 lb-ft (190 Nm) @ 2200 rpm (144 lb-ft (195 Nm) with premium fuel)
Bore	81.0 mm
Stroke	95.5 mm
Compression ratio	10.0:1
Firing order	1-2-4-5-3
Management	Digifant, Tier 1

Engine Code
1Z

General

Vehicles listed below are equipped with engine code **1Z**. This diesel engine uses the **TDI** (**T**urbo-**D**irect **I**njection) engine management system. Features of this 1.9 liter inline 4-cylinder engine include a turbo-charger with inter-cooler and electronic throttle (drive-by-wire) technology.

Engine Code 1Z Vehicles

Engine Code 1Z	Model Years
Passat	1996

Scan tool, connecting

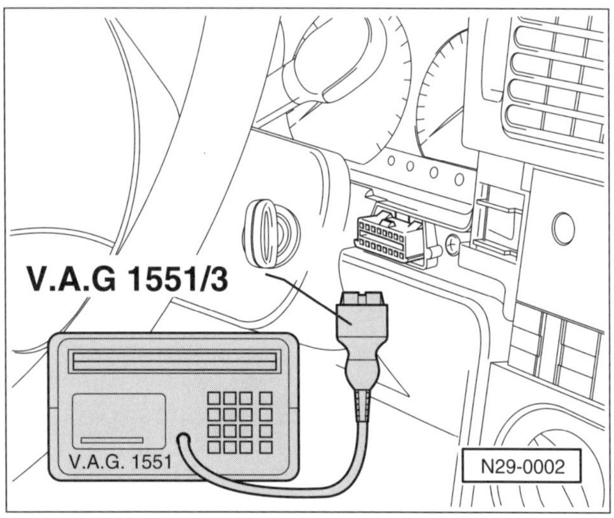

The scan tool is connected through the DLC (Data Link Connector) in the instrument panel, to right side of steering column behind cover.

Scan tool, functions available

	Scan Tool Functions Available	Ignition on, not running	Engine at idle	Page
✔	Control unit version (01)	Yes	Yes	Appendix A
✔	Check DTC memory (02)	Yes	Yes	Appendix A
✔	Output diagnostic test mode (03)	Yes	Yes	136
✔	Basic settings (04)	No	Yes	131
✔	Erase DTC memory (05)	Yes	Yes	Appendix A
✔	End output (06)	Yes	Yes	Appendix A
✗	Code control module (07)	No	No	139
✔	Read measuring value blocks (08)	Yes	Yes	117
✗	Read indiv. measuring value blocks (09)	No	No	Appendix A

Read Measuring Value Blocks (Function 08)

```
Read Measuring Value Blocks     HELP
Input Display Group Number       XXX
```

◀ Measuring value blocks are assembled and displayed in sets called display groups. For the 1Z engine, display groups start with 000 and continue with 001 on up to 025. Some display groups within this range however, contain no data or contain data that is undefined or unavailable.

Display group overview, 1Z engine

Engine Code 1Z, Display Group Overview 000[OV-1]										
Display Field	**1**	**2**	**3**	**4**	**5**	**6**	**7**	**8**	**9**	**10**
	RPM	Cold start injection	TPS	Injection quantity	Manifold pressure (boost)	Barometric pressure (atmospheric)	ECT	IAT	Fuel temperature	Air mass

OV-1) Some data is not relevant or is unavailable.

Function 08 Display Group Overview 001 - 025[OV-2]				
Display Field	**1**	**2**	**3**	**4**
Display Group 001 Injection quantity	RPM	Injection quantity	MPDS voltage	ECT
Display Group 002 Throttle position	RPM	TPS	Operating mode 1 (A/C input signals)	ECT
Display Group 003 EGR	RPM	Air mass inducted (specified)	Air mass inducted (actual)	EGR
Display Group 004 Cold start injection timing	RPM	Cold start injection timing (specified)	Cold start injection timing (actual)	Cold start injection duty cycle
Display Group 005 Start conditions	RPM	Start quantity	Cold start injection timing (actual)	ECT
Display Group 006 Input signals	VSS	Operating mode 2 (pedal position input signals)	Operating mode 3 (cruise control input signals)	System status (cruise control)
Display Group 007 Temperatures	Fuel temperature	n/a	IAT	ECT
Display Group 008 Injection quantity limits 1	RPM	Injection quantity (TPS specified)	Injection quantity limit (torque map)	Injection quantity limit (opacity [smoke] map)

Continued

1Z

Read Measuring Value Blocks (Function 08)

Function 08
Display Group Overview 001 - 025[OV-2] (Continued)

Display Field	1	2	3	4
Display Group 009 Injection quantity limits 2	RPM	Injection quantity (cruise control specified)	Injection quantity limit (automatic trans. torque limit)	MPDS voltage
Display Group 010 Air quantities	Air mass inducted (actual)	Barometric pressure	Manifold pressure	TPS
Display Group 011 Boost pressure control	RPM	Manifold pressure (boost pressure - specified)	Manifold pressure (boost pressure - actual)	Wastegate Bypass Regulator Valve
Display Group 012 Ignition (glow plug) system	n/a	Glow plug time	ECM voltage	ECT
Display Group 013 Idle speed smooth running controls	Injection quantity cylinder #4 (deviation from cylinder #3)	Injection quantity cylinder #2 (deviation from cylinder #3)	Injection quantity cylinder #1 (deviation from cylinder #3)	n/a
Display Group 014 through **Display Group 016**	n/a	n/a	n/a	n/a
Display Group 017 Supplemental fuel metering	Catalyst temperature 2	Catalyst temperature 1	Operating mode 4 (catalyst input signals)	Catalyst temperature difference value
Display Group 018 through **Display Group 025**	n/a	n/a	n/a	n/a

OV-2) Some data is not relevant or is unavailable. This data is identified as n/a.

Function 08
Display Group 000

Engine running at idle speed, coolant temperature above 80°C (176°F).

Display field	Display Fields	Range:[000-1]	Remarks:
10	Air mass	69 - 111[000-2]	Requires EGR operation
9	Fuel temperature	91 - 201[000-3]	—
8	Intake air temperature	50 - 182[000-4]	—
7	Engine coolant temperature	35 - 80[000-5]	Above 80, engine too cold
6	Barometric pressure (atmospheric)	__[000-6]	—
5	Manifold pressure (boost)	__[000-7]	—
4	Injection quantity	11 - 45[000-8]	—
3	Throttle position	0[000-9]	—
2	Cold start injection	0 - 88[000-10]	—
1	Engine speed (RPM)	41 - 45 (m/t) 39 - 43 (a/t)[000-11]	m/t = manual trans. a/t = auto. trans.

000-1) Overall range of values is 0 - 255.

000-2) Values greater than 111 or less than 69, see Display group 003. EGR is automatically switched off after 10 minutes idling; briefly increase engine speed to reset.

000-3) Values greater than 201 or less than 91, see Display group 007.

000-4) Values greater than 182 or less than 50, see Display group 007.

000-5) Lower numbers are hotter. Temperature must rise (value will decrease) smoothly during engine warm-up. See Display group 007.

000-6) No specification available in this display field. Value depends on altitude and local weather conditions.

000-7) No specification available in this display field.

000-8) Values greater than 45 or less than 11, see Display group 001.

000-9) Values above 0, see Display group 002.

000-10) Values above 88, see Display group 004.

000-11) Either transmission in neutral or park.

Read Measuring Value Blocks (Function 08)

Function 08
Display Group 000

Test driven in 3rd gear, at WIDE open Throttle (WOT), coolant temperature above 80°C (176°F).

Display Fields		Range:[000-1]	Remarks:
10	**Air mass**	225 - 255[000-2]	Requires EGR operation
9	**Fuel temperature**	91 - 201[000-3]	—
8	**Intake air temperature**	50 - 182[000-4]	—
7	**Engine coolant temperature**	35 - 80[000-5]	Above 80, engine too cold
6	**Barometric pressure (atmospheric)**	__[000-6]	—
5	**Manifold pressure (boost)**	165 - 189[000-7]	—
4	**Injection quantity**	174 - 180[000-8]	—
3	**Throttle position**	255[000-9]	—
2	**Cold start injection**	138 - 188 (m/t) 150 - 202 (a/t)[000-11]	m/t = manual trans. a/t =auto. trans.
1	Engine speed (RPM)	136 - 150[000-11]	Above 150, engine speed too high

000-1) Overall range of values is 0 - 255.

000-2) Values less than 225, see Display group 010.

000-3) Values greater than 201 or less than 91, see Display group 007.

000-4) Values greater than 182 or less than 50, see Display group 007.

000-5) Lower numbers are hotter. See Display group 007.

000-6) No specification available in this display field. Value depends on altitude and local weather conditions.

000-7) Values greater than 238 or less than 165, see Display group 011

000-8) Values below 174, see Display group 008. Constantly displayed 125 indicates emergency running mode, read DTCs.

000-9) Values below 255, not Wide Open Throttle, see Display group 004.

000-10) Values below 138 (150 a/t), see Display group 007.

000-11) Transmission in 3rd gear (a/t manually selected).

Function 08 Display Group 001				
Engine running at idle, coolant temperature above 176°F (80°C).				
	1	**2**	**3**	**4**
Display	xxxx /min	xx.x mg/H	x.xxx V	xx.x °C
Indicated	Engine speed	Injection quantity	Modulating Piston Displacement Sensor (G149) voltage	Coolant temperature
Specification	861 – 945 (m/t) 819 – 903 (a/t) idle rpm	2.2 – 9 mg/H[001-2]	1.16 – 1.54 V[001-3]	80 – 110°C[001-4]
Working range	819 – 4650 rpm[001-1]		0.0 – 5.0 V	-40 to +141°C

001-1) Approximate maximum governed rpm.

001-2) Values below 2.2 mg/H indicate injection pump too rich or restricted fuel return lines. Values above 9.0 mg/H indicate injection pump too lean or restricted fuel feed lines; also due to engine too cold during test.

001-3) Values below 1.16 V indicate injection pump too rich or restricted fuel return lines. Values above 1.54 V indicate injection pump too lean or restricted fuel feed lines; also due to engine too cold during test.

001-4) Coolant temperature must be between 80 - 110°C for other values in this group to be valid. Temperature must rise smoothly during engine warm-up. Will default to fuel temperature value in the event of a malfunction.

Read Measuring Value Blocks (Function 08)

Function 08 Display Group 002				
Engine running at idle, coolant temperature above 176°F (80°C).				
	1	**2**	**3**	**4**
Display	xxxx /min	xx.x %	x x x	xx.x °C
Indicated	Engine speed	Throttle position	Operating mode 1 (A/C input signals)	Coolant temperature
Specification	861 - 945 (m/t) 819 - 903 (a/t) idle rpm	0 % [002-1]	varies [002-2] See Operating Mode 1 table below	80 - 110°C [002-3]
Working range	819 – 4650 rpm	0 – 100%		-40 to +141°C

[002-1)] Values between 1 - 100% indicate TPS (G79) malfunction or mis-adjustment or open circuit.

[002-2)] Display will usually be 111 or 010.

[002-3)] Coolant temperature must be between 80 - 110°C for other values in this group to be valid. Temperature must rise smoothly during engine warm-up. Will default to fuel temperature value in the event of a malfunction.

Operating Mode 1 - A/C Input Signals (see Display Group 002, Field 3)

Displayed: (1 = recognized/ enabled 0 = not)			**Signal recognized or function enabled**
X			Air conditioner compressor on
	X		Undefined data (always 1)
		X	Air conditioner system on

Function 08
Display Group 003

Engine running at idle, coolant temperature above 176°F (80°C).

	1	2	3	4
Display	xxxx /min	xxx mg/H	xxx mg/H	xx %
Indicated	Engine speed	Air mass inducted (specified)	Air mass inducted (actual)	Exhaust Gas Recirculation duty cycle
Specification	861 - 945 (m/t) 819 - 903 (a/t) idle rpm	230 - 420 mg/H[003-1]	230 - 370 mg/H[003-2]	10 - 90%[003-3]
Working range	819...4650 rpm			0...100%

003-1) Values above 420 mg/H indicate engine too cold or electrical consumers or air conditioning switched on, (daytime runnings lights on are OK).

003-2) Values below 230 mg/H indicate intake air system leak (unmeasured air) or excessive EGR. Values above 370 mg/H indicate engine too cold, insufficient EGR or MAF Sensor (G70) malfunction.

003-3) Duty cycle sent to EGR Vacuum Regulator Solenoid Valve (N18). EGR is automatically switched off after 10 minutes idling; briefly increase engine speed to reset.

Function 08
Display Group 004

Engine running at idle, coolant temperature above 176°F (80°C).

	1	2	3	4
Display	xxxx /min	x.x° n.OT or x.x° v.OT	x.x° n.OT or x.x° v.OT	xx %
Indicated	Engine speed	Cold start injection timing (specified)	Cold start injection timing (actual)	Cold start injection duty cycle
Specification	861 – 945 (m/t) 819 – 903 (a/t)	3° n.OT - 4° v.OT[004-1]	3° n.OT - 4° v.OT[004-2]	2 – 10%[004-3]
Working range	819 – 4650 rpm			0 – 100%

004-1) Values above 4° v.OT indicate engine too cold.

004-2) Values above 4° v.OT indicate engine too cold, Diesel injection pump basic setting too far advanced, or Cold Start Injector (N108) malfunction. Values below 3° n.OT indicate Diesel injection pump basic setting too far retarded, restriction in Diesel injection cold start injector fuel passage, or Cold Start Injector (N108) malfunction.

004-3) Values above 10% can be normal due to new vehicle or new engine. Values above 10%, if not due to new vehicle/new engine, indicate Diesel injection pump basic setting too far retarded.

Read Measuring Value Blocks (Function 08)

Function 08 Display Group 005				
Engine running at idle, coolant temperature above 176°F (80°C).				
	1	**2**	**3**	**4**
Display	xxxx /min	xx.x mg/H	x.x° n.OT or x.x° v.OT	xx.x °C
Indicated	Engine speed	Start quantity	Cold start injection timing (actual)	Coolant temperature
Specification	861 - 945 (m/t) 819 - 903 (a/t) idle rpm	not available[005-1]	3° n.OT - 4° v.OT[005-2]	80 - 110°C[005-3]
Working range	819 – 4,650 rpm			-40 to +141°C

005-1) No specification available.

005-2) Values above 4° v.OT indicate engine too cold, Diesel injection pump basic setting too far advanced, or Cold Start Injector (N108) malfunction. Values below 3° n.OT indicate Diesel injection pump basic setting too far retarded, restriction in Diesel injection cold start injector fuel passage, or Cold Start Injector (N108) malfunction.

005-3) Coolant temperature must be between 80 - 110°C for other values in this group to be valid. Temperature must rise smoothly during engine warm-up. Will default to fuel temperature value in the event of a malfunction.

Function 08 Display Group 006				
Test driven.				
	1	**2**	**3**	**4**
Display	xxx.x km/h	X X X	XXXX X	XXX
Indicated	Vehicle speed	Operating mode 2 (pedal position input signals)	Operating mode 3 (cruise control input signals)	System status (cruise control)
Specification	Not available	varies[006-2]	varies[006-3]	varies0[06-4]
		See Operating Mode 2 table below	See Operating Mode 3 table below	See Operating Mode 4 table below
Working range	0 – 210 km/h006-1			

006-1) Approximate maximum governed top speed.

006-2) Displayed value will be either a 1 or a 0.

006-3) Displayed valued will be either a 1 or a 0.

006-4) Values are added together in some instances. If value 256 is observed, vehicle is not equipped with cruise control or ECM has not been coded to enable cruise control operation. Contact an Authorized Volkswagen Dealer for current codes and procedures.

Operating Mode 2 - Pedal Position Input Signals (see Display Group 006, Field 2)

Displayed: (1= recognized/enabled 0 = not)					Signal recognized or function enabled
X					Brake light switch (F) closed (pedal operated)
		X			Brake vacuum vent valve switch (F47) opened (pedal operated)
				X	Clutch vacuum vent valve switch (F36) opened (pedal operated)

Operating Mode 3 - Cruise Control Input Signals (see Display Group 006, Field 3)

Displayed: (1 = recognized/ enabled 0 = not)						Signal recognized or function enabled
X						Clutch vacuum vent valve switch (F36) opened (pedal operated)
	X					Brake vacuum vent valve switch (F47) opened (pedal operated)
		X				Cruise control switch (E45) ***RESUME*** contact closed
			X			Cruise control switch (E45) ***SET*** contact closed
					X	Cruise control switch (E45) ***ON*** contact closed

System Status - Cruise Control (see Display Group 006, Field 4)

Displayed	Signal recognized or function enabled
0	Cruise control off
1	Cruise control on
2	Accelerating (with ***SET*** button)
4	Decelerating (not observed to be active with this type of system)
8	***RESUME*** contact closed (after having been set)
16	Brake pedal operated (in addition to cruise control on, 1 + 16 = 17)
32	Hold (maintain) speed
64	Not used (undefined data)
128	Not used (undefined data)
256	Cruise control blocked (ECM not coded to enabled operation)

Read Measuring Value Blocks (Function 08)

Function 08
Display Group 007

Ignition switched on, engine cold and not running.

	1	2	3	4
Display	xx.x °C		xx.x °C	xx.x °C
Indicated	Fuel temperature	Not used, no display	Intake air temperature	Coolant temperature
Specification	ambient[007-1]		ambient[007-2]	ambient[007-3]
	Values in display fields 1, 3,& 4 must all be approximately equal when cold		Values in display fields 1, 3,& 4 must all be approximately equal when cold	Values in display fields 1, 3,& 4 must all be approximately equal when cold
Working range	-40 to +141°C		-40 to +141°C	-40 to +141°C

007-1) Continuous value of approximately -5.6°C (21.9°F) is default and indicates short circuit or Fuel Temperature Sensor malfunction.

007-2) Continuous value of approximately 19°C (66.2°F) is default and indicates Intake Air Temperature Sensor malfunction.

007-3) Large deviation from other values on a cold engine indicates short circuit or Coolant Temperature Sensor malfunction.

Function 08
Display Group 008

Test driven in 3rd gear (a/t manually selected), at Wide Open Throttle (WOT), coolant temperature above 176°F (80°C); values are only valid at 3000 RPM (+/– 150 RPM). Do not activate kickdown on automatic transmission.

	1	2	3	4
Display	xxxx /min	xx.x mg/H	xx.x mg/H	xx.x mg/H
Indicated	Engine speed	Injection quantity (TPS specified)	Injection quantity (torque map)	Injection quantity (opacity [smoke] map)
Specification	3000 rpm	36 - 42 mg/H[008-1]	34.8 - 35.8 mg/H[008-2]	35 - 38 mg/H[008-3]
Working range	2850 - 3150 rpm			

008-1) Values below 36 mg/H indicate not WOT or mis-adjusted or malfunctioning TPS.

008-2) Values below 34.8 mg/H indicate speed out of range.

008-3) Values below 35 mg/H indicate air mass inducted too low, intake air system leak (unmeasured air) or excessive EGR.

Function 08
Display Group 009

No test conditions given.

	1	2	3	4
Display	xxxx /min	xx.x mg/H	xx.x mg/H	x.xxx V
Indicated	Engine speed	Injection quantity (cruise control specified)	Injection quantity (automatic trans. torque limit)	Modulating Piston Displacement Sensor (G149) voltage
Specification	not available[009-1]	not available[009-1]	not available[009-1]	1.16 - 1.54 V[009-2]
Working range				

009-1) No specification available.

009-2) As in Display group 001, field 3 if same conditions. May not be displayed with some ECM versions.

Function 08
Display Group 010

Test driven in 3rd gear (a/t manually selected), at Wide Open Throttle (WOT), coolant temperature above 176°F (80°C); values are only valid at 3000 RPM (+/– 150 RPM). Do not activate kickdown on automatic transmission.

	1	2	3	4
Display	xxx mg/H	xxxx mbar	xxxx mbar	xx.x %
Indicated	Air mass inducted (actual)	BARO pressure	Manifold pressure (boost pressure - actual)	Throttle position
Specification	750 - 850 mg/H[010-1]	not available[010-2]	1720 - 1950 mbar[010-3]	100%[010-4]
Working range				0...100%

010-1) Values below 750 mg/H indicate engine speed too low or too high, boost pressure to low, or MAF Sensor (G70) malfunction. Constant display of approximately 425 mg/H also indicates MAF malfunction.

010-2) No specification available. Value depends on altitude and local weather conditions.

010-3) Values below 1720 mbar indicate Wastegate Bypass Regulator Valve (N75) malfunction or turbocharger malfunction. Values that match display field 2 indicate a disconnected sensing hose between the manifold and ECM. Values above 1950 mbar indicate Wastegate Bypass Regulator Valve (N75) malfunction or restriction or blockage in sensing hose between the manifold and ECM.

010-4) Values below 100% indicate not WOT or mis-adjusted or malfunctioning TPS. Must be 100% for test to be valid.

Read Measuring Value Blocks (Function 08)

Function 08 **Display Group 011**				
Test driven in 3rd gear, at Wide Open Throttle (WOT), coolant temperature above 176°F (80°C); values are only valid at 3000 RPM (+/– 150 RPM). Do not activate kickdown on automatic transmission.				
	1	**2**	**3**	**4**
Display	xxxx /min	xxx mbar	xxx mbar	xx.x %
Indicated	Engine speed	Manifold pressure (boost pressure - specified)	Manifold pressure (boost pressure - actual)	Wastegate Bypass Regulator Valve duty cycle
Specification	3000 rpm	1750 - 1950 mbar[011-1]	1720 - 1950 mbar[011-2]	30 - 75%
Working range	2850 - 3150 rpm			0 - 100%

[011-1)] ECM calculated value.

[011-2)] As in Display group 010, field 3. Values below 1720 mbar indicate Wastegate Bypass Regulator Valve (N75) malfunction or turbocharger malfunction. Values that match Display group 010, field 2 indicate a disconnected sensing hose between the manifold and ECM. Values above 1950 mbar indicate Wastegate Bypass Regulator Valve (N75) malfunction or restriction or blockage in sensing hose between the manifold and ECM.

Function 08 **Display Group 012**				
No test conditions given.				
	1	**2**	**3**	**4**
Display	XXXXXXXX	x.xx	xx.x V	xx.x °C
Indicated	Not used[012-1]	Glow plug time	ECM supply voltage	Coolant temperature
Specification		Not available	not available[012-2] VAG 1551 scan tool operates 10V - 16V	
Working range			Maximum 14.5V	-40 to +141°C

[012-1)] Display may be a combination of 1 and 0. No specification available.

[012-2)] No specification available. Experience indicates that ECM supply voltage should be approximate electrical system voltage.

Function 08 Display Group 013				
Engine running at idle, coolant temperature above 176°F (80°C).				
	1	**2**	**3**	**4**
Display	(+/–) xx.x mg/H	(+/–) xx.x mg/H	(+/–) xx.x mg/H	
Indicated	Injection quantity cylinder #4 (deviation from #3)	Injection quantity cylinder #2 (deviation from #3)	Injection quantity cylinder #1 (deviation from #3)	Not used, no display
Specification	013-1	013-1	013-1	
Working range				

013-1) No exact specifications available. Experience indicates that differences generally range from +1.00 to –1.00 mg/H.
This display group shows ECM idle speed smooth running compensation control. Individual cylinders are compared to cylinder #3 which is equipped with the Needle Lift Sensor (G80). Signal is derived from G80 and RPM Sensor, G28, and a time factor. More or less fuel is delivered to each cylinder based on this calculation.
(+) values indicate that relevant cylinder is less powerful than cylinder #3 and is supplied slightly more fuel.
(–) values indicate that relevant cylinder is more powerful than cylinder #3 and is supplied slightly less fuel.
A positive value is also shown as no (+) sign.

Read Measuring Value Blocks (Function 08)

Function 08 **Display Group 017**[017-1]				
Engine running at idle, coolant temperature above 176°F (80°C).				
	1	**2**	**3**	**4**
Display	x.xxx V	x.xxx V	XXXXXXX	XX
Indicated	Catalyst temperature 2	Catalyst temperature 1	See Operating Mode 4 table	Catalyst temperature difference
Specification	1.300 - 3.000 V[017-2]	1.300 - 3.000 V[017-2]	00000000[017-3]	–10 to +10[017-4]
Working range	0...5.00 V	0...5.00 V		

017-1) Some 1Z engines are not equipped with Temperature Sensor I (G20) for Catalyst, Temperature Sensor II (G132) for Catalyst, or Metering Pump (V54). If these components are not installed, this display fields will be blank.

017-2) For values below 1.300 V or above 3.000 V, see display field 3. See relevance table.

017-3) Display may be a combination of 1 and 0. 00000000 indicates all systems/functions OK.

017-4) For values below –10 or above +10, see display field 3.

Operating Mode 4 - Catalyst Input Signals (see Display Group 017, Field 3)

Displayed: (1 = recognized, 0 = OK)								**Signal recognized or function enabled**
X								Voltage value from Temperature Sensor I (G20) too low.
	X							Voltage value from Temperature Sensor I (G20) too high.
		X						Voltage value from Temperature Sensor II (G132) too low.
			X					Voltage value from Temperature Sensor II (G132) too high.
				X				Catalyst malfunction.
					X			EGR Vacuum Regulator Solenoid Valve (N18) or wiring, open circuit or short to positive.
						X		Metering Pump (V54) or wiring has open circuit or short to positive.
							X	EGR Vacuum Regulator Solenoid Valve (N18), Metering Pump (V54) or wiring, short to ground.
0	0	0	0	0	0	0	0	All systems/functions OK

Function 08 Display Groups 014 - 016, 018 - 025[025-1]				
No conditions.				
	1	2	3	4
Display	n/a	n/a	n/a	n/a
Indicated				
Specification				
Working range				

025-1) Groups 014 and 025 are usually blank. Groups 15,16, 18 - 24, usually contain information that is repeated from other Display Groups or contain information with unavailable specifications.

BASIC SETTINGS (FUNCTION 04)

1Z engines do not have provisions for adjustment of idle speed or mixture. All major engine operating parameters are pre-programmed into the ECM as baseline values to be modified as operating conditions change.

The system does, however, require a starting point for injection timing, which is also ignition timing. This adjustment is made by physically moving the Diesel injection pump in the mounting bracket. The specified injection timing value is derived from fuel temperature as displayed on a scan tool.

Failure to properly set injection pump timing will result in hard starting, poor performance, poor fuel economy, excessive noise, smoking and increased emissions. The vehicle may not be drivable.

Normally, dynamic checking and/or adjustment of the injection timing is not required unless any of the following are repairs are required:

- Toothed spur (timing) belt is removed or replaced.
- Toothed spur (timing) belt sprockets are loosened or removed.
- Diesel injection pump is loosened in the mount or replaced.
- A performance problem exists.

Checking and/or adjustment is not required if the battery is disconnected during repairs since this is primarily a mechanical adjustment.

Initiating basic settings

Begin the basic settings/ignition timing procedure by observing the preliminary requirements.

Preliminary requirements

- Insure that basic mechanical engine settings are correct.
- Insure that toothed (timing) belt is properly tensioned.

Checking and adjusting basic settings

NOTE
Engine temperature is not critical for checking and adjusting basic settings.

- Connect scan tool to vehicle.
- With Vehicle stationary, automatic transmission in **P** or **N**, and handbrake on, start engine and allow to idle.

```
Start Basic Setting                HELP
Input Display Group Number          XXX
```

< Access **01 Engine Electronics**. Select 04 **Basic settings**.

- Input display group **000** (or 00 if applicable).

```
System in Basic Setting             000
XX 53 XX XX XX XX XX XX 90 XX
```

< Display will show 10 data display fields. Pertinent information appears in fields **9** and **2**, all other information can be ignored.

- Use the graph below to determine correct injection timing value. Display field 9 is a fuel temperature value and is assigned **B** in the table. Display field 2 is the timing value and is assigned **C** in the table.
- The timing value must fall within the shaded area (**C**) of the table based on fuel temperature. Consult the example given below, as required.
- If the value in scan tool field 2 does **NOT** fall within the appropriate range, adjust the injection pump timing as close to the center of the range as possible.

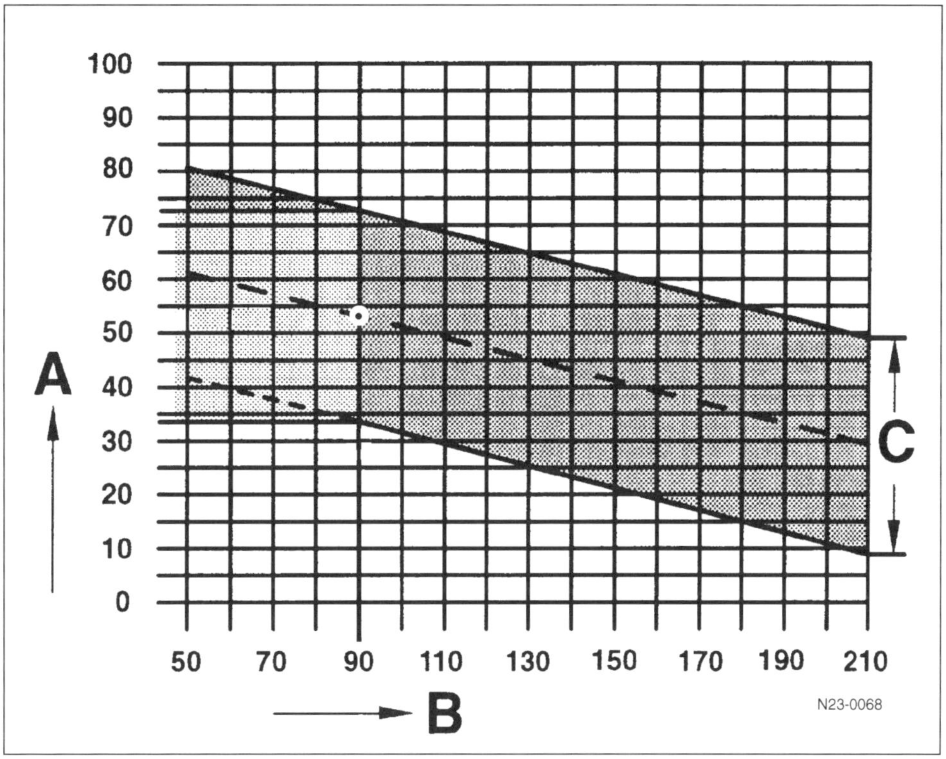

Adjusting injection pump timing

- Switch off ignition.

- Loosen diesel injection pump mounting bolts just enough to allow movement of pump.

- Start engine and repeat checking procedure given earlier. Rotate pump on shaft axis until appropriate value is shown in display field 2 with the engine running.

NOTE
Rotating the pump closer to the cylinder head advances the timing (higher number). Rotating the pump away from the cylinder head retards the timing (lower numbers).

- When correct values are attained, switch off ignition. Tighten all loosened injection pump mounting bolts.

Tightening torques

- Fuel injector pipe union nuts . . 25 Nm (18 ft-lb)
- Injection pump mounting bolts . 25 Nm (18 ft-lb)
- Injection pump mounting nuts . 25 Nm (18 ft-lb)

• Verify that timing value A still falls within range of values specified in graph.

• Loosen all 8 fuel pipe connections at injectors and injection pump and then re-tighten. This relieves the strain on the pipes that developed when the injection pump was moved.

> ***CAUTION—***
> *Failure to relieve the strain on the fuel pipes after moving the Diesel injection pump will almost always result in fuel pipe breakage due to vibration.*

• Verify that all fasteners, electrical connectors, and components previously removed have been properly re-installed and tightened.

• Verify that all fuel lines are secure and that there are no fuel leaks.

Example:

The following example uses the graph on the previous page and the data displayed in the illustration to the left.

◄ With the engine running at idle, the fuel temperature value in display field 9 is 90. This is value **B**. Look on the graph (given earlier) along axis B until you see the value 90. Follow the line up from 90 into the shaded area **C**. Look to the left for the range of values on the **A** axis. In this example, the range is approximately 34 to 73. The value displayed in scan tool field 2 is 53 which is still within the range. No adjustment is required.

• If injection timing requires adjustment, switch off ignition.

• Loosen Diesel injection pump mounting bolts just enough to allow movement of pump. Start engine and repeat checking procedure. Rotate pump on shaft axis until appropriate value is shown in display field 2 with the engine running.

• Rotating the pump so that the upper part is closer to the cylinder head increases the numbers, (advances the timing),

• Rotating the pump so that the upper part moves away from the cylinder head decreases the numbers, (retards the timing),

- When correct values are attained, switch off ignition.

- Tighten all loosened injection pump mounting bolts.

Tightening torques

- Fuel injector pipe union nuts . . 25 Nm (18 ft-lb)
- Injection pump mounting bolts. 25 Nm (18 ft-lb)
- Injection pump mounting nuts . 25 Nm (18 ft-lb)

- Verify that timing value A still falls within the range of values as specified in the previous graph.

- Loosen all 8 connections of the fuel pipes at the injectors and the injection pump and then re-tighten all 8. This relieves the strain on the pipes that developed when the injection pump was moved.

> ***CAUTION—***
> *Failure or relieve the strain on the fuel pipes after moving the Diesel injection pump will always result in fuel pipe breakage due to vibration.*

- Verify that all fasteners, electrical connectors, and components that were removed to gain access have been properly re-installed and tightened.

- Verify that all fuel lines are secure and that there are no fuel leaks.

Output Diagnostic Test Mode (Function 03)

Troubleshooting electrical faults on 1Z engines is facilitated by the Output Diagnostic Test Mode or Function 03. When this function is activated, the scan tool instructs the ECM to operate certain electrical components in a pre-determined sequence. The output diagnostic test mode can only be used when the ignition is switched on, but the engine is not running.

The following is a list of components checked during the output diagnostic test mode and the order in which they are tested:

- Cold Start Injector (N108)
- Exhaust Gas Recirculation (EGR) Vacuum Regulator Solenoid Valve (N18)
- Air Conditioner Compressor Clutch (N25) interruption
- Fuel Cut-Off Valve (N109)
- Wastegate Bypass Regulator Valve (N75)
- Glow Plug Relay (J235)
- Glow Plug Indicator Light (K29)
- Coolant Glow Plug Relay (J325) high heat output
- Coolant Glow Plug Relay (J325) low heat output

```
Rapid data transfer                Q
03 - Output Diagnostic Test Mode
```

◀ Scan tool display from VAG 1551 showing start of Function 03.

```
Output Diagnostic Test Mode      -->
Cold-start injector - N108
```

◀ Screen display from VAG 1551 showing first test.

Testing in Function 03

Testing TDI Diesel engines with a scan tool in Function 03 is different from all other gasoline engines covered in this handbook because the engine must be running at the start of the test. It will shut itself off during this procedure; continue with the test as directed. The following steps should be observed:

- Vehicle stationary, automatic transmission in **P** or **N**, handbrake on.
- Start engine and allow to idle.
- Switch A/C system on; select the highest fan speed and the coldest temperature setting.
- Proper application of the procedure requires coolant temperature of at least 59°F (15°C) or higher.

Output Diagnostic Test Mode (Function 03)

After the scan tool has been connected and Function 03 selected, proceed with the test as indicated on the scan tool noting the following:

1. **Cold Start Injector (N108) –** Cold Start Injector, as previously noted, changes injection timing on a cold engine. When activated, the Cold Start Injector will change the injection timing resulting in an audible change in engine (combustion) noise at idle.

2. **Exhaust Gas Recirculation (EGR) Vacuum Regulator Solenoid Valve (N18) –** EGR Vacuum Regulator Solenoid Valve will be switched on and off (opened and closed) resulting in an audible click.

3. **A/C Compressor Clutch Interruption –** A/C Compressor Clutch (N25) will be switched off and on, disengaging and re-engaging the compressor. The resulting noise is easily heard over ambient engine noise.

4. **Fuel Cut-Off Valve (N109) –** Fuel Cut-Off Valve will be switched off causing the idling engine to stop. Do not re-start the engine, but continue the output diagnostic test mode with the ignition switched on, and the engine off.

5. **Wastegate Bypass Regulator Valve (N75) –** Wastegate Bypass Regulator Valve will be switched on and off (opened and closed) resulting in an audible click.

6. **Glow Plug Relay (J52) –** Glow Plug Relay near the fuse/relay panel will be switched on and off with an audible clicking sound. The engine glow plugs will be energized.

7. **Glow Plug Indicator Light (K29) –** Glow Plug Indicator Light in the instrument cluster will blink on and off.

8. **Coolant Glow Plug Relay (J325), high heat output –** Coolant Glow Plug Relay on the bulkhead in the engine compartment will be switched on and off in the high heat output mode. The relay will make an audible clicking sound. In this mode, two of the coolant glow plugs in the coolant outlet flange on the end of the cylinder head will be switched on and off.

9. **Coolant Glow Plug Relay (J325), low heat output –** Coolant Glow Plug Relay on the bulkhead in the engine compartment will be switched on and off in the low heat output mode. The relay will make an audible clicking sound. In this mode, the remaining coolant glow plug will be switched on and off.

Output Diagnostic Test Mode (Function 03)

```
Output Diagnostic Test Mode

Cold-start injector-N108
EGR vacuum regulator solenoid valve-N18
A/C compressor interruption
Fuel cut-off valve-N109
Wastegate bypass regulator valve-N75
Glow plug relay-J52
Glow plug indicator light-K29
Low heat output relay-J325
High heat output relay-J325
```

◄ When the VAG 1551 printer is switched on, the tape will be printed with all of the tests in sequence.

The Output Diagnostic Test Mode is helpful in checking the electrical operation of a given component. It can also be helpful in diagnosing mechanical malfunctions as well.

If, for example, the Cold Start Injector (N108) was suspected of not changing the injection timing on a cold 1Z engine, and there are no electrical malfunctions with the valve, the wiring, or the connections; than the valve could be suspected of a mechanical malfunction or restriction simply by listening to it work. Similar tests can be devised with many of the other components.

In the event of a component failing to operate, the component and the wiring should be checked for continuity, open circuits, and short circuits, including short circuits to ground. Always consult the appropriate wiring diagram.

```
028 906 021 GQ 1.91 R4 EDC  SG   D00
CODING   00000                WSC00000
```

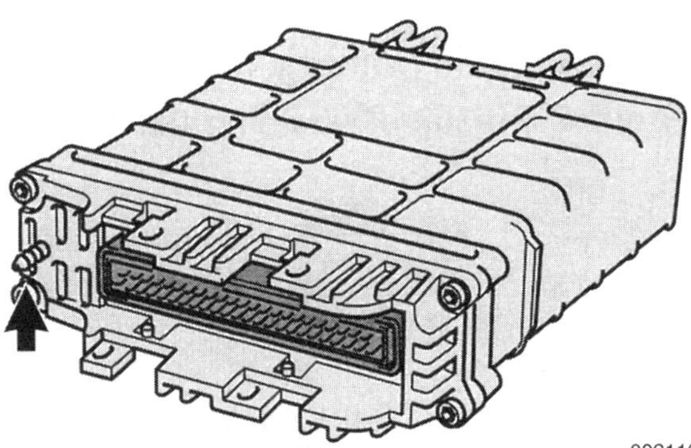

0021105

CODE CONTROL MODULE (FUNCTION 03)

Control module coding by means of the scan tool is not a supported function with TDI ECMs in 1Z coded engines. Coding information does appear, however, in Function 01 (control unit versions). The correct ECM is determined by VIN.

< VAG 1551 scan tool display for Engine Control Module from a 1996 Passat. Part number on ECM label will match Scan Tool display in Function 01.

< ECM for 1Z TDI engine. Note hose connection (arrow) to intake manifold for pressure sensing. Part number information will be printed directly on the housing or on a sticker affixed to the housing.

Part numbers can change within the Volkswagen Parts system for several reasons and are not, therefore, listed here.

> ***NOTE***
> *Always consult with your Volkswagen Parts Department or aftermarket parts specialist for the latest parts information.*

COMPONENT AND SIGNAL OVERVIEW, 1Z ENGINE

The 1Z engine uses the TDI engine management system also known as Electronic Diesel Control (EDC) or Diesel Direct Fuel Injection (DFI). This Diesel Engine Management System closely resembles gasoline engine management systems.

Signals from sensors and other input sources are processed by the ECM. Signals to control the engine are sent to actuators along with engine information needed by other systems or functions.

Component and Signal Overview, 1Z Engine

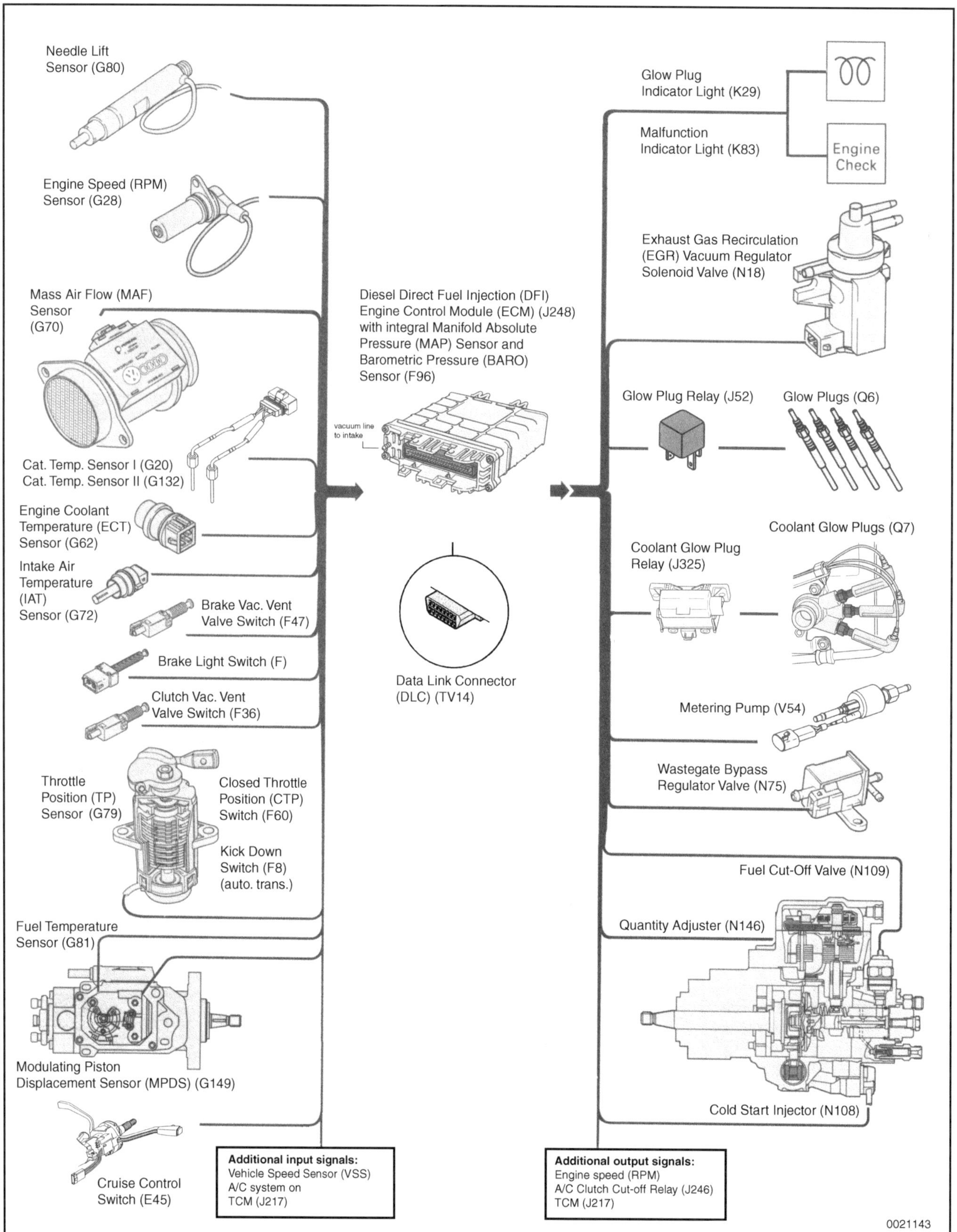

Component and Signal Overview (1Z)

Volkswagen TDI Diesel, 4-cylinder	
Fuel injection	Diesel, Turbo Direct Injection (TDI) Direct cylinder fuel injection with turbo-charger and charge-air cooler (intercooler), OBD-D
Fuel delivery	ECM controlled distributor-type high pressure multi-stage mechanical injection pump, 2-stage pressure operated mechanical fuel injectors, drive-by-wire throttle control
Ignition system	Compression ignition via distributor-type injection pump, ECM controlled
Emission control	Oxidation-type (two-way) catalytic converter, positive crankcase ventilation,
Diagnostics	On-Board Diagnostics via scan tool, Rapid data transfer, Non-volatile memory
Control Module	Single 68-pin Diesel Direct Fuel Injection (DFI) Engine Control Module (ECM) (J248) with integral Manifold Absolute Pressure (MAP) Sensor (G71) and Barometric Pressure (BARO) Sensor (F96); supplied by Power Supply Relay (J317)
Sensors	Engine Speed (RPM) Sensor (G28)
	Throttle Position (TP) Sensor (G79)[1]
	Closed Throttle Position (CTP) Switch (F60)[1]
	Kick Down Switch (F8)[2]
	Brake Light Switch (F)
	Brake Vacuum Vent Valve Switch (F47)[3]
	Clutch Vacuum Vent Valve Switch (F36)[3]
	Cruise Control Switch (E45)
	Temperature Sensor I for Catalyst (G20)
	Temperature Sensor II for Catalyst (G132)
	Mass Air Flow (MAF) Sensor (G70)
	Needle Lift Sensor (G80)[4]
	Modulating Piston Displacement Sensor (MPDS) (G149)
	Fuel Temperature Sensor (G81)[5]
	Engine Coolant Temperature (ECT) Sensor (G62)
	Intake Air Temperature (IAT) Sensor (G72)
Input signals	Vehicle speed (VSS)
	Air conditioner, system on
	Automatic Transmission Control Module (TCM) (J217)

Continued

Component and Signal Overview, 1Z Engine

Component and Signal Overview

Actuators	Quantity Adjuster (N146)
	Exhaust Gas Recirculation (EGR) Vacuum Regulator Solenoid Valve (N18)
	Wastegate Bypass Regulator Valve (N75)
	Glow Plug Relay (J52), and Glow Plugs (Q6)
	Coolant Glow Plug Relay (J325), and Coolant Glow Plugs (Q7)
	Cold Start Injector (N108)[6]
	Fuel Cut-Off Valve (N109)
	Metering Pump (V54)[7]
	Malfunction Indicator Light (MIL) (K83)
	Glow Plug Indicator Light (K29)
Output signals	Engine speed (rpm)
	Automatic Transmission Control Module (TCM) (J217)
	Air Conditioner Clutch Cut-Off Relay (J246)

[1] Throttle Position (TP) Sensor and Closed Throttle Position (CTP) Switch are combined in a single housing within the vehicle interior near the accelerator pedal.

[2] Vehicles with automatic transmission only. Combined in housing with TPS and CTP switch.

[3] Brake Vacuum and Clutch Vacuum Vent Valve Switches retain their names from their use in older vacuum operated cruise control systems. In 1Z engines, only the electrical section is used.

[4] Integral with fuel injector number 3.

[5] Located within the Diesel fuel injection pump.

[6] Cold Start Injector (N108) does not inject fuel into the cylinders as in gasoline engines. This valve is part of the Diesel fuel injection pump and allows for automatic injection timing changes on a cold engine. This valve is also known (more correctly) as the Start of Injection Solenoid Valve.

[7] Not installed on some later 1Z engines.

TECHNICAL DATA

Technical data is compiled from several Volkswagen publications. In some instances, the information from these sources differed slightly. In these cases, the most current specifications are listed.

1Z (Passat)	**Technical Data**
Type	4-cylinder in-line (R4), turbo direct injection (TDI) with charge air cooler, Diesel fuel
Construction	Cast iron block, aluminum 2V cylinder head, belt driven single overhead camshaft
Displacement	1.9 Liters (1896 cc), (116 cid)
Horsepower	90 hp (66 Kw) @ 4000 rpm
Torque	149 lb-ft (202 Nm) @ 1900 rpm
Bore	79.5 mm
Stroke	95.5 mm
Compression ratio	19.5:1
Firing order	1-3-4-2
Management	Diesel Turbo Direct Injection

Notes

Engine Code
2H

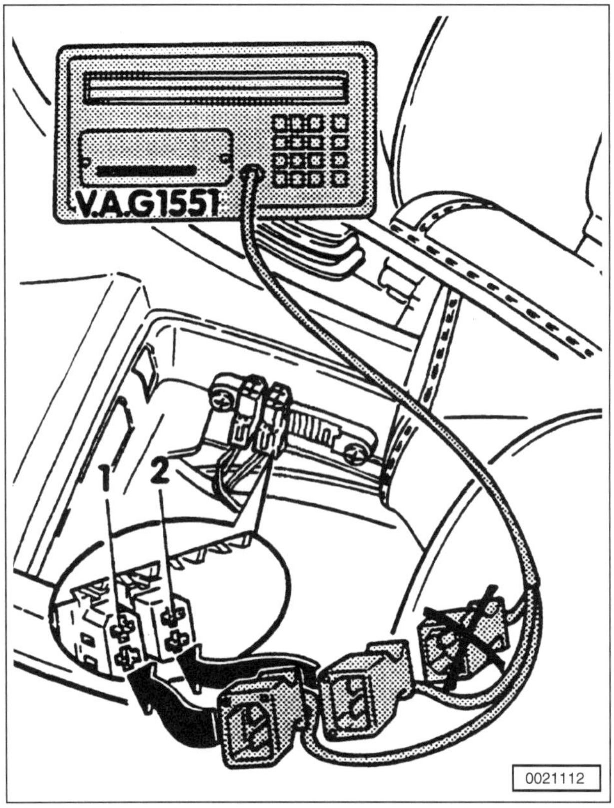

GENERAL

The **2H** engine is installed in the Volkswagen Cabriolet for all 50 States and Canada for model years 1990 through 1993. Only engines originally certified for sale in California for model years 1991 through 1993 are equipped with the scan tool capability detailed in this section.

Engine Code 2H Vehicles

Engine Code 2H	Model Years
Cabriolet	1991, 1992, 1993 (California certified only)

Scan tool, connecting

The scan tool is connected through the DLC (Data Link Connector).

◄ **Cabriolet, 1991 - 1993 (California only):**
Manual transmission: center console under shifter boot.
Automatic transmission: center console under selector indicator cover.
Black connector on scan tool harness is connected to black connection on vehicle (**1**) and provides scan tool power. White connector is connected to white connection on vehicle (**2**) for data transfer. Other connectors (blue and red) are not used.

Scan tool, functions available

	Scan Tool Functions Available	Ignition on, not running	Engine at idle	Page
✔	Control unit version (01)	Yes	Yes	Appendix A
✔	Check DTC memory (02)	Yes	Yes	Appendix A
✔	Output diagnostic test mode (03)	No	No	153
✔	Basic settings (04)	No	Yes	152
✔	Erase DTC memory (05)	Yes	Yes	Appendix A
✔	End output (06)	Yes	Yes	Appendix A
✗	Code control module (07)	No	No	154
✔	Read measuring value blocks (08)	Yes	Yes	147
✗	Read indiv. measuring value blocks (09)	No	No	Appendix A

Read Measuring Value Blocks (Function 08)

Measuring value blocks are assembled and displayed in sets called display groups. For the 2H engine, display groups are numbered starting with 000 and continuing with 001 on up to 005.

```
Read Measuring Value Blocks        HELP
Input Display Group Number          XXX
```

◄ Scan tool display from VAG 1551 requesting Measuring Value Block Display Group information (XXX).

Display group overview, 2H engine (Cabriolet - California only)

Function 08, (Cabriolet) Display Group Overview 000[OV-1]										
Display Field	**1**	**2**	**3**	**4**	**5**	**6**	**7**	**8**	**9**	**10**
	n/a	n/a	ECT	n/a	HO2S	n/a	n/a	n/a	n/a	n/a

OV-1) Some data is not relevant, or is unavailable. This data is identified as n/a.

Function 08 (Cabriolet) Display Group Overview 001 - 005[OV-2]				
Display Field	**1**	**2**	**3**	**4**
Display Group 001	RPM	VAF	ECT	Injector duration
Display Group 002	RPM	IAT	n/a	Injector duration
Display Group 003	RPM	ECT	n/a	Injector duration
Display Group 004	RPM	VAF	n/a	Injector duration
Display Group 005	RPM	TPS	n/a	Injector duration

OV-2) Some data is not relevant, or is unavailable. This data is identified as n/a.

Read Measuring Value Blocks (Function 08)

Function 08
Display Group 000

Engine running at idle speed, coolant temperature above 176°C, ECM in **Read Measuring Value Block** (Function 08)

Display Field	Display Fields	Observed range: [000-1]	Corresponds to:
10	**Undefined data**[000-2]	—	—
9	**Undefined data**	—	—
8	**Undefined data**	—	—
7	**Undefined data**	—	—
6	**Undefined data**	—	—
5	**Heated Oxygen Sensor (HO2S) signal**	must vary by at least 14[000-3]	operation OK
4	**Undefined data**	—	—
3	**Engine Coolant Temperature (ECT) Sensor**	less than 11[000-4]	176°C
2	**Undefined data**	—	—
1	**Undefined data**	—	—

[000-1] Overall range of values is 0 - 255.

[000-2] Undefined data means that information is displayed on the scan tool but information to interpret or define it's meaning is unavailable.

[000-3] Values between 0 - 5 indicate short circuit to positive in HO2S wiring to ECM
Values between 164 - 168 indicate open circuit in HO2S wiring to ECM.
Values between 230 and 255 indicate short circuit to ground in HO2S wiring to ECM.

[000-4] Lower numbers are hotter. Temperature must rise (value will decrease) smoothly during engine warm-up.

Function 08 Display Group 001				
	1	2	3	4
Display	xxxx /min	xx%	xx.x °C	xx.x ms
Indicated	Engine speed	VAF signal	Coolant temperature	Fuel injector duration
Specification	750-850 idle rpm[001-1]	16%-26%	none given[001-4]	none given[001-5]
		At idle with coolant temperature at least 80°C (176°F)	Open circuit shows a constant -40° Short circuit shows a constant 80°C	
Working range	750...6300 rpm[001-2]	0%...100%[001-3]	-40°C...141°C (approximately)	

001-1) Valid with coolant temperature of at least 80° (176°F).

001-2) Approximate maximum governed rpm.

001-3) Values in this display field are valid only at idle with a coolant temperature of at least 80°C (176°F).
Values between 16 - 26% indicate VAF Sensor and ECM control OK.
Values between 5 - 15% indicate intake air leaks.
Values between 0 - 2% indicate open circuit in VAF Sensor wiring to ECM.

001-4) No specification available. Experience indicates that at idle, temperature will vary between approximately 86°C and 105°C depending on radiator fan operating cycle. Temperature must rise smoothly during engine warm-up. If value displayed does not increase jumps up by 2°C to 5°C in display, ECM is raising temperature based on running time due to a faulty ECT Sensor.

001-5) No idle specification available. Increase engine speed above 3000 rpm at least 3 times and let speed return to idle for at least 2 minutes. Note value. Again increase engine speed above 3000 rpm; fuel injector duration display must increase. Allow engine speed to return to idle. Value must drop to 0.00 mS to indicate deceleration fuel shut-off as speed decreases. Previously displayed idle value should again be shown.

Read Measuring Value Blocks (Function 08)

Function 08
Display Group 002

	1	2	3	4
Display	xxxx /min	xx.x °C	xxx	xx.x ms
Indicated	Engine speed	Intake air temperature	n/a[002-3]	Fuel injector duration
Specification	750-850 idle rpm[002-1]	none given[002-2]		none given[002-4]
		Open circuit shows a constant 19.6°		
Working range	750...6300 rpm[002-1]	-46.5°C...141.0°C		

002-1) As in Display Group 001, Field 1.

002-2) No specification given. Experience indicates that at idle, temperature will be approximately ambient air temperature. Intake air pre-heater will generally keep incoming air temperature to around 30°C, but may be substantially higher on a very hot day. Very high temperatures suggest a malfunctioning intake air pre-heater.

002-3) Data is not relevant, is undefined, or is unsupported by the factory.

002-4) As in Display Group 001, Field 4.

Function 08
Display Group 003

	1	2	3	4
Display	xxxx /min	xx.x °C	xxx	xx.x ms
Indicated	Engine speed	Coolant temperature	n/a[003-3]	Fuel injector duration
Specification	750-850 idle rpm[003-1]	none given[003-2]		none given[003-4]
		Open circuit shows a constant -40° Short circuit shows a constant 80°C		
Working range	750...6300 rpm[003-1]	-40°C...141°C (approximately)		

003-1) As in Display Group 001, Field 1.

003-2) As in Display Group 001, Field 3.

003-3) As in Display Group 002, Field 3.

003-4) As in Display Group 001, Field 4.

Function 08 Display Group 004				
	1	**2**	**3**	**4**
Display	xxxx /min	xx%	xxx	xx.x ms
Indicated	Engine speed	VAF signal	n/a[004-3]	Fuel injector duration
Specification	750-850 idle rpm[004-1]	16%-26%		none given[004-4]
		At idle with coolant temperature at least 80°C (176°F)		
Working range	750...6300 rpm[004-1]	0%...100%[004-2]		

004-1) As in Display Group 001, Field 1.

004-2) As in Display Group 001, Field 2.

004-3) As in Display Group 002, Field 3.

004-4) As in Display Group 001, Field 4.

Function 08 Display Group 005				
	1	**2**	**3**	**4**
Display	xxxx /min	xx.x ∠°	xxx	xx.x ms
Indicated	Engine speed	TPS angle	n/a[005-3]	Fuel injector duration
Specification	750-850 idle rpm[005-1]	5-50°		none given[005-4]
		At CTP		
Working range	750...6300 rpm[005-1]	0°...to over 90°[005-2]		

005-1) As in Display Group 001, Field 1.

005-2) Momentarily operate throttle to WOT. Value displayed should be 90.0 ∠° or greater.
0.0 ∠° indicates open circuit in TPS wiring to ECM.
90.0 ∠° or greater at idle indicates short circuit to positive in TPS wiring to ECM.
Value must increase uniformly and without interruption when throttle is opened.

005-3) As in Display Group 002, Field 3.

005-4) As in Display Group 001, Field 4.

Basic Settings (Function 04)

Adjustment of engine settings through the use of Function 04 (basic settings) is not a supported function in this version of Digifant. Baseline values for ignition timing, idle speed, and CO (carbon monoxide) content require manual adjustment.

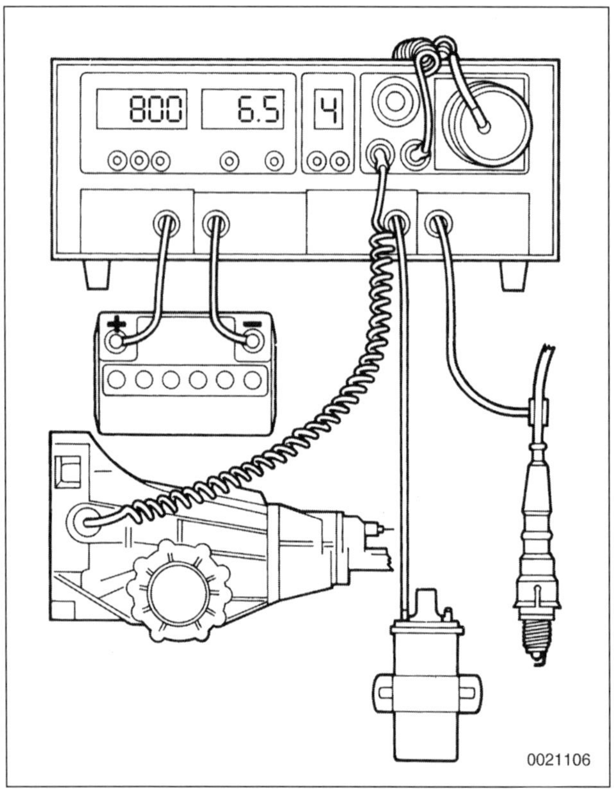

Adjustment of engine settings does not require use of a scan tool, but does requires the connection of several other pieces of test equipment. After adjustment of engine settings, it will, however, be necessary to connect a scan tool and erase DTCs that are recorded during the normal adjusting procedures.

Test equipment required to adjust engine settings includes the following:

- An engine tester such as the VAG 1367 must be connected to the engine to measure ignition timing and engine speed.
- An exhaust gas analyzer must be attached to the CO pick-up or sampling tube located ahead of the catalytic converter to measure CO (carbon monoxide) content.

◄ Engine tester such as the VAG 1367 must used in conjunction with an exhaust gas analyzer to properly adjust engine settings.

Output Diagnostic Test Mode (Function 03)

Troubleshooting electrical faults in Cabriolets with 2H Digifant I engines must be done with a test harness such as the Volkswagen supplied VAG 1598. The ability of the scan tool to instruct the ECM to operate certain electrical components is not a supported function in this version of Digifant.

Use of a test harness on Digifant I systems requires that the ECM be disconnected during continuity and resistance checks and re-connected to test voltages.

In the event of a suspected component malfunction, the component and the wiring should be checked for continuity, open circuits, and short circuits, including short circuits to ground. Always consult the appropriate wiring diagram.

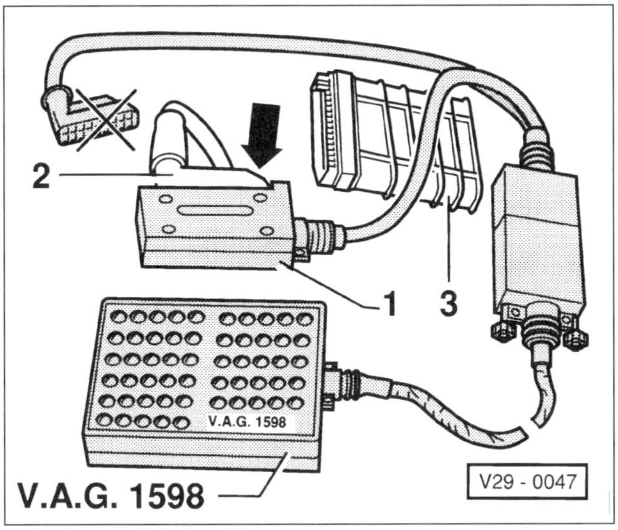

Test box VAG 1598 shown attached to Digifant I vehicle wiring harness (arrow) with appropriate adapter (1). ECM harness connector (2) must remain disconnected from the ECM (3) during resistance checks to insure accuracy.

Code Control Module (Function 07)

Control module coding by means of the scan tool is not a supported function with California Digifant I ECMs. Coding information does appear, however, in Function 01 (control unit versions). ECM coding is generally accomplished through the use of specific part number ECMs.

Engine Control Module from a 1991 California Cabriolet. Part number on ECM label matches Scan Tool display in Function 01. Coding information does not, however, appear externally

NOTE
Always consult with your Volkswagen Parts Department or aftermarket parts specialist for the latest parts information.

Component and Signal Overview, 2H Engine

Signals from sensors and other input sources are processed by the ECM. Signals to control the engine are sent to actuators.

Component and Signal Overview, 2H Engine

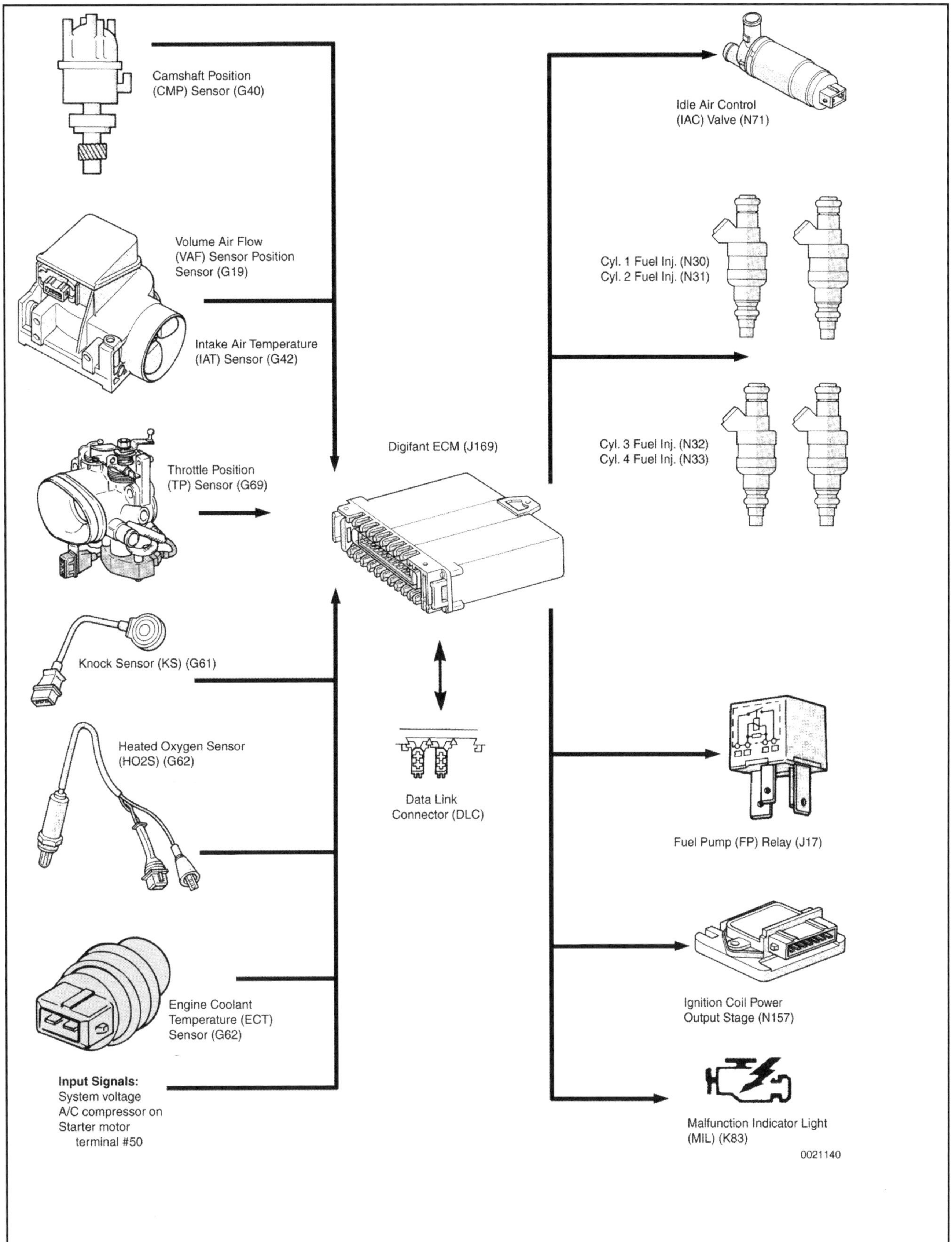

Component and Signal Overview, 2H Engine

Component and Signal Overview (2H)

Volkswagen California Digifant I, 4-cylinder	
Fuel injection	Non-sequential (simultaneous) Multi-Point Fuel Injection with Lambda (Oxygen Sensor) Control, OBD-I
Fuel delivery	Tank-mounted electric transfer fuel pump, externally-mounted electric fuel pump, load-sensing mechanical pressure regulator
Ignition system	Distributor, power output stage and ignition coil, single knock sensor, ECM controlled
Emission control	3-Way catalytic converter, carbon canister with mechanical (vacuum) control valve, positive crankcase ventilation
Diagnostics	On-Board Diagnostics via scan tool, Rapid data transfer, Non-volatile memory
Control Module	Single 38-pin Digifant Engine Control Module (ECM) (J169) supplied by Digifant ECM Power Supply Relay (J176)
Sensors	Camshaft Position (CMP) Sensor (G40)
	Volume Air Flow (VAF) Sensor Position Sensor (G19)[1]
	Intake Air Temperature (IAT) Sensor (G42)
	Throttle Position (TP) Sensor (G69)
	Knock Sensor (KS) (G61)
	Heated Oxygen Sensor (H2OS) (G39)
	Engine Coolant Temperature (ECT) Sensor (G62)
Input signals	System voltage
	Starter motor (terminal 50)
	Air conditioner, compressor on
Actuators	Idle Air Control (IAC) Valve (N71)
	Fuel Injectors: Cylinder 1 (N30), Cylinder 2 (N31), Cylinder 3 (N32), Cylinder 4 (N33)
	Ignition Coil Power Output Stage (N157), and Ignition Coil (N152)
	Fuel Pump (FP) Relay (J17), Transfer Fuel Pump (FP) (G23), Fuel Pump (FP) (G6)
	Malfunction Indicator Light (MIL) (K83)
Output signals	No additional output signals

[1] Built into VAF Sensor Position Sensor housing.

Technical Data

Technical data is compiled from several Volkswagen publications. In some instances, the information from these sources differed slightly. In these cases, the most current specifications are listed.

2H (Cabriolet, California)	**Technical Data**
Type	4-cylinder in-line (R4), gasoline fuel
Construction	Cast iron block, aluminum 2V cylinder head, belt driven single overhead camshaft
Displacement	1.8 Liters (1781 cc), (109 cid)
Horsepower	100 hp (75 Kw) @ 5400 rpm
Torque	107 lb-ft (145 Nm) @ 3400 rpm
Bore	81.0 mm
Stroke	86.4 mm
Compression ratio	10.0:1
Firing order	1-3-4-2
Management	Digifant I

Notes

Engine Code
9A

0021123

General

The vehicles listed below are equipped with engine code **9A**. This engine uses the Bosch® **CIS-E Motronic** engine management system. The displacement of this inline 4-cylinder, 16 valve engine is 2.0 liters.

Engine Code 9A Vehicles

Engine Code 9A	Model Years
Golf GTI	1990, 1991, 1992
Jetta GLI	1990, 1991, 1992
Passat GL	1990, 1991, 1992, 1993

Scan tool, connecting

The scan tool is connected through the DLC (Data Link Connector).

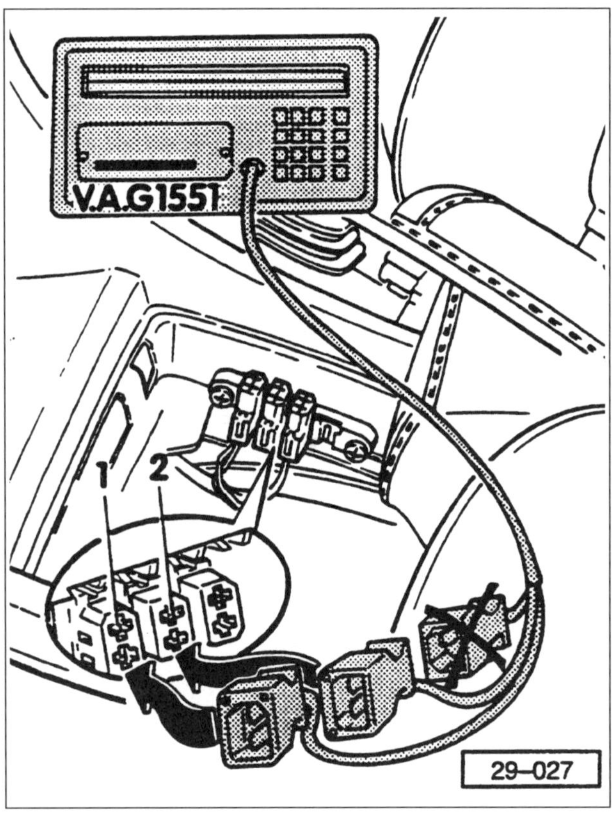

◀ **Golf GTI, Jetta GLI, 1990-1992**:
Manual transmission: center console under shift boot.
Automatic transmission: center console under selector indicator cover.

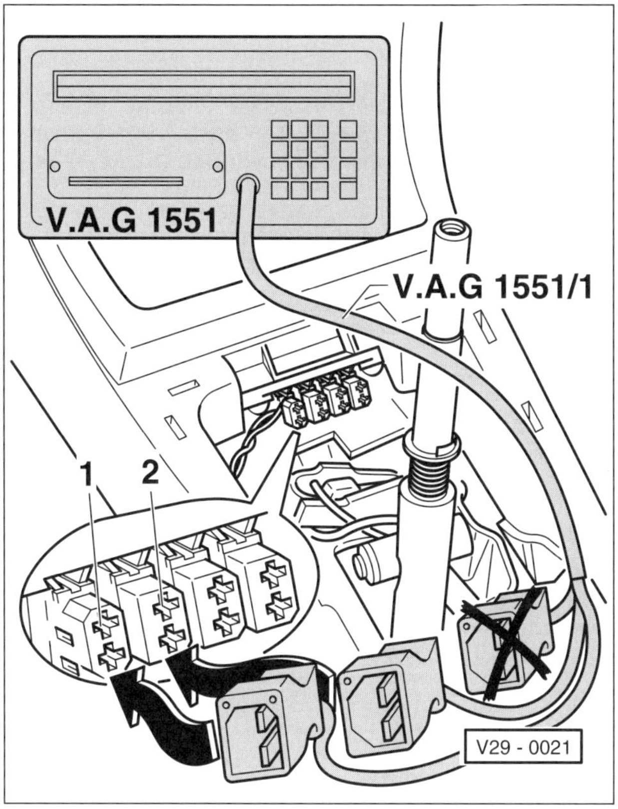

Passat GL, 1990-1993:
Manual transmission: center console under shift boot.
Automatic transmission: center console under selector indicator cover.

Scan tool, functions available

	Scan Tool Functions Available	Ignition on, not running	Engine at idle	Page
✔	Control unit version (01)	Yes	Yes	Appendix A
✔	Check DTC memory (02)	Yes	Yes	Appendix A
✔	Output diagnostic test mode (03)	Yes	No	174
✔	Basic settings (04)	No	Yes	169
✔	Erase DTC memory (05)	Yes	Yes	Appendix A
✔	End output (06)	Yes	Yes	Appendix A
✗	Code control module (07)	No	No	176
✔	Read measuring value blocks (08)	Yes	Yes	162
✗	Read indiv. measuring value blocks (09)	No	No	Appendix A

READ MEASURING VALUE BLOCKS (FUNCTION 08)

```
Read Measuring Value Blocks     HELP
Input Display Group Number       XXX
```

Measuring value blocks are assembled and displayed in sets called display groups. Display Group 000 (or 00) with 10 data fields is the only supported Display Group.

◄ Scan tool display from VAG 1551 requesting Measuring Value Block Display Group information (XXX).

Display group overview, 9A engine

Engine Code 9A, Display Group Overview 000[OV-1]										
Display Field	**1**	**2**	**3**	**4**	**5**	**6**	**7**	**8**	**9**	**10**
	ECT	Load	RPM	IAC adaptive	IAC working	Diff. fuel pressure regulator working	Diff. fuel pressure regulator adaptive	KPH	Input signals	Ignition timing

OV-1) All values are shown in decimal format and require interpretation.

Function 08
Display Group 000

Engine running at idle speed, ECM in Read Measuring Value Blocks, **Function 08** or Basic Settings, **Function 04**

Field	Display Fields	Range:[000-1]	Corresponds to:[000-2]
10	**Ignition timing (calculated by ECM)**[000-3]	48 - 230	43.13° BTDC to 21.86° ATDC
9	**ECM input signals**	0 - 110	—
8	**Vehicle speed**	0 - 50[000-4]	—
7	**Differential fuel pressure regulator (adaptive value)**	28 - 128 or 128 - 228	+10 mA to -10 mA
6	**Differential fuel pressure regulator (working value)**	0 - 50 or 255 - 206	+10 mA to -10mA
5	**Idle air control (working value)**	0 - 48 or 255 - 206	—
4	**Idle air control (adaptive value)**	0 - 24 or 255 - 232	—
3	**Engine speed (RPM)**	20 - 250	480 RPM to 6000 RPM[000-5]
2	**Engine load**	40 - 64 255[000-6]	—
1	**Engine coolant temperature**	220 - 35[000-7]	32.1°F to 223.8°F (0.2°C to 106.6°C)

000-1) Overall range of values is 0 - 255.

000-2) Display group 000, all values must use field interpretation tables shown below

000-3) Some ECM versions display timing in function 08 only.

000-4) Digital signal.

000-5) Some ECM versions limit maximum displayed to 2000 RPM.

000-6) Warm engine at idle and full load values are only values defined.

000-7) Lower numbers are hotter. Temperature must rise (value will decrease) smoothly during engine warm-up.

Read Measuring Value Blocks (Function 08)

Engine Coolant Temperature (see Display Group 000, Field 1)

Scan tool display	° Centigrade	° Fahrenheit
35	106.6	223.8
40	100.5	212.9
50	90.5	194.9
60	82.2	179.9
70	75.1	167.1
80	68.8	155.8
90	63.1	145.6
100	57.9	136.2
110	53.0	127.4
120	48.3	118.9
130	43.8	110.8
140	39.4	102.9
150	35.0	95.0
160	30.6	87.0
170	26.2	79.2
180	21.6	70.9
190	16.8	62.2
200	11.6	52.9
210	6.0	42.8
220	0.2	32.1

Engine Load (see Display Group 000, Field 2)

Scan tool specification	
40 to 64	This value must fluctuate. The average value at warm idle must be within the range.
255	This constant value must be displayed at full load
If adjustments are required, appropriate repair/service manual procedures must be followed. Adjustment cannot be made using a scan tool alone.	

Engine Speed (RPM)
(see Display Group 000, Field 3)

Scan tool display	RPM	Scan tool display	RPM
20	480	41	984
21	504	42	1008
22	528	43	1032
23	552	44	1056
24	576	45	1080
25	600	46	1104
26	624	47	1128
27	648	48	1152
28	672	49	1176
29	696	50	1200
30	720	64	1536
31	744	75	1800
32	768	84	2040
33	792	105	2520
34	816	125	3000
35	840	146	3504
36	864	167	4008
37	888	188	4512
38	912	209	5016
39	936	230	5520
40	960	250	6000

Idle Air Control - Adaptive Value
(see Display Group 000, Field 4)

Scan tool specification	
0 to 24	Upper adaptive range
255 to 232	Lower adaptive range
A value within either range is OK	
This value is not adjustable. If not within adaptive range, check all other engine adjustments, air/vacuum leaks, and engine mechanical condition. Due to adaptive nature of this value, allow a minimum of 4 minutes for corrections to take effect.	

Idle Air Control - Working Value (see Display Group 000, Field 5)

Scan tool specification	
0 to 48	Upper working range
255 to 206	Lower working range
A value within either range is OK	
This value is not adjustable. If not within working range, check all other engine adjustments, air/vacuum leaks, and engine mechanical condition.	

Differential Fuel Pressure Regulator - Working Value (see Display Group 000, Field 6)

Scan tool specification	
0 to 50	Upper working range
255 to 206	Lower working range
A value within either range is OK	
• A value of 50 = +10 mA (+ 0.010 A) of Differential Fuel Pressure Regulator current. • A value of 0 = 0 mA of Differential Fuel Pressure Regulator current. • A value of 206 = -10 mA (- 0.010 A) of Differential Fuel Pressure Regulator current. • If adjustments are required, appropriate repair/service manual procedures must be followed. Adjustment cannot be made using a scan tool alone.	

Differential Fuel Pressure Regulator - Adaptive Value (see Display Group 000, Field 7)

Scan tool specification	
28 to 128	Lower working range
128 to 228	Upper working range
A value within either range is OK	
• A value of 228 = +10 mA (+ 0.010 A) of Differential Fuel Pressure Regulator current. • A value of 128 = 0 mA of Differential Fuel Pressure Regulator current. • A value of 28 = -10 mA (- 0.010 A) of Differential Fuel Pressure Regulator current.	

Vehicle Speed Sensor signal (see Display Group 000, Field 8)

Scan tool specification	
0	Vehicle stationary
1 to 50	Vehicle in motion
Value must rise as vehicle speed increases. May fluctuate slightly at a constant speed. Digital signal cannot be readily converted to road speed.	

Input signals to ECM (see Display Group 000, Field 9)

Value	Input signal description
*Value displayed will depend on vehicle equipment and engine operating status. Values are added together to obtain specification. **Add values to obtain specification**: A vehicle at idle with an automatic transmission in park should display a value of **5** (1 + 4 = 5). Switching on A/C should change display to **13** (1 + 4 + 8 = 13). Missing signals, conditions, or components are assigned a value of 0.	
0	Automatic transmission in gear
1	CTP Switch (F60) closed
2	WOT Switch (F81) closed
4	Manual transmission in gear or in neutral
4	Automatic transmission in **P**ark or **N**eutral
8	Air conditioner compressor on
32	Shift signal from 4-speed automatic transmission
64	Fuel enrichment
110 (128)	Deceleration fuel shut-off

Ignition Timing
(see Display Group 000, Field 10)

Scan tool display	Ignition timing	Scan tool display	Ignition timing
48	+43.13	164	+2.34
63	+37.85	165	+1.99
79	+32.23	166	+1.64
95	+26.60	167	+1.29
111	+20.98	168	+0.94
127	+15.35	169	+0.59
143	+9.73	170	+0.23
144	+9.38	171	-0.12
145	+9.02	172	-0.47
146	+8.67	173	-0.82
147	+8.32	174	-1.17
148	+7.97	175	-1.57
149	+7.62	176	-1.18
150	+7.27	177	-2.22
151	+6.91	178	-2.58
152	+6.56	179	-2.93
153	+6.21	180	-3.28
154	+5.86	185	-4.69
155	+5.51	190	-6.45
156	+5.16	195	-8.55
157	+4.80	200	-10.31
158	+4.45	205	-12.07
159	+4.10	210	-13.83
160	+3.75	215	-15.59
161	+3.40	220	-17.34
162	+3.05	225	-19.10
163	+2.70	230	-20.86-

Ignition timing values preceded by a plus (+) sign are **B**efore **T**op **D**ead **C**enter (**BTDC**).
Ignition timing values preceded by a minus (-) sign are **A**fter **T**op **D**ead **C**enter (**ATDC**).

BASIC SETTINGS (FUNCTION 04)

9A engines have provisions for adjustment of base ignition timing, idle mixture (CO), and idle speed. These operating parameters must be manually set to baseline values. During engine operation, data is received from the various sensors and corrections are made as required. These “adaptive” settings are retained in the ECM’s memory when the ignition is switched off and become the starting point for subsequent engine operation.

If the ECM is disconnected from the battery during repairs for any reason, the adaptive values are erased and the ECM will revert to the default values allowing the engine to run. The default values may not match the current needs of the engine, which can result in poor performance and driveability. Also, when repairs have been made, such as repair of a vacuum leak, the default values will not match the current needs of the engine.

In order to provide the Engine Management System (EMS) with the greatest possible range of adaptation, engine basic settings must be adjusted to allow an optimal starting point. Use of a scan tool set to Function 04, Basic Settings, is required for these adjustments.

When an appropriate scan tool is properly connected to the CIS-E Motronic ECM and set to Function 04 (basic settings), the ECM is instructed to:

- Stabilize ignition timing
- Stabilize idle speed
- Disable EVAP system
- Allow for mixture (CO) adjustment

Initiating basic settings

Begin the basic settings/ignition timing procedure by observing the following preliminary requirements:

Preliminary requirements:

- If adjustments are being performed as the result of a performance issue, insure that all pertinent information regarding the situation is available.
- Insure that any outstanding Volkswagen Campaigns have been completed.
- Visually inspect all ground connections on engine, transmission and battery. Insure that wiring harnesses are routed correctly and are undamaged. Check for air/vacuum leaks from the following: oil cap, dipstick, intake air boot, connecting hoses/ducts, crankcase vent hoses, vacuum hoses and lines.
- Insure that correct version ECM and related components are installed.
- Check ignition system components for condition and correct application.
- Check knock sensors for correct application, torque, and wire routing.
- Check throttle linkage for correct gap between idle switch actuation arm and throttle arm. Check throttle cable for proper adjustment.
- Check CTP and WOT Switches for proper operation.

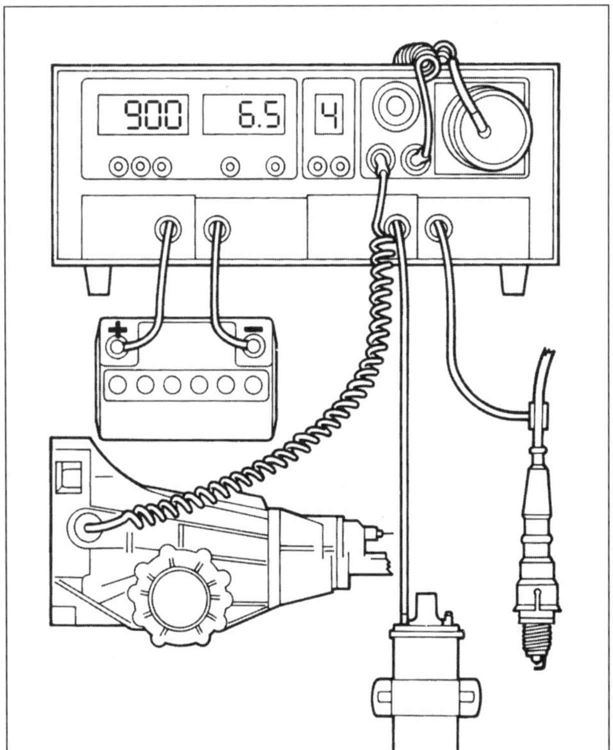

0021115

Test conditions

- Ignition switched off.
- Remove all fuel pressure testing equipment (if previously installed).
- Connect engine tester VAG 1367 or equivalent.

◄ Engine tester such as the VAG 1367 must be used in conjunction with an exhaust gas analyzer to properly adjust engine settings.

- Remove tamper-proof plug from air sensor housing assembly.

- Connect exhaust gas analyzer to sampling tube (upstream of Three Way Catalytic Converter) insuring an airtight connection.

- Disconnect crankcase breather/vent hoses from housing on lower cylinder block. Position so that only fresh air can be drawn in.

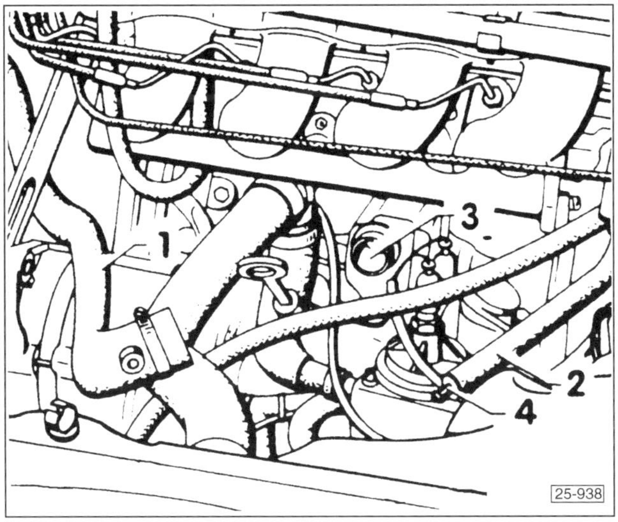

< Disconnect crankcase breather/vent hoses (**1** and **2**) from breather housing (**3**) on lower cylinder block. Position hoses so that they cannot draw vented fumes back into engine, only fresh air. Calibrated orifice (**4**) must remain in hose (**2**).

- Disconnect harness connector from differential fuel pressure regulator and connect harness test adaptor VAG 1315A/1 or equivalent and digital multimeter. Set digital multimeter to read milliamps ranging to 200mA.

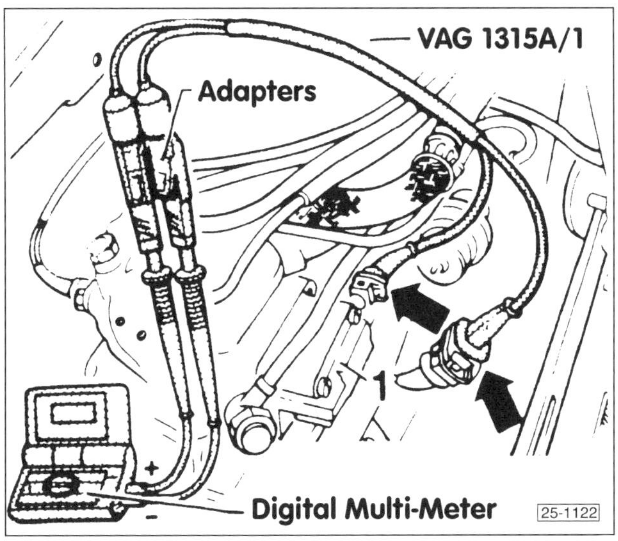

< Disconnect harness connector from differential fuel pressure regulator and connect harness test adaptor VAG 1315A/1 and Digital Multi-Meter into vehicle wiring harness (**arrows**) at differential fuel pressure regulator (**1**). Switch meter to read milliamps ranging to 200mA.

- Switch ignition on, but do not start engine. Observe multimeter display.

NOTE
Displayed value must be positive polarity (+) 90 mA to (+) 110 mA. If minus polarity (-) is displayed, reverse meter leads.

- Vehicle stationary, automatic transmission in **P** or **N**, handbrake on.

- Start engine and allow to warm up until engine oil temperature is at least 176°F (80°C). Accelerate engine to approximately 3000 rpm several times to insure removal of any fuel vapors trapped in fuel lines.

- Radiator fan must have cycled on at least one time, but must not run while taking measurements.

- All electrical consumers including air conditioner must be switched off.

- Exhaust system must be free from leaks.

Basic Settings (Function 04)

- Connect scan tool as previously detailed and allow engine to run at idle.

Adjusting Basic Settings:

- Allow engine to remain at idle speed.
- From the initial Menu select:
  1 Rapid Data
- From the address word Menu select:
  01 Engine Electronics
- Advance to the Function Menu when the ECM responds with the version information.
- From the Function Menu select:
  02 Check DTC memory.
  (Read and erase any DTCs recorded)

```
Start Basic Setting                 HELP
Input Display Group Number           XXX
```

◄ From the Function Menu select:
04 Basic settings.

- From the Start Basic Settings display, input:
  display group 000 (or 00 if applicable).

```
System in Basic Setting              000
XX XX XX XX XX XX XX XX 5 XX
```

◄ Observe value in display field 9. Value must be **5**. If any other value is displayed, see Input signals to ECM, Display Group 000, Field 9 for interpretation).

- Scan tool must remain in Basic Settings for remainder of procedure.
- Observe ignition timing on engine tester:
  Specification:
  checking. . . . . 4° - 8°BTDC
  adjusting . . . . 5° - 7°BTDC
- Adjust timing and re-test as required (loosen ignition distributor and rotate to adjust timing).
- Observe idle speed on engine tester (not scan tool):
  Specification:. . . . . 800 - 1000 RPM
  (Idle speed cannot be adjusted.)
- Observe differential fuel pressure regulator control current:
  Specification: . . . .+2.5 mA (±2.5 mA)
  (Value must fluctuate at idle.)

NOTE
If differential fuel pressure regulator control current does not fluctuate slightly at idle, check Heated Oxygen Sensor operation and control.

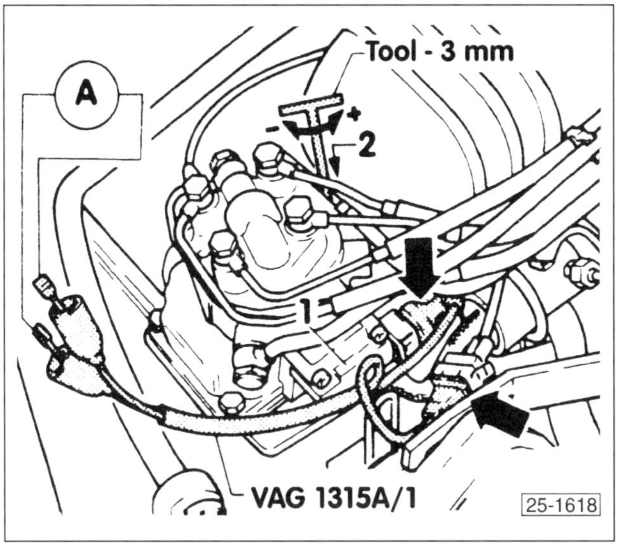

Adjust differential fuel pressure regulator control current as required at CO adjusting screw. Remove anti-tamper plug above screw as necessary.
- Do not push down on 3 mm allen wrench while adjusting.
- Do not accelerate engine with adjusting tool in place.
- Remove wrench after each adjustment, accelerate engine slightly and allow to stabilize before observing multimeter.

NOTE
Turning adjuster to the plus (+) side increases the value, turning to the minus (-) decreases it.

- Observe CO content on exhaust gas analyzer:
  Specification: . . . . 0.2 - 1.2% (by volume)
- If operating data is within specification and radiator coolant fan is not running, exit basic settings.
- Switch off ignition and disconnect all test equipment.
- Install new tamper-proof plug in air sensor housing assembly. (Legally required and also keeps dirt out of sensor adjustment mechanism).
- Reconnect all removed hoses and lines, inspect for tightness.
- Reconnect all removed electrical connectors, inspect for tightness.
- Reinstall cap on CO sampling tube.
- Road test/test drive vehicle.
- Connect scan tool and recheck for DTCs as required.

If operating data on exhaust gas analyzer and/or engine tester does not fall within listed specification, determine the malfunction and re-test. Idle speed and CO content are not adjustable.

Output Diagnostic Test Mode (Function 03)

The output diagnostic test mode can only be used when the ignition is switched on, but with the engine not running. The following is a list of components checked during the output diagnostic test mode and the order in which they are tested:

- Differential Fuel Pressure Regulator (N73)
- Evaporative Emission (EVAP) Canister Purge Regulator Valve (N80)
- Idle Air Control (IAC) Valve (N71)
- Cold Start Injector (N17)

```
Rapid data transfer                 Q
03 - Output Diagnostic Test Mode
```

◄ Scan tool display from VAG 1551 identifying start of Function 03.

Testing with Function 03

Testing CIS-E Motronic equipped engines with a scan tool in Function 03 is a relatively straight forward operation. Items to consider before beginning include:

- The Closed Throttle Position (CTP) Switch must function properly.
- All engine system fuses and grounds must be good.
- The engine temperature is not a critical factor for this function

```
Output Diagnostic Test Mode      -->
Differential pressure regulator-N73
```

◄ Display for Function 03 as shown on a VAG 1551 showing first Output Diagnostic Mode test.

After the scan tool has been connected and Function 03 selected, proceed with the test as indicated on the scan tool noting the following points:

1. **Differential Fuel Pressure Regulator (N73)** – The Differential Fuel Pressure Regulator control current will be cycled from 0 mA to 100 mA. Measurement of this value will require the insertion of special tool VAG 1315A/1 or equivalent into the wiring to measure mA with a digital multimeter. The program is advanced with the right arrow button (-->).

2. **Evaporative Emission (EVAP) Canister Purge Regulator Valve (N80)** – The EVAP Canister Purge regulator Valve will be switched off and on (opened and closed). The resulting noise is faint and may be difficult to hear, but operation of the valve can usually be felt. Advance the program with the right arrow button (-->).

3. **Idle Air Control (IAC) Valve (N71)** – The IAC Valve will be operated through a range of positions with a clicking sound. The vibrations from operation can be heard and felt. Advance the program with the right arrow button (-->).

4. **Cold Start Injector (N17)** – The Cold Start Injector will be activated a maximum of 10 times in short bursts when the throttle is opened slightly. The Injector valve can be heard to click. Advance the program with the right arrow button (-->).

The Output Diagnostic Test Mode is helpful in checking the electrical operation of a given component. It can also be helpful in diagnosing mechanical malfunctions as well. If, for example, an EVAP Canister Purge Regulator Valve was suspected of a malfunction, the hoses could be disconnected and the Output Diagnostic Test Mode run while blowing through the valve. This would help determine if it worked properly. Similar tests can be devised with many of the other components.

In the event of a component failing to operate, the component and the wiring should be checked for continuity, open circuits, and short circuits, including short circuits to ground. Always consult the appropriate wiring diagram.

```
Output Diagnostic Test Mode

Differential pressure regulator-N73
Evap canister purge valve-N80
Idle air control valve-N71
Cold-start injector-N17
```

◄ When the VAG 1551 printer is switched on, the tape will be printed with all of the tests in sequence.

NOTE
Different ECM and/or scan tool software versions may identify components with slightly different names. Alpha-numeric designation (e.g. N80) will be correct in all cases.

```
8A0 907 404 CC                     MOTOR

CODING   00
```

Code Control Module (Function 07)

Control module coding by means of the scan tool is not a supported function with CIS-E Motronic ECMs in 9A coded engines. Coding information does appear, however, in Function 01 (control unit versions).

Different ECMs are used based on installed equipment and market variations:

- Transmission type (manual or automatic).
- Market area (California or 49 States/Canada).
- Transmission Control Module EPROM version.
- Automatic Transmission Range Switch type (push button or rotary).

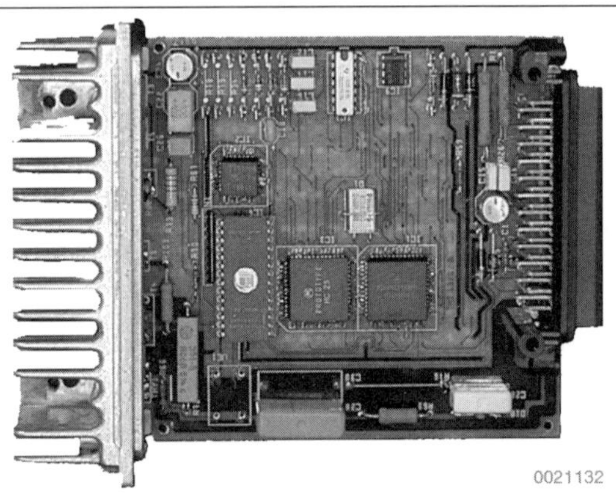

0021132

ECM for 9A 16V engine shown with housing removed. Note large aluminum heatsink on one end. Part number information will be printed directly on the housing or on a sticker affixed to the housing.

NOTE

Part numbers can change within the Volkswagen Parts system for several reasons and are not, therefore, listed here. Always consult with your Volkswagen Parts Department or aftermarket parts specialist for the latest parts information.

Component and Signal Overview, 9A Engine

9A engines use the Bosch CIS-E Motronic engine management system. This system is based on the mechanical Bosch Continuous Injection System (CIS) where fuel is metered in a continuous supply proportional to the quantity of air drawn into the engine.

Signals from sensors and other input sources are processed by the ECM. Signals to control the engine are sent to actuators along with engine information needed by other systems or functions.

Component and Signal Overview, 9A Engine

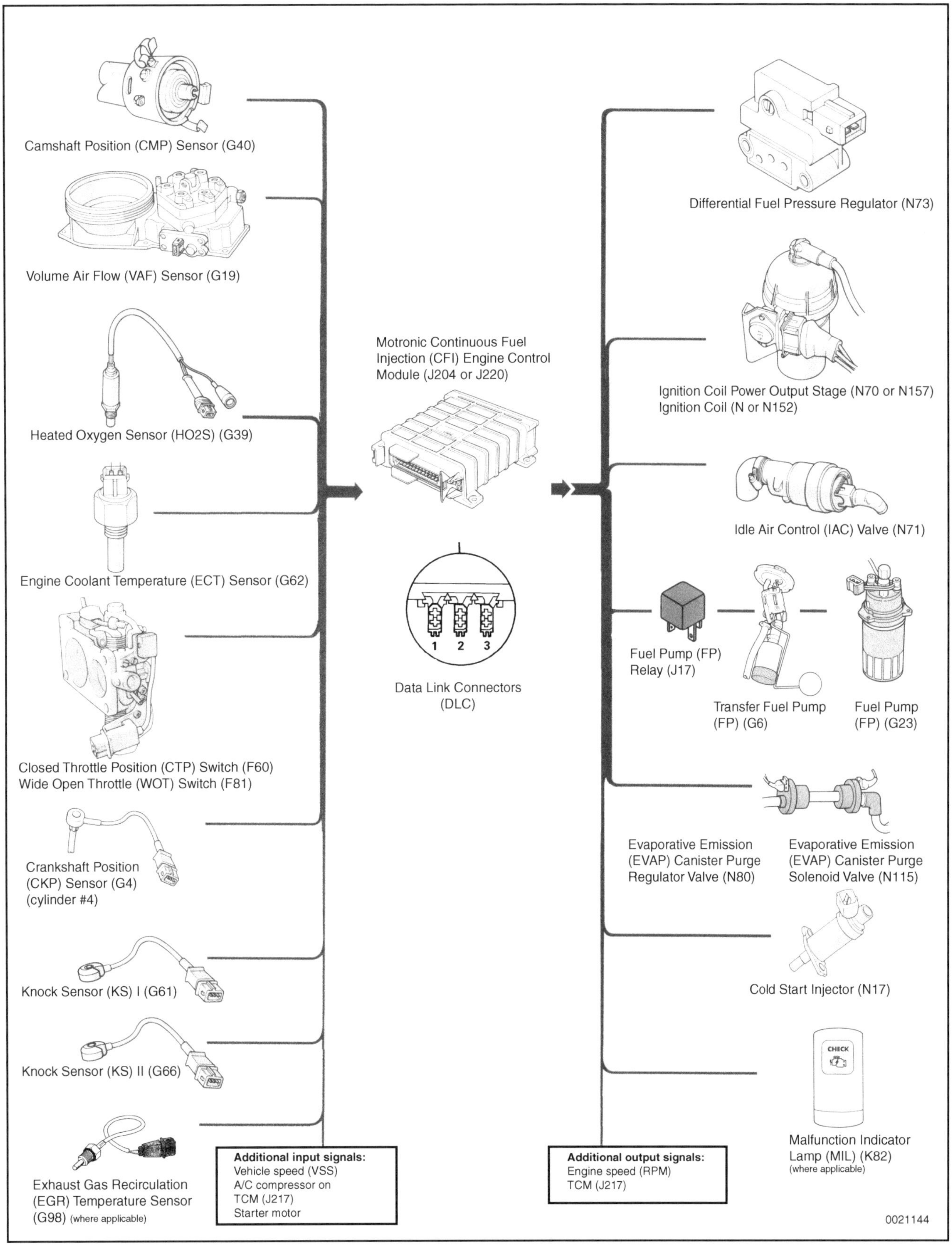

Component and Signal Overview, 9A Engine

Component and Signal Overview (9A)

Volkswagen 16V 2.0 CIS-E Motronic, 4-cylinder	
Fuel injection	Continuous Injection System (CIS) with Lambda (Oxygen Sensor) Control
Fuel delivery	Tank-mounted electric fuel transfer pump, reservoir-mounted electric fuel pump, fuel pressure accumulator, mechanical pressure regulator, pressure operated fuel injectors
Ignition system	Distributor, with power output stage and ignition coil, ECM controlled
Emission control	3-Way catalytic converter, evaporative emissions with carbon canister, positive crankcase ventilation, mechanical (pneumatic) exhaust gas recirculation valve
Diagnostics	On-Board Diagnostics via scan tool, Rapid data transfer, Non-volatile memory
Control Module	Single 35-pin CIS-E Motronic Engine Control Module (ECM) (J204 or J220)
Sensors	Camshaft Position (CMP) Sensor (G40)
	Wide Open Throttle (WOT) Switch (F81)
	Closed Throttle Position (CTP) Switch (F60) [1]
	Heated Oxygen Sensor (H2OS) (G39)
	Engine Coolant Temperature (ECT) Sensor (G62)
	Crankshaft Position (CKP) Sensor (G4)
	Volume Air Flow (VAF) Sensor (G19)
	Knock Sensor (KS) 1 (G61)
	Knock Sensor (KS) 2 (G66)
	Exhaust Gas Recirculation (EGR) Temperature Sensor (G98)[2]
Input signals	Vehicle speed (VSS)
	Air conditioner, compressor on
	Automatic Transmission Control Module (TCM) (J217)
	Starter motor
Actuators	Idle Air Control Valve (IAC) (N71)
	Evaporative Emission (EVAP) Canister Purge Regulator Valve (N80)
	Evaporative Emissions (EVAP) Canister Purge Solenoid Valve (N115)
	Differential Fuel Pressure Regulator (N73)
	Cold Start Injector (N17)
	Ignition Coil Power Output Stage (N70 or N157), and Ignition Coil (N or N152)
	Fuel Pump (FP) Relay (J17), Transfer Fuel Pump (FP) (G6), and Fuel Pump (FP) (G23)
	Malfunction Indicator Lamp (MIL) and Switch (K82)[3]
Output signals	Engine speed (rpm)
	Automatic Transmission Control Module (TCM) (J217)

[1] Vehicles with automatic transmissions also use a TP Sensor. The TP Sensor is combined in a common housing with the CTP and WOT Switches.

[2] EGR only installed on vehicles originally intended for sale in California.

[3] MIL only functional on vehicles with EGR.

Technical Data

Technical data is compiled from several Volkswagen publications. In some instances, the information from these sources differed slightly. In these cases, the most current specifications are listed.

9A (Passat, Golf, Jetta)	**Technical Data**
Type	4-cylinder in-line (R4), gasoline fuel
Construction	Cast iron block, aluminum 4V cylinder head, belt/chain driven double overhead camshafts
Displacement	2.0 Liters (1984 cc), (121 cid)
Horsepower	134 hp (100 Kw) @ 5800 rpm
Torque	133 lb-ft (180 Nm) @ 4400 rpm
Bore	82.5 mm
Stroke	92.8 mm
Compression ratio	10.8:1
Firing order	1-3-4-2
Management	CIS-E Motronic

Notes

Engine Code
PG

General

The vehicles listed below are equipped with engine code **PG**. This 1.8 liter engine uses a Volkswagen's **Digifant** engine management system.

The **PG** engine is installed in the Volkswagen Corrado for all 50 States and Canada for model years 1990, 1991, and 1992. Only PG engines originally certified for sale in California for model years 1991 and 1992 are equipped with the scan tool capability detailed in this section.

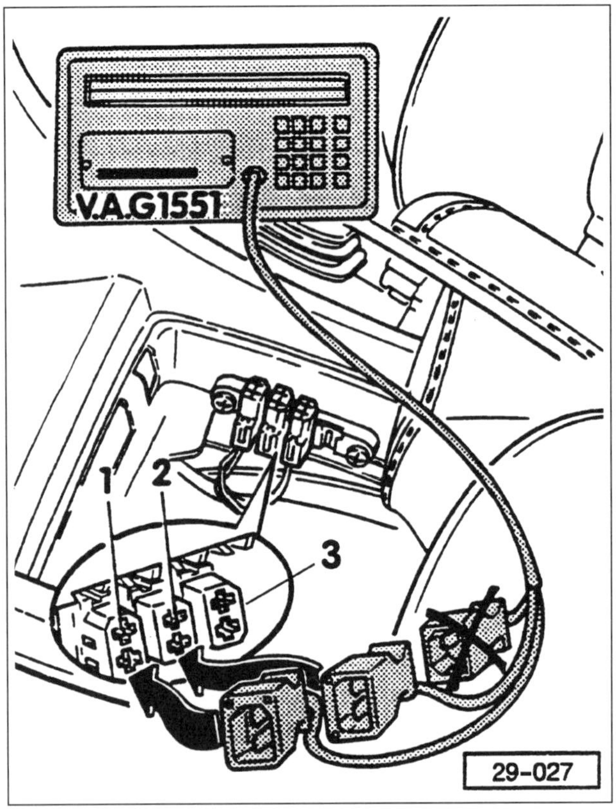

Engine Code PG Vehicles

Engine Code PG	Model Years
Corrado	1991, 1992, (California certified only)

Scan tool, connecting

The scan tool is connected through the DLC (Data Link Connector).

Corrado, 1991-1992:
Manual transmission: center console under shifter boot.
Automatic transmission: center console under selector indicator cover
Black connector on scan tool harness is connected to black connection on vehicle (**1**) and provides scan tool power. White connector is connected to the white connection on the vehicle (**2**) for data transfer. Blue connector (**3**) is not used.

Scan tool, functions available

	Scan Tool Functions Available	Ignition on, not running	Engine at idle	Page
✔	Control unit version (01)	Yes	Yes	Appendix A
✔	Check DTC memory (02)	Yes	Yes	Appendix A
✔	Output diagnostic test mode (03)	No	No	189
✔	Basic settings (04)	No	No	188
✔	Erase DTC memory (05)	Yes	Yes	Appendix A
✔	End output (06)	Yes	Yes	Appendix A
✗	Code control module (07)	No	No	190
✔	Read measuring value blocks (08)	Yes	Yes	183

READ MEASURING VALUE BLOCKS (FUNCTION 08)

Measuring value blocks are assembled and displayed in sets called display groups. For the PG engine, display groups are numbered starting with 000 and continuing with 001 on up to 005.

```
Read Measuring Value Blocks        HELP
Input Display Group Number         XXX
```

◄ Scan tool display from VAG 1551 requesting Measuring Value Block Display Group information (XXX).

Display group overview, PG engine (Corrado - California only)

Function 08, (Corrado - California only) Display Group Overview 000[OV-1]										
Display Field	**1**	**2**	**3**	**4**	**5**	**6**	**7**	**8**	**9**	**10**
	IAT	CO FT	ECT	n/a	HO2S	n/a	n/a	n/a	n/a	n/a

OV-1) Some data is not relevant, or is unavailable. This data is identified as n/a.

Function 08 (Corrado - California only) Display Group Overview 001 - 005[OV-2]				
Display Field	**1**	**2**	**3**	**4**
Display Group 001	RPM	MAP	ECT	Injector duration
Display Group 002	RPM	n/a	n/a	Injector duration
Display Group 003	RPM	ECT	n/a	Injector duration
Display Group 004	RPM	MAP	n/a	Injector duration
Display Group 005	RPM	TPS	n/a	Injector duration

OV-2) Some data is not relevant, or is unavailable. This data is identified as n/a.

Read Measuring Value Blocks (Function 08)

Function 08
Display Group 000

Engine running at idle speed, coolant temperature above 80°C (176°F), ECM in **Read Measuring Value Block** (Function 08)

Display Field	Display Fields	Observed range:[000-1]	Corresponds to:
10	**Undefined data**[000-2]	—	—
9	**Undefined data**	—	—
8	**Undefined data**	—	—
7	**Undefined data**	—	—
6	**Undefined data**	—	—
5	**Heated Oxygen Sensor (HO2S) signal**	must vary by at least 14[000-3]	operation OK
4	**Undefined data**	—	—
3	**Engine Coolant Temperature (ECT) Sensor**	less than 11[000-4]	80°C (176°F)
2	**CO Fuel Trim(FT) Potentiometer**	40 - 140[000-5]	operation OK
1	**Intake Air Temperature (IAT)**	10 - 190[000-6]	operation OK

000-1) Overall range of values is 0 - 255.

000-2) Undefined data means that information is displayed on the scan tool but information to interpret or define it's meaning is unavailable.

000-3) Values between 0 - 5 indicate short circuit to positive in HO2S wiring to ECM
Values between 164 - 168 indicate open circuit in HO2S wiring to ECM.
Values between 230 and 255 indicate short circuit to ground in HO2S wiring to ECM.

000-4) Lower numbers are hotter. Temperature must rise (value will decrease) smoothly during engine warm-up.

000-5) Values between 250 - 255 indicate open circuit in CO FT Potentiometer wiring to ECM.
Value between 0 - 2 indicate short circuit to ground in CO FT Potentiometer wiring to ECM.

000-6) Values between 250 - 255 indicate open circuit in IAT Sensor wiring to ECM.
Value of 0 indicates short circuit to positive in IAT Sensor wiring to ECM.

Function 08 Display Group 001				
	1	**2**	**3**	**4**
Display	xxxx /min	xx%	xx.x °C	xx.x ms
Indicated	Engine speed	MAP signal	Coolant temperature	Fuel injector duration
Specification	750-850 idle rpm[001-1]	20%-40%	not available[001-4]	not available[001-5]
		At idle with coolant temperature at least 80°C (176°F) Value must fluctuate	Open circuit shows a constant -40° Short circuit shows a constant 80°C	
Working range	750...6100 rpm[001-2]	0%...100%[001-3]	-40°C...141°C (approximately)	

001-1) Valid with coolant temperature of at least 80° (176°F).

001-2) Approximate maximum governed rpm.

001-3) Values in this display field are valid only at idle with a coolant temperature of at least 80°C (176°F). Values fluctuating slightly in the range between 20 - 40% indicate MAP Sensor in ECM is OK. Constant value of 45% or greater indicates malfunction with vacuum hose connecting intake with ECM.

001-4) No specification available. Experience indicates that at idle, temperature will vary between approximately 86°C and 105°C depending on radiator fan operating cycle. Temperature must rise smoothly during engine warm-up. If value displayed does not increase jumps up by 2°C to 5°C in display, ECM is raising temperature based on running time due to a faulty ECT Sensor.

001-5) No idle specification available. Increase engine speed above 3000 rpm at least 3 times and let speed return to idle for at least 2 minutes. Note value. Again increase engine speed above 3000 rpm; fuel injector duration display must increase. Allow engine speed to return to idle. Value must drop to 0.00 mS to indicate deceleration fuel shut-off as speed decreases. Previously displayed idle value should again be shown.

Function 08 Display Group 002				
	1	**2**	**3**	**4**
Display	xxxx /min	xxx	xxx	xx.x ms
Indicated	Engine speed	n/a[002-2]	n/a[002-2]	Fuel injector duration
Specification	750-850 idle rpm[002-1]			none given[002-3]
Working range	750...6100 rpm[002-1]			

002-1) As in Display Group 001, Field 1.

002-2) Data is not relevant/undefined.

002-3) As in Display Group 001, Field 4.

Read Measuring Value Blocks (Function 08)

Function 08 Display Group 003				
	1	2	3	4
Display	xxxx /min	xx.x °C	xxx	xx.x ms
Indicated	Engine speed	Coolant temperature	n/a[003-3]	Fuel injector duration
Specification	750-850 idle rpm[003-1]	not available[003-2]		not available[003-4]
		Open circuit shows a constant -40° Short circuit shows a constant 80°C		
Working range	750...6100 rpm[003-1]	-40°C...141°C (approximately)		

003-1) As in Display Group 001, Field 1.

003-2) As in Display Group 001, Field 3.

003-3) As in Display Group 002, Field 2.

003-4) As in Display Group 001, Field 4.

Function 08 Display Group 004				
	1	2	3	4
Display	xxxx /min	xx%	xxx	xx.x ms
Indicated	Engine speed	MAP signal	n/a[004-3]	Fuel injector duration
Specification	750-850 idle rpm[004-1]	20%-40%		none given[004-4]
		At idle with coolant temperature at least 80°C (176°F) Value must fluctuate		
Working range	750...6100 rpm[004-1]	0%...100%[004-2]		

004-1) As in Display Group 001, Field 1.

004-2) As in Display Group 001, Field 2.

004-3) As in Display Group 002, Field 2.

004-4) As in Display Group 001, Field 4.

Function 08 Display Group 005				
	1	2	3	4
Display	xxxx /min	xx.x ∠°	xxx	xx.x ms
Indicated	Engine speed	TPS angle	n/a[005-3]	Fuel injector duration
Specification	750-850 idle rpm[005-1]	5-50°		not available[005-4]
		At CTP		
Working range	750...6100 rpm[005-1]	0°...to over 90°[005-2]		

005-1) As in Display Group 001, Field 1.

005-2) Momentarily operate throttle to WOT. Value displayed should be 90.0 ∠° or greater.
0.0 ∠° indicates open circuit in TPS wiring to ECM.
90.0 ∠° or greater at idle indicates short circuit to positive in TPS wiring to ECM.
Value must increase uniformly and without interruption when throttle is opened.

005-3) As in Display Group 002, Field 2.

005-4) As in Display Group 001, Field 4.

BASIC SETTINGS (FUNCTION 04)

Adjustment of engine settings through the use of Function 04 (basic settings) is not a supported function in this version of Digifant. Baseline values for ignition timing, idle speed, and CO (carbon monoxide) content require manual adjustment.

Adjustment of engine settings does not require use of a scan tool, but does requires the connection of several other pieces of test equipment. After adjustment of engine settings, it will, however, be necessary to connect a scan tool and erase DTCs that are recorded during the normal adjusting procedures.

Test equipment required to adjust engine settings includes the following:

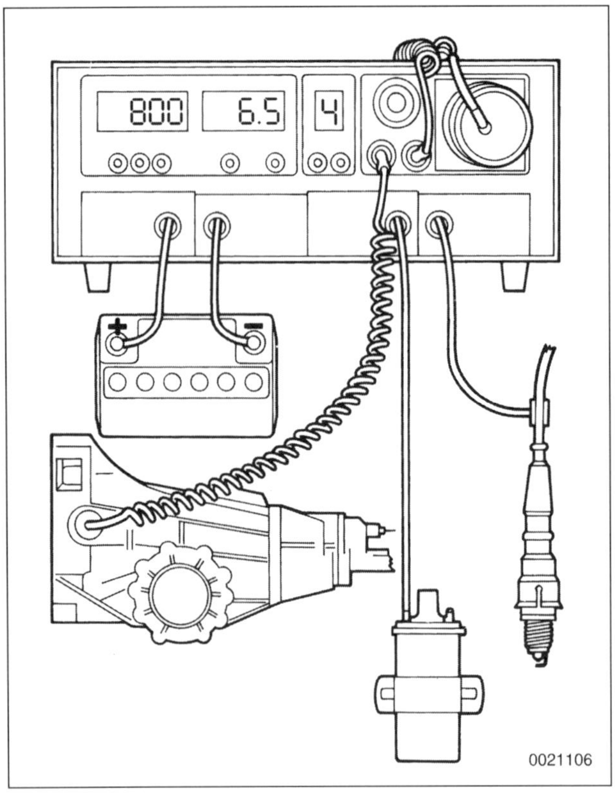

- ◀ An engine tester such as the VAG 1367 must be connected to the engine to measure ignition timing and engine speed.

- An exhaust gas analyzer must be attached to the CO pick-up or sampling tube located ahead of the catalytic converter to measure CO (carbon monoxide) content.

OUTPUT DIAGNOSTIC TEST MODE (FUNCTION 03)

The ability of the scan tool to instruct the ECM to operate certain electrical components is not a supported function in this version of Digifant.

CODE CONTROL MODULE (FUNCTION 07)

Control module coding by means of the scan tool is not a supported function with California Digifant I ECMs. Coding information does appear, however, in Function 01 (control unit versions). ECM coding is generally accomplished through the use of specific part number ECMs.

Several part number supersessions have resulted in 2 ECMs covering all applications with the determining factor being only if equipped with manual or automatic transmission.

```
037 906 023 S        DIGIFANT        0883
CODING   00000
```

◄ VAG 1551 scan tool display for Engine Control Module from a 1991 California Corrado. Part number on ECM label will match Scan Tool display in Function 01.

NOTE
Always consult with your Volkswagen Parts Department or aftermarket parts specialist for the latest parts information.

COMPONENT AND SIGNAL OVERVIEW, PG ENGINE

PG engines use a version of the Volkswagen-developed **Digifant** engine management system. This version of Digifant is generally known as Digifant with G-Charger except in California where it is designated Digifant I due to legal requirements.

Signals from sensors and other input sources are processed by the ECM. Signals to control the engine are sent to the actuators.

Component and Signal Overview, PG Engine

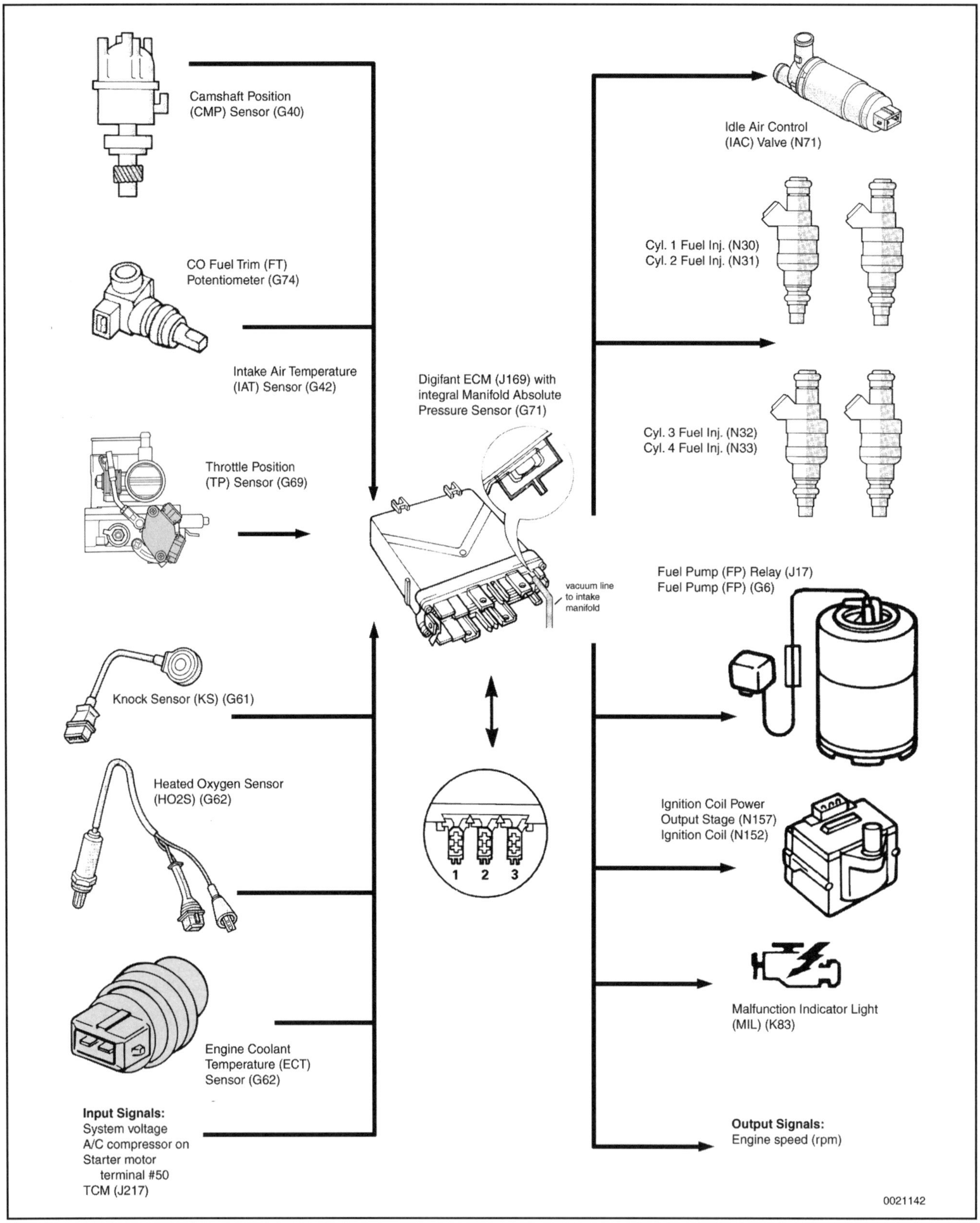

Component and Signal Overview (PG)

Volkswagen California Digifant 1, 4-cylinder	
Fuel injection	Non-sequential (simultaneous) Multi-Point Fuel Injection with Lambda (Oxygen Sensor) Control, belt driven supercharger and charge-air cooler (intercooler), OBD-I
Fuel delivery	Tank-mounted 2-stage electric fuel pump, load-sensing mechanical pressure regulator
Ignition system	Distributor, power output stage and ignition coil, single knock sensor, ECM controlled
Emission control	3-Way catalytic converter, carbon canister with mechanical (vacuum) control valve, positive crankcase ventilation
Diagnostics	On-Board Diagnostics via scan tool, Rapid data transfer, Non-volatile memory
Control Module	Single 38-pin Digifant Engine Control Module (ECM) (J169) with integral Manifold Absolute Pressure (MAP) Sensor (G71), supplied by Digifant ECM Power Supply Relay (J176)
Sensors	Camshaft Position (CMP) Sensor (G40)
	Intake Air Temperature (IAT) Sensor (G42)
	Throttle Position (TP) Sensor (G69)[1]
	Heated Oxygen Sensor (H2OS) (G39)
	Engine Coolant Temperature (ECT) Sensor (G62)
	Knock Sensor (KS) (G61)
	CO Fuel Trim (FT) Potentiometer (G74)[2]
Input signals	System voltage
	Starter motor (terminal 50)
	Air conditioner, compressor on
	Automatic Transmission Control Module (TCM) (J217)
Actuators	Idle Air Control (IAC) Valve (N71)
	Fuel Injectors: Cylinder 1 (N30), Cylinder 2 (N31), Cylinder 3 (N32), Cylinder 4 (N33)
	Ignition Coil Power Output Stage (N157), and Ignition Coil (N152)
	Fuel Pump (FP) Relay (J17), and Fuel Pump (FP) (G6)[3]
	Malfunction Indicator Light (MIL) (K83)
Output signals	Engine speed (rpm)

[1] Vehicles with automatic transmissions use separate TP Sensors combined in a single housing.

[2] Built into IAT Sensor housing.

[3] All vehicles also use a Fuel Pump (FP) After-Run Control Module (J206) and Fuel Pump (FP) After-Run Pressure Switch (F130). Operation of these components is essentially independent of the Digifant system.

TECHNICAL DATA

Technical data is compiled from several Volkswagen publications. In some instances, the information from these sources differed slightly. In these cases, the most current specifications are listed.

PG (Corrado, California)	**Technical Data**
Type	4-cylinder in-line (R4), belt-driven supercharger (G-60) with charge air cooler, gasoline fuel
Construction	Cast iron block, aluminum 2V cylinder head, belt driven single overhead camshaft
Displacement	1.8 Liters (1781 cc), (109 cid)
Horsepower	158 hp (118 Kw) @ 5600 rpm
Torque	166 lb-ft (225 Nm) @ 4000 rpm
Bore	81.0 mm
Stroke	86.4 mm
Compression ratio	8.0:1
Firing order	1-3-4-2
Management	Digifant I

Engine Code

RV

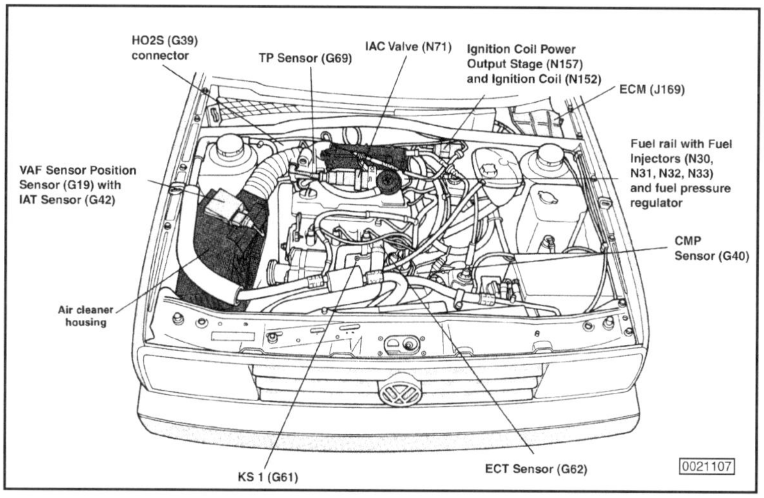

GENERAL

The vehicles listed below are equipped with engine code **RV**. This engine uses a version of Volkswagen's **Digifant** engine management system. The displacement of this inline 4-cylinder engine is 1.8 liters.

The **RV** engine is installed in the Volkswagen Golf and Jetta for all 50 States and Canada for model years 1987 through 1992. Only engines originally certified for sale in California for model years 1991 and 1992 are equipped with the scan tool capability detailed in this section.

Engine Code RV Vehicles

Engine Code RV	Model Years
Golf and Jetta	1991, 1992 (California certified only)

Scan tool, connecting

The scan tool is connected through the DLC (Data Link Connector).

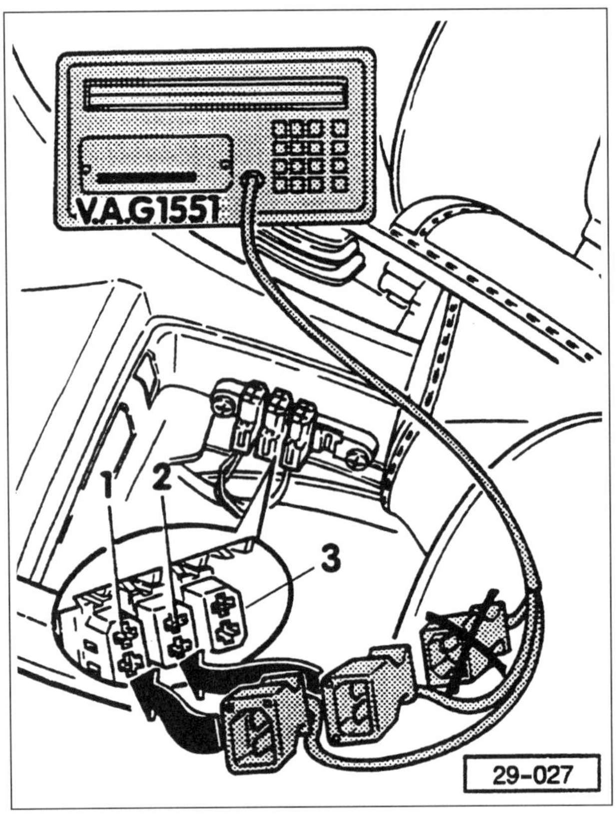

◄ **Golf and Jetta, 1991-1992 (California only)**:
Manual transmission: center console under shifter boot.
Automatic transmission: center console under selector indicator cover.
Black connector on scan tool harness is connected to black connection on vehicle (**1**) and provides scan tool power. White connector is connected to the white connection on the vehicle (**2**) for data transfer. Blue connector (**3**) is not used.

Scan tool, functions available

	Scan Tool Functions Available	Ignition on, not running	Engine at idle	Page
✔	Control unit version (01)	Yes	Yes	Appendix A
✔	Check DTC memory (02)	Yes	Yes	Appendix A
✔	Output diagnostic test mode (03)	No	No	201
✔	Basic settings (04)	No	No	200
✔	Erase DTC memory (05)	Yes	Yes	Appendix A
✔	End output (06)	Yes	Yes	Appendix A
✗	Code control module (07)	No	No	201
✔	Read measuring value blocks (08)	Yes	Yes	195

READ MEASURING VALUE BLOCKS (FUNCTION 08)

Measuring value blocks are assembled and displayed in sets called display groups. For the RV engine, display groups are numbered starting with 000 and continuing with 001 on up to 005.

```
Read Measuring Value Blocks        HELP
Input Display Group Number          XXX
```

◀ Scan tool display from VAG 1551 requesting Measuring Value Block Display Group information (XXX).

Display group overview, RV engine (Golf/Jetta - California only)

Function 08 RV, (Golf/Jetta - California only) Display Group Overview 000[OV-1]										
Display Field	**1**	**2**	**3**	**4**	**5**	**6**	**7**	**8**	**9**	**10**
	n/a	n/a	ECT	n/a	HO2S	n/a	n/a	n/a	n/a	n/a

OV-1) Some data is not relevant, or is unavailable. This data is identified as n/a.

Function 08 RV (Golf/Jetta - California only) Display Group Overview 001 - 005[OV-2]				
Display Field	**1**	**2**	**3**	**4**
Display Group 001	RPM	VAF	ECT	Injector duration
Display Group 002	RPM	IAT	n/a	Injector duration
Display Group 003	RPM	ECT	n/a	Injector duration
Display Group 004	RPM	VAF	n/a	Injector duration
Display Group 005	RPM	TPS	n/a	Injector duration

OV-2) Some data is not relevant, or is unavailable. This data is identified as n/a.

Read Measuring Value Blocks (Function 08)

Function 08 **Display Group 000**		
Engine running at idle speed, coolant temperature above 80°C (176°F), ECM in **Read Measuring Value Block** (Function 08)		
Display Fields	**Observed range:** 000-1	**Corresponds to:**
10: **Undefined data** 000-2	—	—
9: **Undefined data**	—	—
8: **Undefined data**	—	—
7: **Undefined data**	—	—
6: **Undefined data**	—	—
5: **Heated Oxygen Sensor (HO2S) signal**	must vary by at least 14 000-3	operation OK
4: **Undefined data**	—	—
3: **Engine Coolant Temperature (ECT) Sensor**	less than 11 000-4	80°C (176°F)
2: **Undefined data**	—	—
1: **Undefined data**	—	—

000-1) Overall range of values is 0 - 255.

000-2) Undefined data means that information is displayed on the scan tool but to interpret or define it's meaning is unavailable.

000-3) Values between 0 - 5 indicate short circuit to positive in HO2S wiring to ECM.
Values between 164 - 168 indicate open circuit in HO2S wiring to ECM.
Values between 230 and 255 indicate short circuit to ground in HO2S wiring to ECM.

000-4) Lower numbers are hotter. Temperature must rise (value will decrease) smoothly during engine warm-up.

Function 08 Display Group 001				
	1	**2**	**3**	**4**
Display	xxxx /min	xx%	xx.x °C	xx.x ms
Indicated	Engine speed	VAF signal	Coolant temperature	Fuel injector duration
Specification	750-850 idle rpm[001-1]	16%-26%	not available[001-4]	not available[001-5]
		At idle with coolant temperature at least 80°C (176°F)	Open circuit shows a constant -40° Short circuit shows a constant 80°C	
Working range	750...6300 rpm[001-2]	0%...100%[001-3]	-40°C...141°C (approximately)	

001-1) Valid with coolant temperature of at least 80° (176°F).

001-2) Approximate maximum governed rpm.

001-3) Values in this display field are valid only at idle with a coolant temperature greater than 80°C (176°F).
Values between 16 - 26% indicate VAF Sensor and ECM control OK.
Values between 5 - 15% indicate intake air leaks.
Values between 0 - 2% indicate open circuit in VAF Sensor wiring to ECM.

001-4) No specification available. Experience indicates that at idle, temperature will vary between approximately 86°C and 105°C depending on radiator fan operating cycle. Temperature must rise smoothly during engine warm-up. If value displayed jumps up by 2°C to 5°C, ECM is raising temperature based on running time due to a faulty ECT Sensor.

001-5) No specification available. Increase engine speed above 3000 rpm at least 3 times and let speed return to idle for at least 2 minutes. Note value. Again increase engine speed above 3000 rpm; fuel injector duration display must increase. Allow engine speed to return to idle. Value must drop to 0.00 mS to indicate deceleration fuel shut-off as speed decreases. Previously displayed idle value should again be shown.

Read Measuring Value Blocks (Function 08)

Function 08
Display Group 002

	1	2	3	4
Display	xxxx /min	xx.x °C	xxx	xx.x ms
Indicated	Engine speed	Intake air temperature	n/a[002-3]	Fuel injector duration
Specification	750-850 idle rpm[002-1]	not available[002-2]		not available[002-4]
		Open circuit shows a constant 19.6°		
Working range	750...6300 rpm[002-1]	-46.5°C...141.0°C		

002-1) As in Display Group 001, Field 1.

002-2) No specification available. Experience indicates that at idle, temperature will be approximately ambient air temperature. Intake air pre-heater will generally keep incoming air temperature to around 30°C, but may be substantially higher on a very hot day. Very high temperatures suggest a malfunctioning intake air pre-heater.

002-3) Data is not relevant or is undefined.

002-4) As in Display Group 001, Field 4.

Function 08
Display Group 003

	1	2	3	4
Display	xxxx /min	xx.x °C	xxx	xx.x ms
Indicated	Engine speed	Coolant temperature	n/a[003-3]	Fuel injector duration
Specification	750-850 idle rpm[003-1]	not available[003-2]		not available[003-4]
		Open circuit shows a constant -40° Short circuit shows a constant 80°C		
Working range	750...6300 rpm[003-1]	-40°C...141°C (approximately)		

003-1) As in Display Group 001, Field 1.

003-2) As in Display Group 001, Field 3.

003-3) As in Display Group 002, Field 3.

003-4) As in Display Group 001, Field 4.

Function 08 Display Group 004				
	1	2	3	4
Display	xxxx /min	xx%	xxx	xx.x ms
Indicated	Engine speed	VAF signal	n/a[004-3]	Fuel injector duration
Specification	750-850 idle rpm[004-1]	16%-26%		not available[004-4]
		At idle with coolant temperature at least 80°C (176°F)		
Working range	750...6300 rpm[004-1]	0%...100%[004-2]		

004-1) As in Display Group 001, Field 1.

004-2) As in Display Group 001, Field 2.

004-3) As in Display Group 002, Field 3.

004-4) As in Display Group 001, Field 4.

Function 08 Display Group 005				
	1	2	3	4
Display	xxxx /min	xx.x ∠°	xxx	xx.x ms
Indicated	Engine speed	TPS angle	n/a[005-3]	Fuel injector duration
Specification	750-850 idle rpm[005-1]	5-50°		not available[005-4]
		At CTP		
Working range	750...6300 rpm[005-1]	0°...to over 90°[005-2]		

005-1) As in Display Group 001, Field 1.

005-2) Momentarily operate throttle to WOT. Value displayed should be 90.0 ∠° or greater.
0.0 ∠° indicates open circuit in TPS wiring to ECM.
90.0 ∠° or greater at idle indicates short circuit to positive in TPS wiring to ECM.
Value must increase uniformly and without interruption when throttle is opened.

005-3) As in Display Group 002, Field 3.

005-4) As in Display Group 001, Field 4.

Basic Settings (Function 04)

Adjustment of engine settings through the use of Function 04 (basic settings) is not a supported function in this version of Digifant. Baseline values for ignition timing, idle speed, and CO (carbon monoxide) content require manual adjustment.

Adjustment of engine settings does not require use of a scan tool, but does require the connection of several other pieces of test equipment. After adjustment of engine settings, it will be necessary to connect a scan tool and erase DTCs that are recorded during the normal adjusting procedures.

Test equipment required to adjust engine settings includes the following:

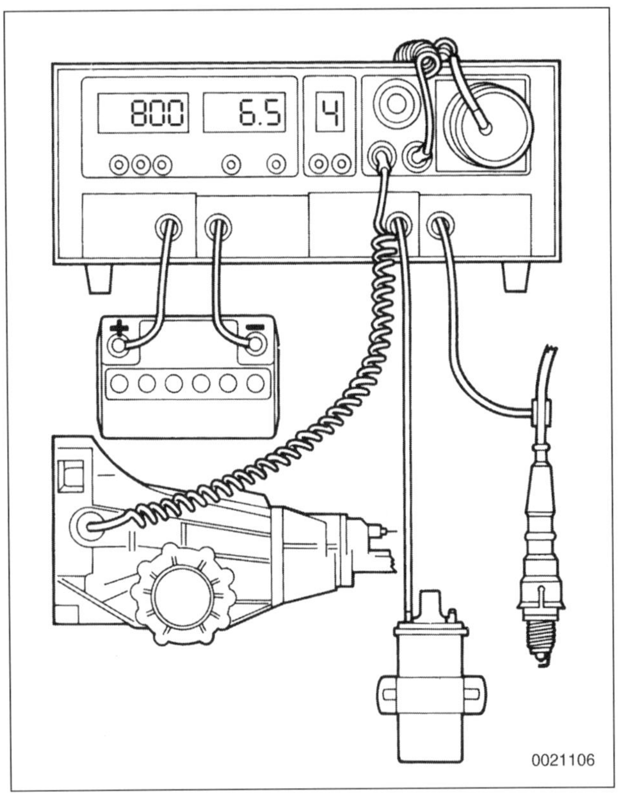

- An engine tester such as the VAG 1367 must be connected to the engine to measure ignition timing and engine speed.
- An exhaust gas analyzer must be attached to the CO pick-up or sampling tube located ahead of the catalytic converter to measure CO (carbon monoxide) content.

Consult appropriate repair manual for ignition timing, idle speed, and CO (carbon monoxide) checking and adjusting procedures.

OUTPUT DIAGNOSTIC TEST MODE (FUNCTION 03)

The ability of the scan tool to instruct the ECM to operate certain electrical components is not a supported function in this version of Digifant.

CODE CONTROL MODULE (FUNCTION 07)

Control module coding by means of the scan tool is not a supported function with California Digifant I ECMs. Coding information does appear, however, in Function 01 (control unit versions). ECM coding is generally accomplished through the use of different ECMs.

Engine Control Module from a 1991 California Golf/Jetta. Part number on ECM label matches Scan Tool display in Function 01. Coding information does not, however, appear externally.

NOTE
Always consult with your Volkswagen Parts Department or aftermarket parts specialist for the latest in parts information.

COMPONENT AND SIGNAL OVERVIEW, RV ENGINE

RV engines use a version of the Volkswagen-developed **Digifant** engine management system. This version of Digifant is generally known as Digifant II except in California where it is designated Digifant I due to legal requirements.

Signals from sensors and other input sources are processed by the ECM. Signals to control the engine are sent to the actuators.

Component and Signal Overview, RV Engine

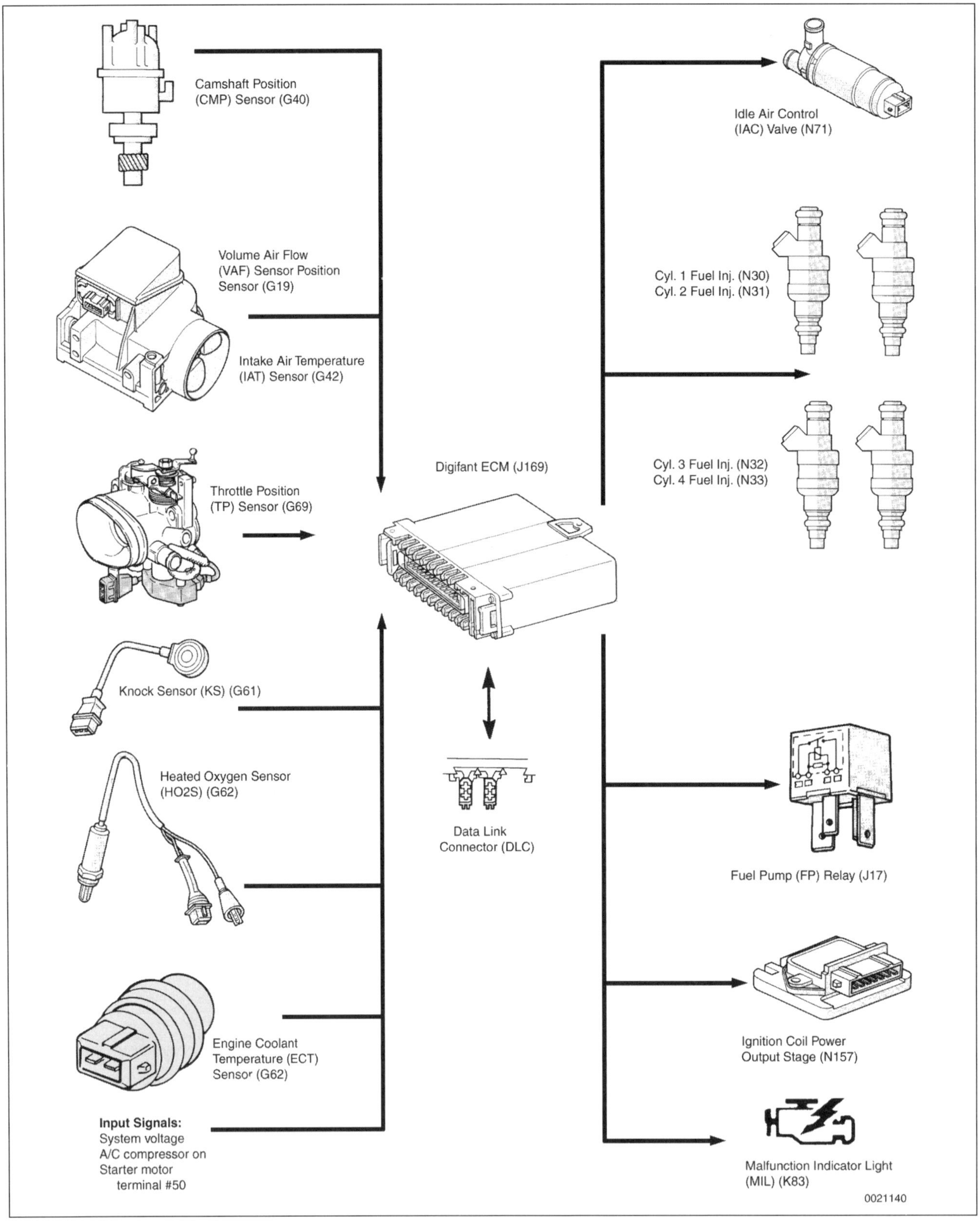

Component and Signal Overview (RV)

Volkswagen California Digifant 1, 4-cylinder	
Fuel injection	Non-sequential (simultaneous) Multi-Point Fuel Injection with Lambda (Oxygen Sensor) Control, OBD-I
Fuel delivery	Tank-mounted electric transfer fuel pump, externally-mounted electric fuel pump, load-sensing mechanical pressure regulator
Ignition system	Distributor, power output stage and ignition coil, single knock sensor, ECM controlled
Emission control	3-Way catalytic converter, carbon canister with mechanical (vacuum) control valve, positive crankcase ventilation
Diagnostics	On-Board Diagnostics via scan tool, Rapid data transfer, Non-volatile memory
Control Module	Single 38-pin Digifant Engine Control Module (ECM) (J169) supplied by Digifant ECM Power Supply Relay (J176)
Sensors	Camshaft Position (CMP) Sensor (G40)
	Volume Air Flow (VAF) Sensor Position Sensor (G19)
	Intake Air Temperature (IAT) Sensor (G42)[1]
	Throttle Position (TP) Sensor (G69)
	Knock Sensor (KS) (G61)
	Heated Oxygen Sensor (H2OS) (G39)
	Engine Coolant Temperature (ECT) Sensor (G62)
Input signals	System voltage
	Starter motor (terminal 50)
	Air conditioner, compressor on
Actuators	Idle Air Control (IAC) Valve (N71)
	Fuel Injectors: Cylinder 1 (N30), Cylinder 2 (N31), Cylinder 3 (N32), Cylinder 4 (N33)
	Ignition Coil Power Output Stage (N157), and Ignition Coil (N152)
	Fuel Pump (FP) Relay (J17), Transfer Fuel Pump (FP) (G23), Fuel Pump (FP) (G6)
	Malfunction Indicator Light (MIL) (K83)
Output signals	No additional output signals

[1] Built into VAF Sensor Position Sensor housing.

Technical Data

Technical data is compiled from several Volkswagen publications. In some instances, the information from these sources differed slightly. In these cases, the most current specifications are listed.

RV (Golf, Jetta, California)	**Technical Data**
Type	4-cylinder in-line (R4), gasoline fuel
Construction	Cast iron block, aluminum 2V cylinder head, belt driven single overhead camshaft
Displacement	1.8 Liters (1781 cc), (109 cid)
Horsepower	94 hp (70 Kw) @ 5400 rpm
Torque	100 lb-ft (136 Nm) @ 3000 rpm
Bore	81.0 mm
Stroke	86.4 mm
Compression ratio	10.0:1
Firing order	1-3-4-2
Management	Digifant I

Appendix A
Scan Tool Fundamentals

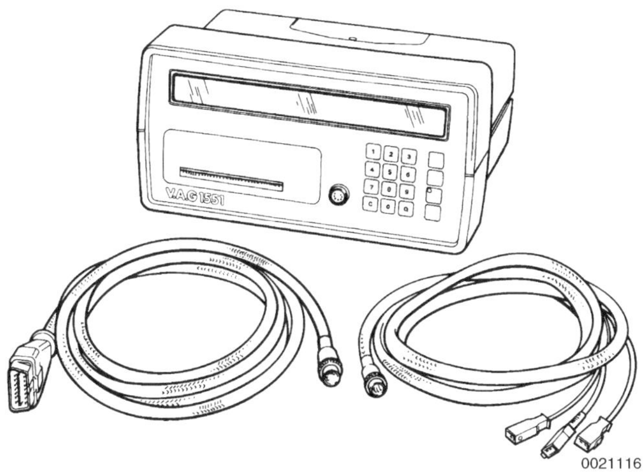

0021116

0021145

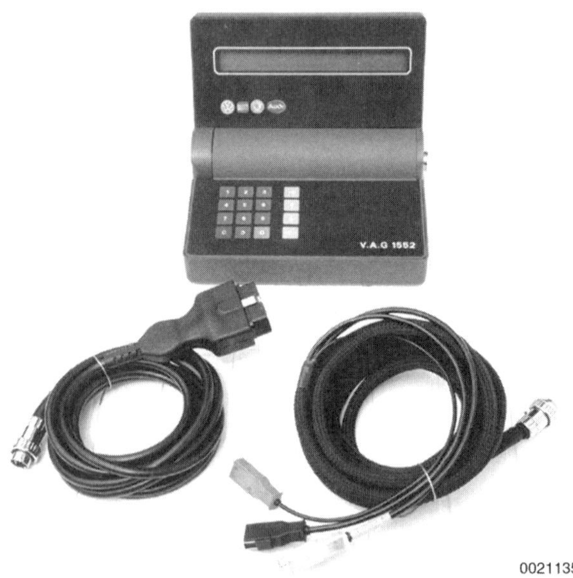

0021135

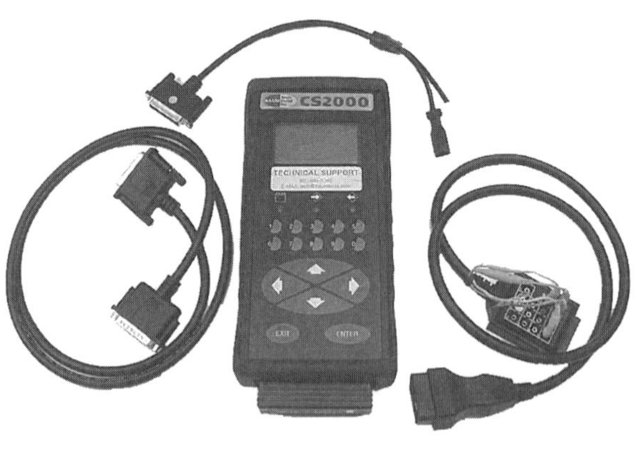

0021134

GENERAL

This chapter outlines the fundamentals of the Volkswagen VAG 1551 scan tool or an aftermarket equivalent. It is not the intention of this manual to teach the technician how to use a scan tool, but instead to familiarize the reader with the tool functions, menu navigation, menu organization and interpretation of displayed data.

< VAG 1551 Scan Tool.

This information in this book must be used in conjunction with the VAG 1551 scan tool (or its equivalent) and the appropriate service and repair information.

< VAG 1552 Scan Tool, the smaller version of the VAG 1551, has the same capabilities (and uses the same cables) but without the printer.

NOTE

This book is organized based on Volkswagen engine codes. A complete listing of the models and engines covered by this book can be found on the inside front cover.

Factory service and repair information is import because it generally includes the following information:

- Component locations and specifications.
- Wiring diagrams.
- Component and system test procedures.
- Removal and installation instructions.
- Exploded views with part identification.
- Torque sequences and specifications.
- Cautions, warnings, and safety concerns.
- Maintenance requirements and intervals.
- Vehicle and model identification guides.

In addition to the factory VAG 1551 and VAG 1552 scan tools, there are a number of high quality scan tools and PC-based programs that perform the same functions of the factory tool.

< CS2000 is one of several high quality Scan Tools available from Baum Tools Unlimited, Inc.

CONTROL UNIT VERSION (FUNCTION 01)

When communications are first established between the scan tool and the control unit, the control unit being tested always responds to the scan tool by identifying itself.

NOTE
Some ECM versions require an engine speed below 2,000 rpm and a closed throttle (closed CTP switch) to initially access the ECM. However, once the ECM is accessed, higher speeds can be used.

Depending on the system, Control Unit Version (Function 0) identification information can include any or all of the following:

- ECM part number and suffix (1H0 907 311 G)
- Basic application (1.8l RE MONO)
- Software version/level (011)
- Specific application coding (CODING 01)
- Work Shop Code number (00356)

NOTE
Although Function 01 is an automatic response to the initial scan tool inquiry, it can be called up from the function menu at any time during the diagnosis.

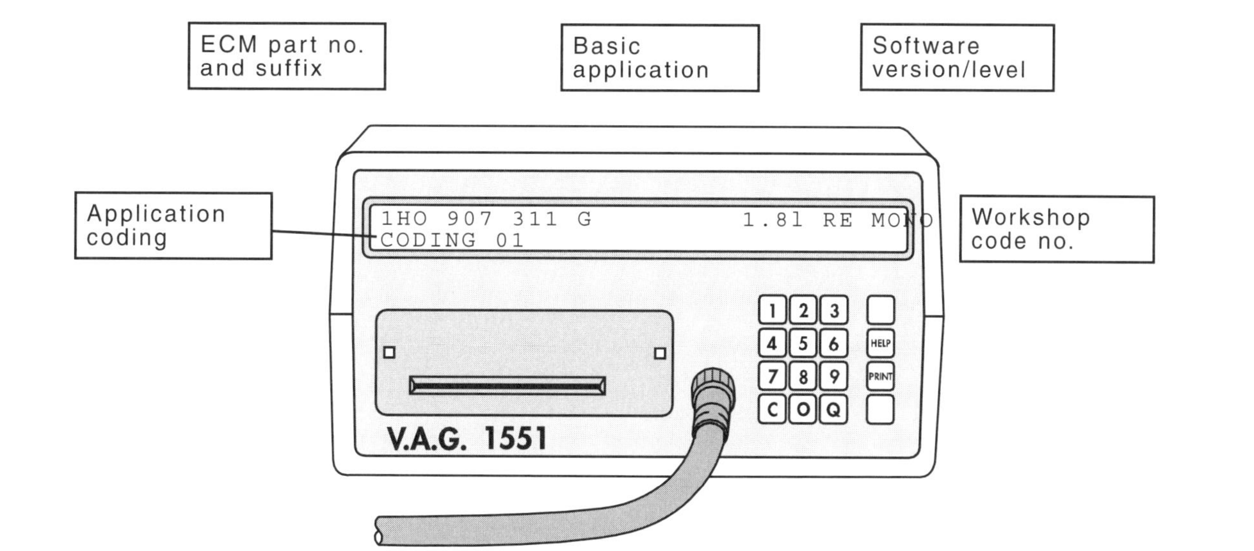

0021133

Part number (**arrow**) on ECM must match number shown in Scan Tool display.

CHECK DTC MEMORY (FUNCTION 02)

All engine management systems covered in this manual have the ability to monitor the operation of certain components and system functions. If a malfunction or fault occurs, it is generally stored as a DTC or Diagnostic Trouble Code. Volkswagen calls this feature "permanent fault memory" because DTCs are retained when the ignition is switched off, unlike some earlier systems that retained fault memory only if the ignition was switched on.

```
2 DTC recognized
```

Function 02 displays DTCs that are currently present or that have recently occurred. When this function is called up from the appropriate menu, the VAG 1551 scan tool will respond with a display indicating the number of DTCs, such as "2 DTC recognized". If there are no DTCs recorded, the scan tool will display "no DTC recognized".

NOTE
Some engine management systems and/or some scan tool program versions may substitute the word "fault" for DTC, such as "2 faults recognized", but the operation is otherwise the same.

Exact functionality from this point varies with the scan tool type or program being used. For example, when using the VAG 1551, if the printer is switched on, the scan tool will print all pertinent data including data that may not appear on the screen. It will continue printing and automatically scrolling through each DTC, returning to the function menu only when all DTCs have been read. If the printer is switched off, however, the function must be advanced manually by use of the **-->** key. In all cases, when the DTC memory has been completely checked, the scan tool returns to the function menu.

Printing DTCs has two benefits as compared to simply viewing them on screen:

- Eliminates losing the data if the memory is accidentally erased. Paper copy also allows the data to be included with other vehicle information for later reference.
- The VAG 1551 usually prints more information on the paper than what is displayed on the screen, resulting in easier DTC identification and troubleshooting.

```
00516          2121
Closed Throttle Position Switch-F60
Open/Short circuit to B+
```

◄ The information printed on the paper tape of a VAG 1551 scan tool generally includes the following:

- VAG code (00516).
- Blink code (2121).
- Failed component name and alpha-numeric designation (Closed Throttle Position Switch - F60).
- Failure mode (Open/Short circuit to B+).

```
00516          2121
Closed Throttle Position Switch F60
Open/Short circuit to B+
sporadic DTC
```

◄ Occasionally, a momentary malfunction may occur within the system. If this temporary fault is short in duration and does not re-occur, it is said to be a sporadic fault. The ECM will detect and store the temporary fault and display it as such when the DTC memory is checked. The paper tape will have the words "sporadic DTC printed on the last line.

```
Closed Throttle Position Switch-F60
Open/Short circuit to B+          /SP
```

◄ A sporadic DTC shown in the VAG 1551 display window will show "/sp" on the right side of the last display line.

OUTPUT DIAGNOSTIC TEST MODE (FUNCTION 03)

Troubleshooting electrical faults is facilitated by the Output Diagnostic Test Mode or Function 03.

```
Output Diagnostic Test Mode         -->
Throttle Position Actuator-V60
```

◄ When this function is activated, the scan tool instructs the ECM to operate certain electrical components in a pre-determined sequence. The output diagnostic test mode can only be used when the ignition is switched on, but the engine is not running.

This ability to remotely operate components can be a valuable resource when troubleshooting although not all of the systems covered by this manual have this capability. Output Diagnostic Test components, sequencing, and procedures vary with each system and specific information appears in the individual engine code sections where applicable.

BASIC SETTINGS (FUNCTION 04)

Most engines covered by this manual do not have provisions for mechanical adjustment of ignition timing, idle speed, or mixture. These operating parameters are preprogrammed into the ECM as default or baseline values. During engine operation, data is received from the various sensors and corrections are made as required.

These corrections are retained in the ECM's memory when the ignition is switched off and become the starting point for subsequent engine operation. These "learned" values and can change or adapt as often as needed.

If the ECM is disconnected from the battery during repairs for any reason, the learned values are erased and the ECM will revert to the default values allowing the engine to run. The default values may not match the current needs of the engine, which can result in poor performance and driveability. Also, when repairs have been made, such as repair of a vacuum leak, the default values will not match the current needs of the engine.

```
System in Basic Setting       01    -->
710 /min     85°C     1.02     6.2° v.OT
```

◄ VAG 1551 Scan Tool display showing Basic Settings display for a typical Motronic M2.9 Engine Management system.

In both situations, the ECM will start from the default or baseline settings and re-learn and adapt to current operating conditions. This process can, however, take some time.

When an appropriate scan tool is properly connected to these systems and set to Basic settings, the ECM can be made to adapt to current operating conditions in several minutes rather than a longer period of time.

In order to facilitate the adaptation process, when Basic Settings is selected, the scan tool signals the ECM to implement pre-programed instructions. This could include switching off the Evaporative Emission Canister Purge Regulator Valve (N80) for example, to eliminate it's influence during the process.

Information in Basic settings is displayed in the same format as in Read measuring value blocks (Function 08) with similar displays on the scan tool, but the functions differ with regard to their interface with the EMS.

ERASE DTC MEMORY (FUNCTION 05)

If a DTC was displayed when Check DTC Memory (Function 02) was accessed, it must then be erased after repairs have been completed.

Before erasing DTCs, all known malfunctions should be repaired. A road test of at least 10 minutes duration is recommended to verify proper completion of the repair.

Erasing DTCs using VAG 1551

- Connect scan tool
- From the initial Menu select:
  1 Rapid Data
- From the address word Menu select:
  01 Engine Electronics 01
- Advance to the Function Menu when the ECM responds with the version information
- From the Function Menu select:
  02 Check DTC memory
  Read DTCs and return to the Function Menu
- From the Function Menu select:
  05 Erase DTC memory
  Scan tool will respond with display to indicate that DTC memory is erased
- Advance to the Function Menu
- From the Function Menu select:
  06 End output
- Disconnect scan tool

```
Attention!

DTC memory was not interrogated
```

While it might seem appropriate to simply dismiss and erase a DTC that was noted on a previous scan tool connection, the safeties built into the engine management and most scan tools will not allow it.

- In order to prevent accidental or unintended erasure of DTCs, all DTCs must be read before Function 05 is allowed. A display will appear with a warning as a reminder if Function 05 is selected before Function 02.

End Output (Function 06)

When diagnostic activities are finished, the safest way to end communication with the ECM is to select function 06 from the Function Menu. This function safely breaks the communications link and allows the scan tool user to access a different vehicle control module without disconnecting the scan tool, thus saving wear and tear on the DLC and the scan tool cable.

Code Control Module (Function 07)

Control module coding by means of the scan tool is not a supported function of the Engine Management Systems covered by this manual. Coding information does appear, however, in Function 01 (control unit versions). ECM coding is generally accomplished through the use of special coding wires in the ECM wiring harness or by system-specific ECMs. Codes are used to identify certain engine equipment levels and transmission types.

Coding information appears in the individual engine code sections where applicable.

READ MEASURING VALUE BLOCKS (FUNCTION 08)

An important feature of all of the Engine Management Systems covered by this manual is their ability to show operating information in real time. This information can be displayed in either raw form or in converted and grouped form. When displayed in converted form, other data that the factory deems as related will also be shown.

```
Read Measuring Value Block        01
710 /min    85°C     1.02     6.2° v.OT
```

◄ Information in Read measuring value blocks (Function 08) is displayed in the same format as in Basic settings (Function 04) with similar displays on the scan tool, but the functions differ with regard to their interface with the EMS.

When Function 04 is selected, the scan tool signals the ECM to implement pre-programed instructions. This could include switching off the Evaporative Emission Canister Purge Regulator Valve (N80) for example. When Function 08 is selected, the Scan Tool does not switch off the valve. Stated another way, 04 alters the EMS and reads it, while 08 only reads it.

These pre-programed instructions are listed in the individual engine code sections for Basic Settings (Function 4) and vary slightly depending on the engine code.

Value block information appears in the individual engine code sections under Read Measuring Value Blocks (Function 08).

```
Read Individual Measuring Value
Channel 1      Measuring value  68
```

READ INDIVIDUAL MEASURING VALUES (FUNCTION 09)

Individual parts of the Display Groups can be separated and shown on the scan tool for some systems. Very little information on this function is available. The preferred method is for the Technician to look at the larger picture shown by the Display Groups instead of the narrow view afforded by the individual measuring value

Individual Measuring values are shown as separate channels ranging from 0 to 255. The data is given in the range format of 0 to 255. Interpretation of the displayed information is not readily apparent.

Individual Measuring Value information appears in the individual engine code sections where applicable.

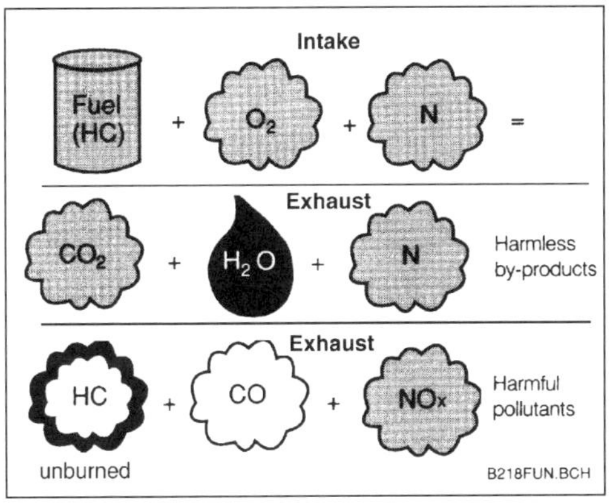

Appendix B
Emissions Basics

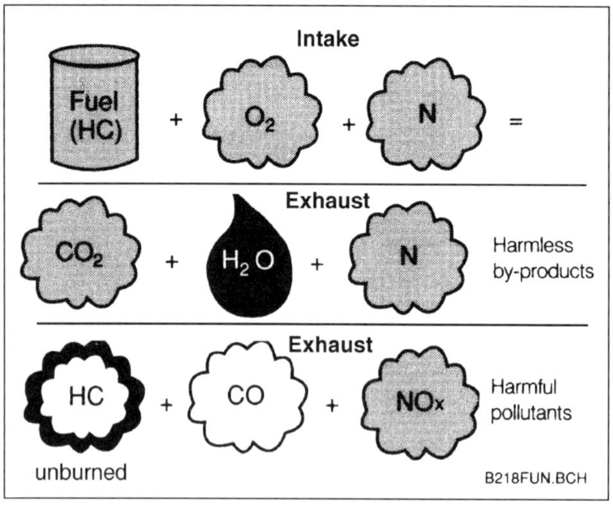

GENERAL

To operate a car, mostly hydrocarbons (HC) derived from crude oil are used. The chemical energy stored in these compounds is freed during the combustion process and transferred via the crankshaft and transmission to the driven wheels of the vehicle.

Combustion of the air-fuel mixture creates gaseous by-products that make up the exhaust gas. Some of the combustion by-products are harmless, while others have been determined to be harmful.

How Emissions are Formed

During "complete combustion," hydrocarbons oxygen, and nitrogen produce carbon dioxide, water, and nitrogen. Incomplete combustion can produce carbon monoxide instead of carbon dioxide, hydrocarbons, and oxides of nitrogen. Complete combustion, however, is only a theoretical value. In the real world we can only talk about the actual combustion.

To discharge as little harmful emissions as possible into the environment and to use the energy in the fuel as much as possible, a precisely adjusted mixture of air and fuel is necessary.

For a complete combustion we need exactly 1 lb. of fuel and 14.7 lbs. of air. This well known ratio of 14.7:1 is also called the "stoichiometric point" and is necessary for optimum exhaust emissions and engine performance.

If this ratio of air and fuel is not precisely maintained, the combustion is not optimal and excessive harmful emissions are emitted into the environment. During the actual combustion, the ratio 14.7:1 is not always maintained and results in a greater output of harmful emissions.

To simplify the understanding of this process, the air number Lambda (λ) will be defined as the stoichiometric point of 1.

Lambda also describes the ratio of the air that is actually available for combustion versus the air that is necessary for combustion.

$$\lambda = \frac{\text{air added}}{\text{air needed}}$$

A value of less than (<) 1 identifies rich air/fuel mixture, or not enough air available for complete combustion. This normally results in unburned fuel in the exhaust gas in the form of carbon monoxide (CO) and hydrocarbons (HC).

A value of greater than (>) 1 identifies lean air/fuel mixture, or too much air. In this case there is excess air available for combustion that cannot be used. There is no unburned fuel in the exhaust gas.

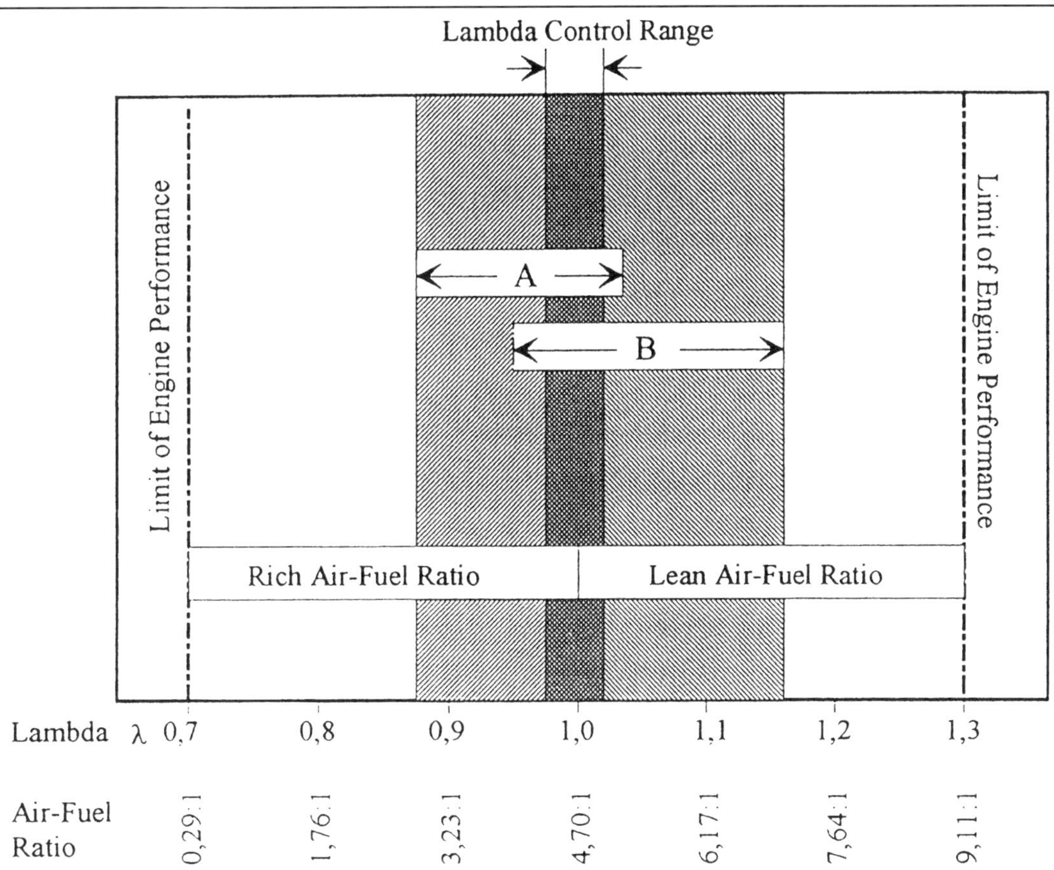

Fuel Injection

A: Older Engine Concepts
B: Later Engine Concepts

The Chemicals Reactions of Oxidation and Reduction

The chemical reactions that occur during engine combustion are very complex and partially not even known. To understand the relationships during the reduction of noxious emissions it is helpful to know two different chemical reactions that occur in the catalytic converter. The chemical reactions we are talking about are Oxidation and Reduction.

Oxidation

Oxidation means that one or more oxygen atoms are added to a chemical compound. The most important chemical oxidation reactions during the treatment of exhaust gases in the catalytic converter are:

1. Carbon monoxide (CO) oxidizes with oxygen from the air (O_2) to form carbon dioxide (CO_2):

$$2\ CO + O_2 \rightarrow 2\ CO_2$$

2. Hydrocarbons (HC) oxidize with oxygen from the air (O_2) to form water (H_2O):

$$2\ H_2 + O_2 \rightarrow 2\ H_2O$$

Reduction

Reduction means that one or more oxygen atoms are deleted from a chemical compound. The most important chemical reduction reactions during the treatment of exhaust gases in the catalytic converter are:

1. Carbon monoxide (CO) extracts from the oxide of nitrogen (NOx) an oxygen atom. The oxygen atom oxidizes itself to carbon dioxide (CO_2) while the oxide of nitrogen (NOx) is reduced to nitrogen (N_2):

$$2\ NOx + 2\ CO \rightarrow N_2 + 2\ CO_2$$

2. Hydrogen (H_2) extracts from the oxide of nitrogen (NOx) an oxygen atom. The oxygen atom oxidizes itself to water (H_2O) while the oxide of nitrogen (NOx) is reduced to nitrogen (N_2):

$$2\ NOx + 2\ H_2 \rightarrow N_2 + 2\ H_2O$$

COMBUSTION BY-PRODUCTS

> ***WARNING —***
> *Never run the engine unless the work area is well ventilated. Exhaust gas emissions are extremely toxic and can kill.*

The exhaust gas from engine combustion consists mainly of the following components:

- Hydrocarbons **HC** (controlled)
- Carbon Monoxide **CO** (controlled)
- Oxides of Nitrogen **NOx** (controlled)
- Carbon Dioxide CO_2 (not controlled)
- Oxygen O_2 (not controlled)
- Water H_2O (not controlled)

There are still other components in the exhaust gas. These are, however, omitted to keep this very complex subject simple.

Hydrocarbons (HC)

> ***WARNING —***
> *Never run the engine unless the work area is well ventilated. Gasoline hydrocarbons are harmful to your health.*

Gasoline is a hydrocarbon mixture. The general description of hydrocarbons is a collective name for organic compounds that consist only of carbon (C) and hydrogen (H) molecules.

If hydrocarbons are detected during an emissions test, unburned or not completely burned fuel is being exhausted from the combustion chamber. Also engine oil—although not easily burned—can get into the combustion chamber and cause high HC readings.

Ignition problems (worn/fouled spark plugs, corroded plug connectors, faulty wiring, incorrectly adjusted ignition, etc.) are the most common cause of high hydrocarbons readings. Another common cause is due to lean fuel/air mixtures. In this case, the fuel/air mixture is so lean that it is hard to ignite and burn. The lean mixture can be caused by poor mixture, but more likely it is due to intake air leaks (leaking vacuum hoses or connections).

Combustion By-Products

The HC emission can also be caused by the so-called "quenching effect" which is a design problem of the combustion chamber. Due to uneven heat distribution, the cylinder charge is not fully burned and this unburned fuel is emitted into the exhaust system.

A reduction of the HC-emission can be chemically produced by oxidation (introducing oxygen into the exhaust gas). This is achieved through one of two ways; either by using a Three-Way Catalytic Converter (TWC) or through Secondary Air Injection (AIR). The TWC has the ability to store oxygen on its large surface. The AIR system pumps air into the exhaust and works together with an oxidation-type catalytic converter.

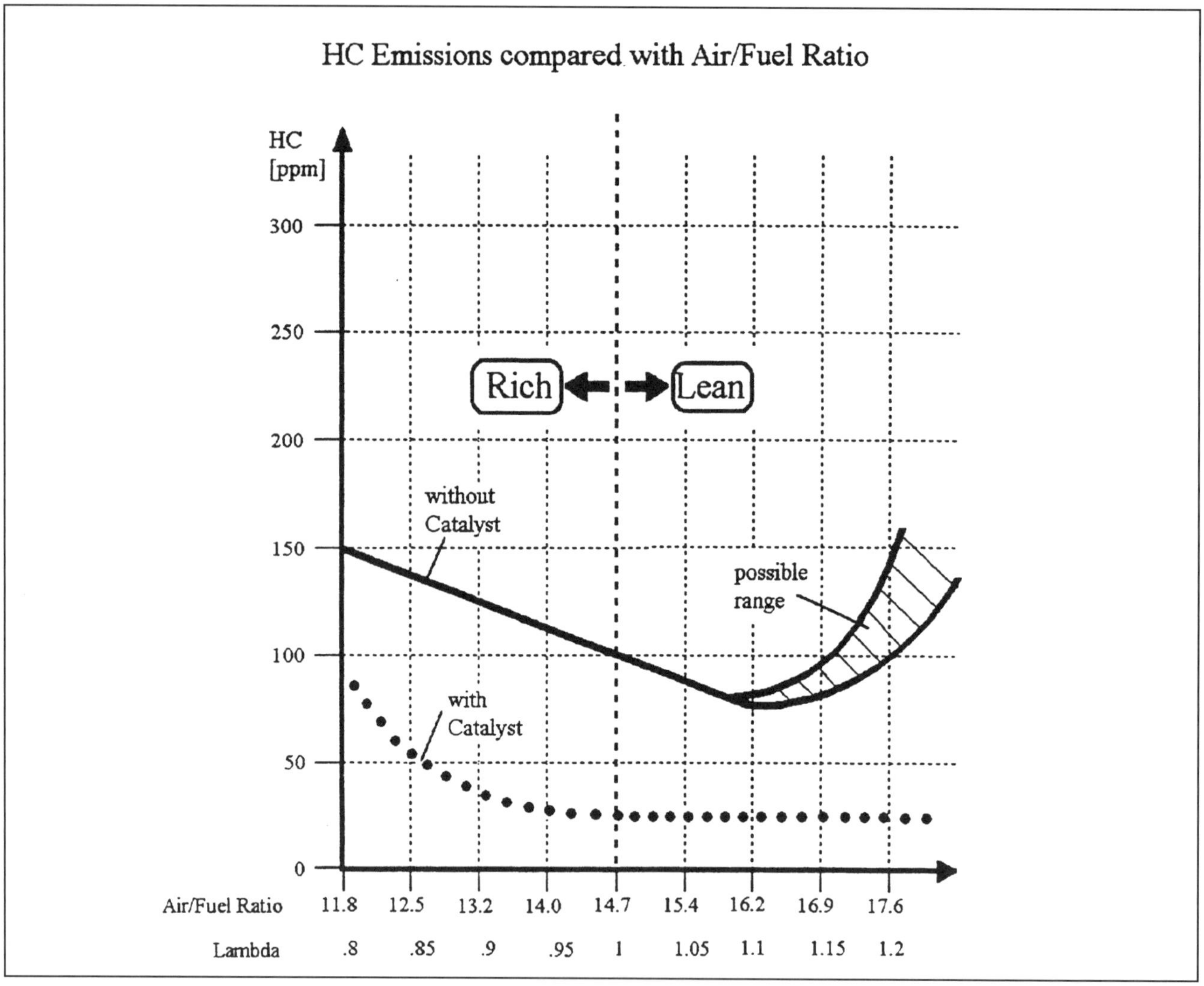

Health effects—

Hydrocarbons irritate the mucous membrane. They can be identified as follows:

Saturated compounds (paraffin) are nearly odorless and have a narcotic effect. Unsaturated compounds (olefin, acetylene) have a slightly sweet smell and together with NO are to a great extent responsible for smog.

The aromatic hydrocarbons have a characteristic, often pleasant smell. They however have a harmful effect on the nervous system and may also produce cancer.

Carbon Monoxide (CO)

WARNING —
- *Never run the engine unless the work area is well ventilated. Carbon monoxide is very toxic and can kill.*
- *Carbon monoxide is easily and quickly absorbed into the bloodstream and takes a long time to leave the bloodstream.*

High CO-values are associated mostly with a mixture that is too rich, or in other words ($\lambda < 1$). This means there is not enough oxygen available for the combustion of fuel. Anything that prevents the supply of fresh air to the combustion chamber can increase the CO emission. We therefore can use the CO content of the exhaust gas as a direct indicator for the air/fuel ratio of the mixture.

A reduction of the CO-emission can also be chemically produced by oxidation (introducing oxygen into the exhaust gas). This is achieved through a Three-Way Catalytic Converter (TWC) or through a Secondary Air Injection (AIR) system.

Health effects—

CO is a very toxic, colorless, tasteless, and odorless gas that combines easily with the blood molecule hemoglobin. This effectively replaces the oxygen in the blood and can quickly lead to toxic poisoning and asphyxiation.

Combustion By-Products

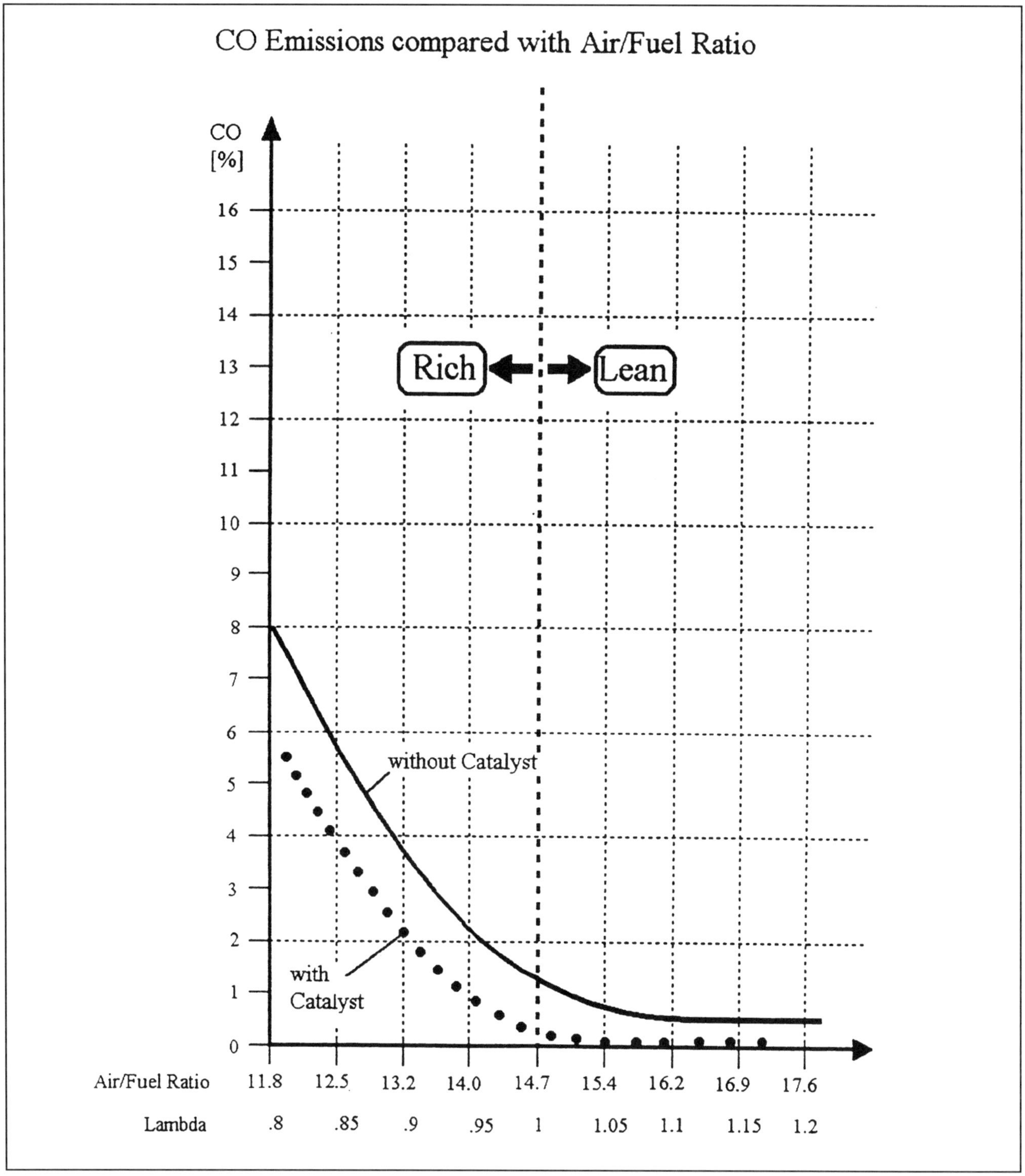

Oxides of Nitrogen (NOx)

> ***WARNING —***
> *Never run the engine unless the work area is well ventilated. Oxides of nitrogen are harmful to your health.*

Oxides of nitrogen (NOx) appear in the form of nitrogen monoxide (NO) and nitrogen dioxide (NO_2) and are also a collective name for many compounds that need not be identified.

NOx are generated during the combustion of nitrogen dioxide (NO_2) under very high temperatures and pressures. Normally, nitrogen (composes 79% of air) is a low reaction gas that combines with the oxygen from the air to form oxides.

High combustion temperatures are created by high compression ratios, very lean fuel/air mixtures and early ignition timing.

NOx emissions are mainly controlled by measures that lower the combustion chamber temperature. This can be done by lowering compression ratios, adjusting ignition timing toward late, applying exhaust gas recirculation, and through control of fuel/air ratios.

> ***Health effects—***
>
> ***NO is a colorless gas that replaces the oxygen of the blood molecule hemoglobin, which can quickly lead to symptoms of paralysis.***
>
> ***NO2 is a reddish-brown gas that has a stinging smell which can lead to tissue damage in the lungs.***
>
> ***In connection with non-saturated hydrocarbons and ultraviolet sun radiation, NOx emissions are main contributors for smog. Because of this reason they are to be considered noxious emissions.***

Combustion By-Products

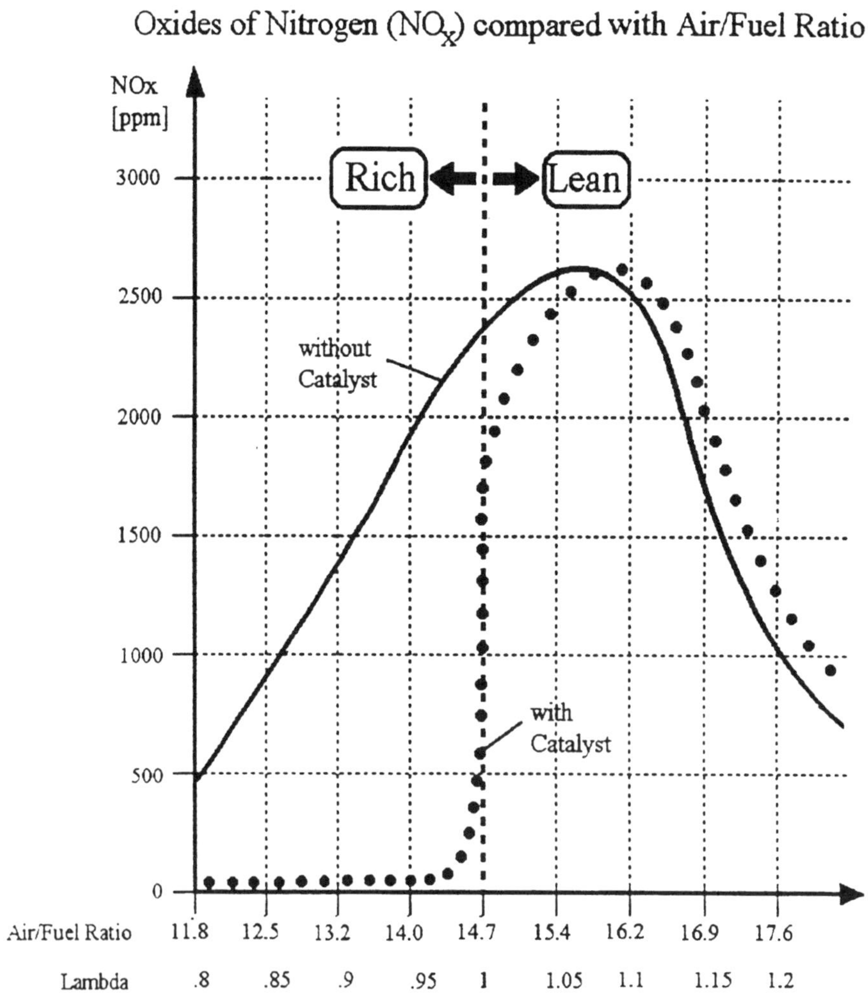

Carbon Dioxide (CO_2)

The value for carbon dioxide is not limited. High values (14% to 15% in the exhaust gas) are reached when $\lambda = 1$ (stoichiometric point). This is an indication that the fuel/air mixture is properly adjusted.

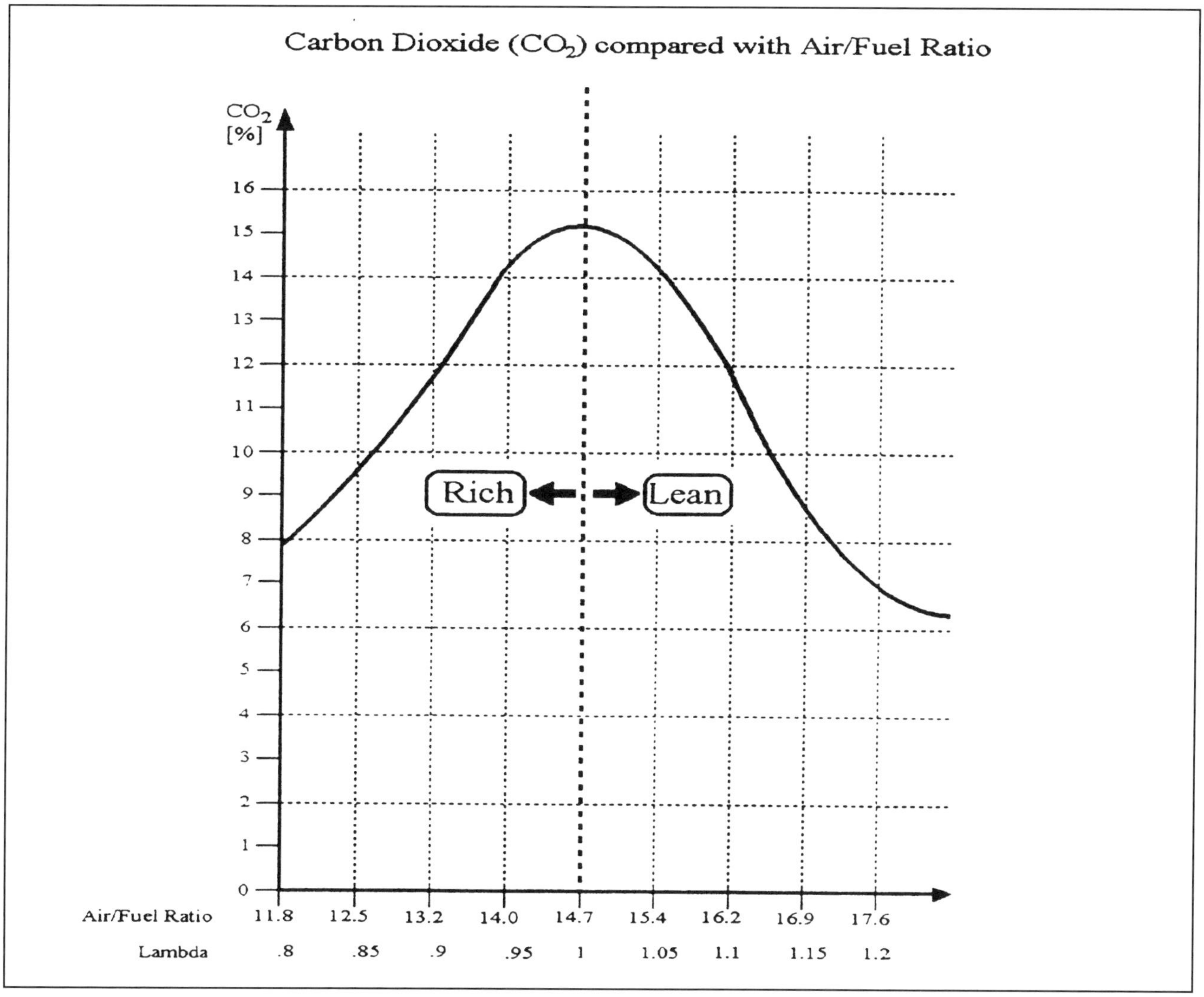

> ***Health effects—***
>
> ***CO2 in normal concentration is not health threatening, however it destroys the ozone layer of the earth and is therefore considered to be harmful to the earth's atmosphere.***

Combustion By-Products

Oxygen (O_2)

Air (which contains up to 21% oxygen) is mixed with fuel for combustion in the combustion chamber. The oxygen content measured in the exhaust gas makes a lean mixture when the oxygen is high and a rich mixture when the oxygen content is low.

Carbon monoxide (CO) behaves exactly opposite to that of oxygen. In other words, a high CO content indicates a rich mixture, and a low content indicates a lean mixture. At the stoichiometric point ($\lambda = 1$), the amount of carbon monoxide and oxygen are about evenly low.

> ***Health effects—***
>
> ***Oxygen is not considered to be a harmful emission. It is an information gas—that by its concentration you can tell whether the exhaust gas is rich or lean.***

Oxygen (O_2) compared with Air/Fuel Ratio

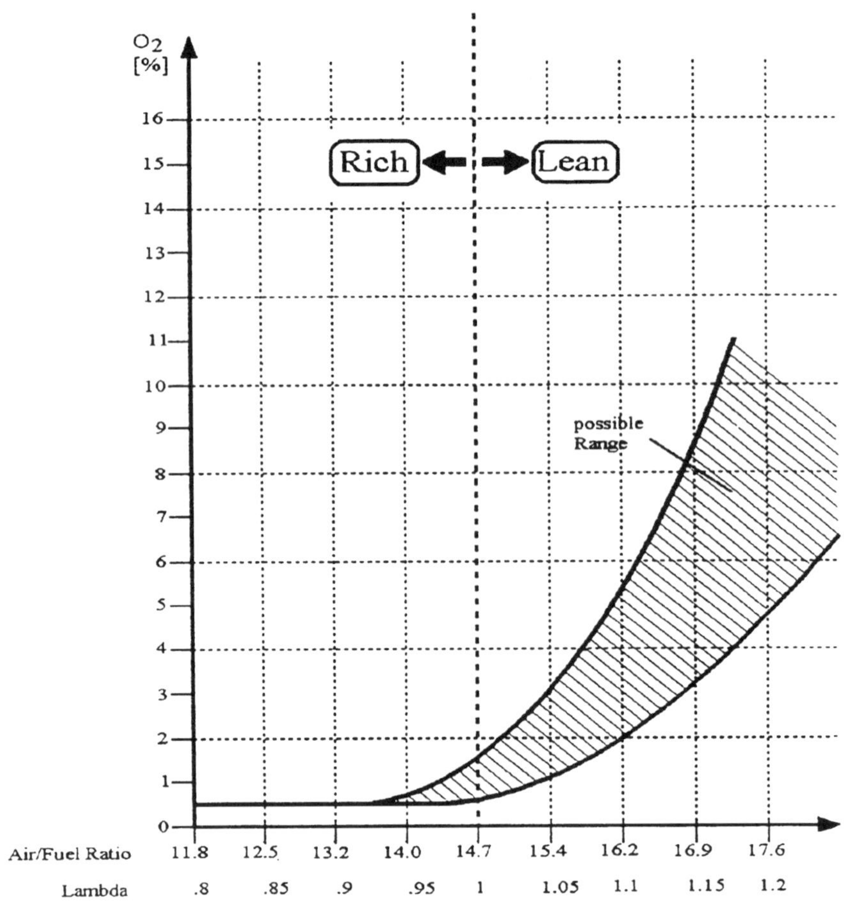

The Lambda Value in the Emission Composition

For the best combustion process, a precisely adjusted fuel/air ratio is very important. At a fuel/air ratio of 14.7:1, $\lambda=1$. This point is also called the "stoichiometric point" and indicates the optimum exhaust and engine operating conditions.

The narrow range of 0.97 to 1.03 is called the "Lambda window" because of its good exhaust and engine operation conditions. In this range a Three-Way Catalytic Converter must be used. The Lambda window can be recognized by the following:

- Low carbon monoxide (CO) and oxygen (O_2) content (0.2 to 1.5%)
- High carbon dioxide (CO_2) (10 to 15%) and oxides of nitrogen (NOx) (2000 to 2500 PPM)
- Low hydrocarbons (HC) (< 200 PPM)

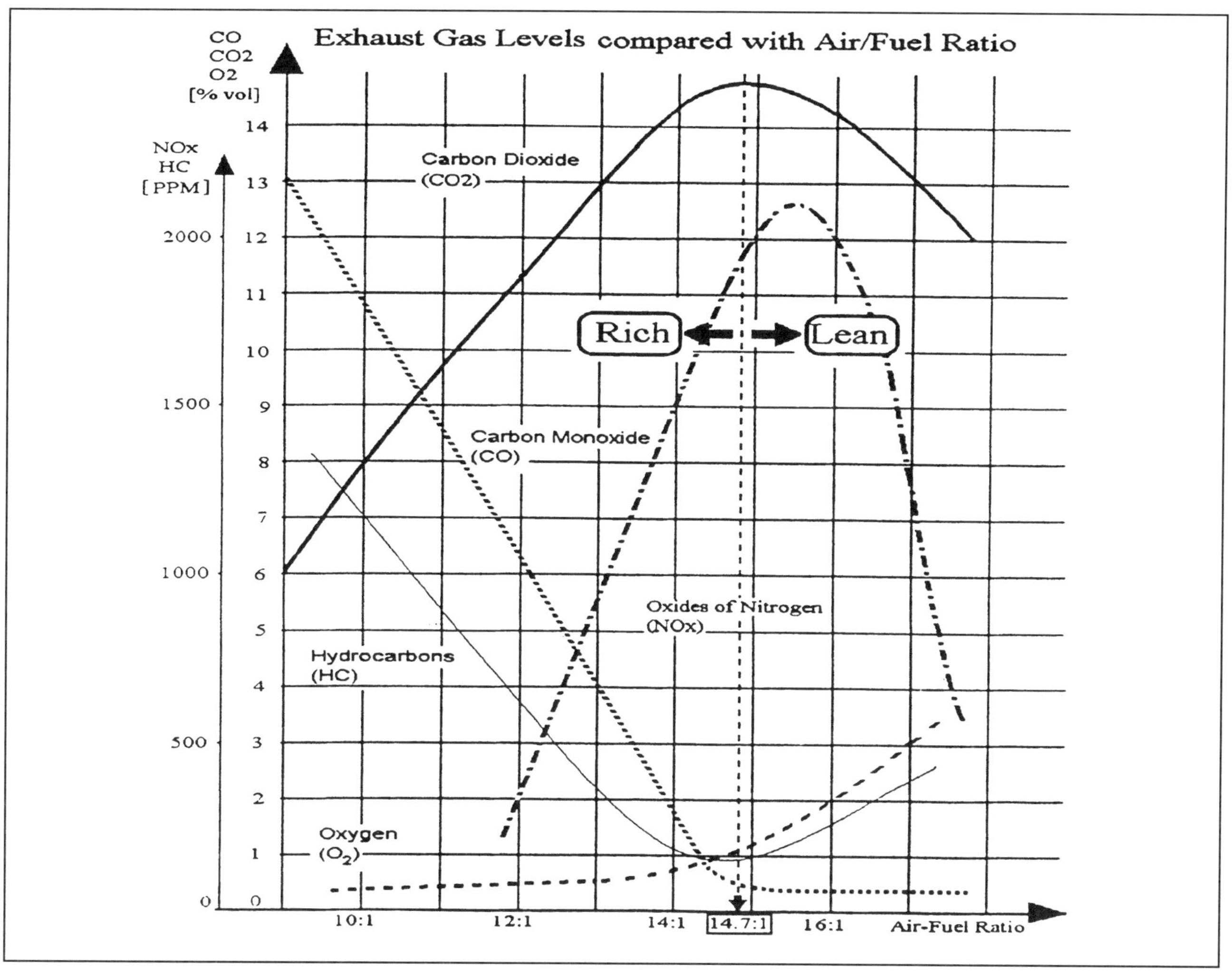

The Lambda Value in the Emission Composition

During engine combustion this "stoichiometric" condition varies to a certain degree because of the changing load and other operating conditions. In this way the fuel/air ratio changes away from the stoichiometric point toward the rich or the lean range and changes the composition of the exhaust gas.

The following table provides a brief overview of how the fuel/air ratio affects engine operation and exhaust emissions.

Fuel /Air Ratio Effects on Engine Operation and Exhaust Emissions

Fuel /Air Ratio	Effect
Too rich (Lambda (λ) window = 0.8 to 0.9)	• high CO-value • high HC-values • black exhaust gas • engine oil thinning • high fuel consumption
Enriched range	• high CO-value • high HC-values • enhanced engine performance • increased fuel consumption • less tendency to knock
Stoichiometry (λ=1, approx.) (Lambda (λ) window = 0.97 to 1.03	• optimal idle • good emission values
Slightly lean range	• low HC-values • low CO-values • maximum NOx-values • reduced engine performance • low fuel consumption • slight tendency to knock
Lean range (Lambda (λ) window = 1.1 to 1.2)	• increased NOx-values • poor engine performance • misfiring • temperature damage to pistons and valves • high tendency to knock

METHODS TO REDUCE EMISSIONS

To reduce harmful emissions the following measures are used:

- Catalytic converters
- Lambda regulation
- Secondary air injection (AIR)
- Exhaust gas recirculation (EGR)
- Crankcase ventilation
- Evaporative canister system (reduction of fuel evaporation)

Catalytic converters and secondary air injection are part of the exhaust gas treatment. This includes all measures that allow additional chemical change of the exhaust gas composition.

In addition to systems that treat the exhaust gas itself, engine design directly affects the composition of the exhaust gas. Primarily, the various types of fuel injection and ignition systems as well as exhaust gas recirculation, crankcase ventilation and the EVAP canister systems.

Catalytic Converters

The catalytic converter is a metal housing filled with a carrier material. The carrier material is normally a ceramic monolith (AL_2O_3) covered by an alloy of precious metals. Precious metals have a very slow chemical reaction without taking part in the reaction, but stimulate chemical reactions in other combustion by-products.

The job of the catalytic converter is to react to the pollutants in the exhaust gas (HC, CO and NOx) and convert them into the non-harmful emissions (H_2O, CO_2 and N_2).

Although the catalytic converter promotes chemical reactions without affecting the catalyst itself, the catalytic converter will age over time due to high temperatures. The converter can also be damaged by knocks to the housing and the use of leaded gasoline.

For the catalytic converter to operate properly, it must be at sufficient operating temperature. Below 300°C (572°F) the conversion does not take place.

The following types of catalytic converters are used:

- Oxidation catalytic converters
- Dual-bed catalytic converters
- Three-way catalytic converters

In addition there are systems that do not affect the oxygen content in the exhaust gas and where the catalytic converter works alternately as a reduction or oxidation converter.

Oxidation Catalytic Converters

Oxidation catalytic converters can only convert the harmful emissions HC and CO into H_2O and CO_2. The conversion requires a lot of oxygen supplied primarily as secondary air.

If the engine runs with a lean mixture ($\lambda > 1$), not all of the oxygen is used for the combustion. This effectively leaves sufficient oxygen for the after-treatment of the exhaust gas.

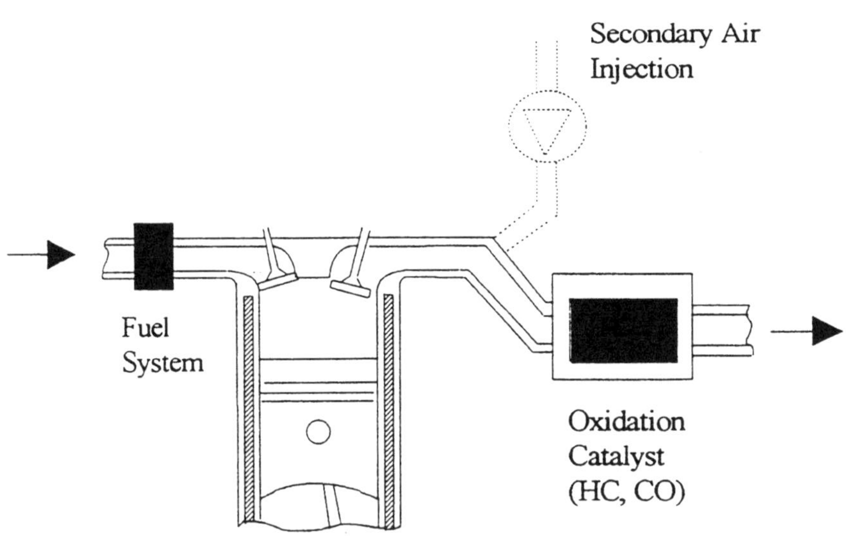

Dual-bed Catalytic Converters

Dual-bed catalytic converters consist of two converters, one positioned behind the other in the same housing.

In the first converter, oxides of nitrogen (NOx) are converted in the exhaust gas. Normally, this reaction can only happen when there is little or no oxygen in the exhaust gas (i.e. a rich fuel mixture). By employing a reduction converter, the result is proper fuel mixtures and low (normal) fuel consumption.

In the second converter, CO and HC are oxidized to H_2O and CO_2. Normally, this reaction can only take place if there is sufficient oxygen in the exhaust gas. For this, additional air is fed between the two converters by means of secondary air injection (see also **Secondary Air Injection**).

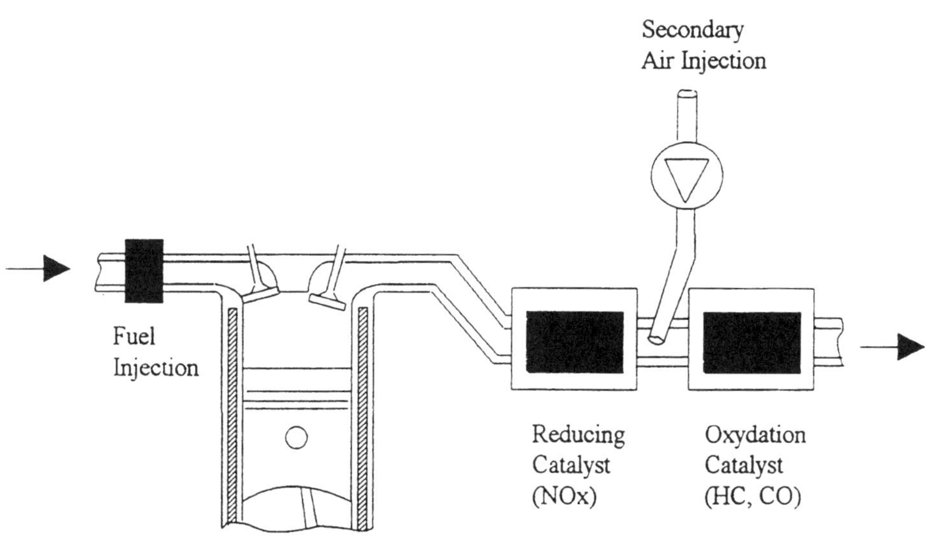

Methods To Reduce Emissions

Three-way Catalytic Converter

The three-way catalytic converter combines the principles of the reduction and oxidation converters. The three harmful emissions HC, CO and NOx are converted in just one converter.

To accomplish this, oxygen is stored by the converter when the exhaust gas is rich in oxygen. This stored oxygen is released as necessary for the oxidation and conversion to H_2O and CO_2 while NOx is reduced.

When the engine runs lean, CO and HC become H_2O and CO_2, however NOx is chemically not converted and passes the converter unchanged.

To function as described, the engine must run with a precisely adjusted mixture of $\lambda = 0.97$ to 1.03. This narrow range is called the "Lambda window." This way, harmful emissions are reduced up to 90%.

To make it possible for an engine to run under almost all load conditions at $\lambda = 1$, a Lambda regulation system is needed. With the aid of an oxygen sensor in the exhaust system ahead of the catalytic converter it can be determined whether there is residual oxygen in the exhaust gas.

The oxygen sensor reports back to the electronic engine control module (ECM), which in turn evaluates the information and initiates a corrective measure. When the exhaust gas is rich, the mixture is adjusted toward lean and when lean the mixture is adjusted toward rich. See **Oxygen Sensor and Lambda Regulation** given below for more information

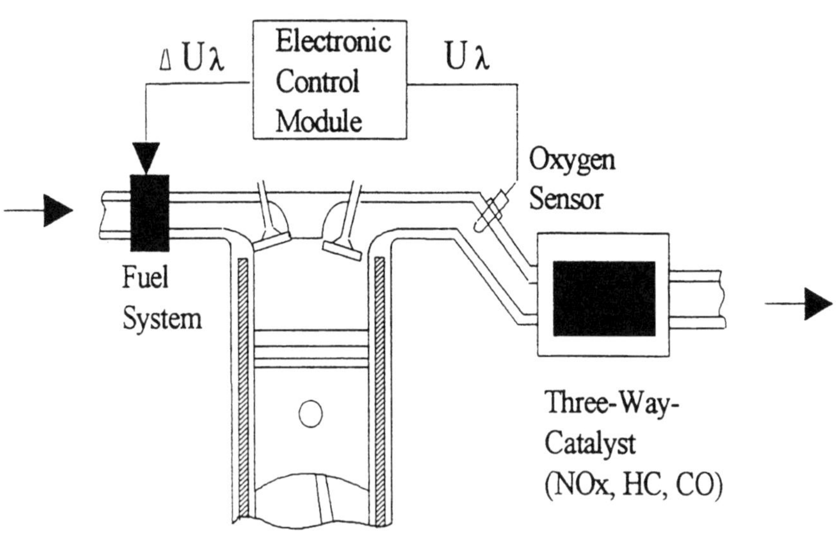

Oxygen Sensor and Lambda Regulation

Precise regulation of the air-fuel mixture can only be accomplished through a reporting procedure regarding the composition of the exhaust gas. This assignment is accomplished by the Lambda regulation system, which operates in a closed control loop. This control loop constantly measures the residual oxygen content in the exhaust gas. The volume of fuel needed is then immediately corrected for optimum combustion.

The oxygen sensor acts as the measuring sensor that creates a current differential at $\lambda = 1$. This current differential allows a judgment whether the exhaust gas is richer or leaner than $\lambda = 1$.

The oxygen sensor is installed into an appropriate location in the exhaust system with its ceramic part protruding into the exhaust gas and with the other part exposed to the outside air. The surface of the ceramic part is permeable to oxygen at approximately 300°C (572°F) and becomes electrically conductive.

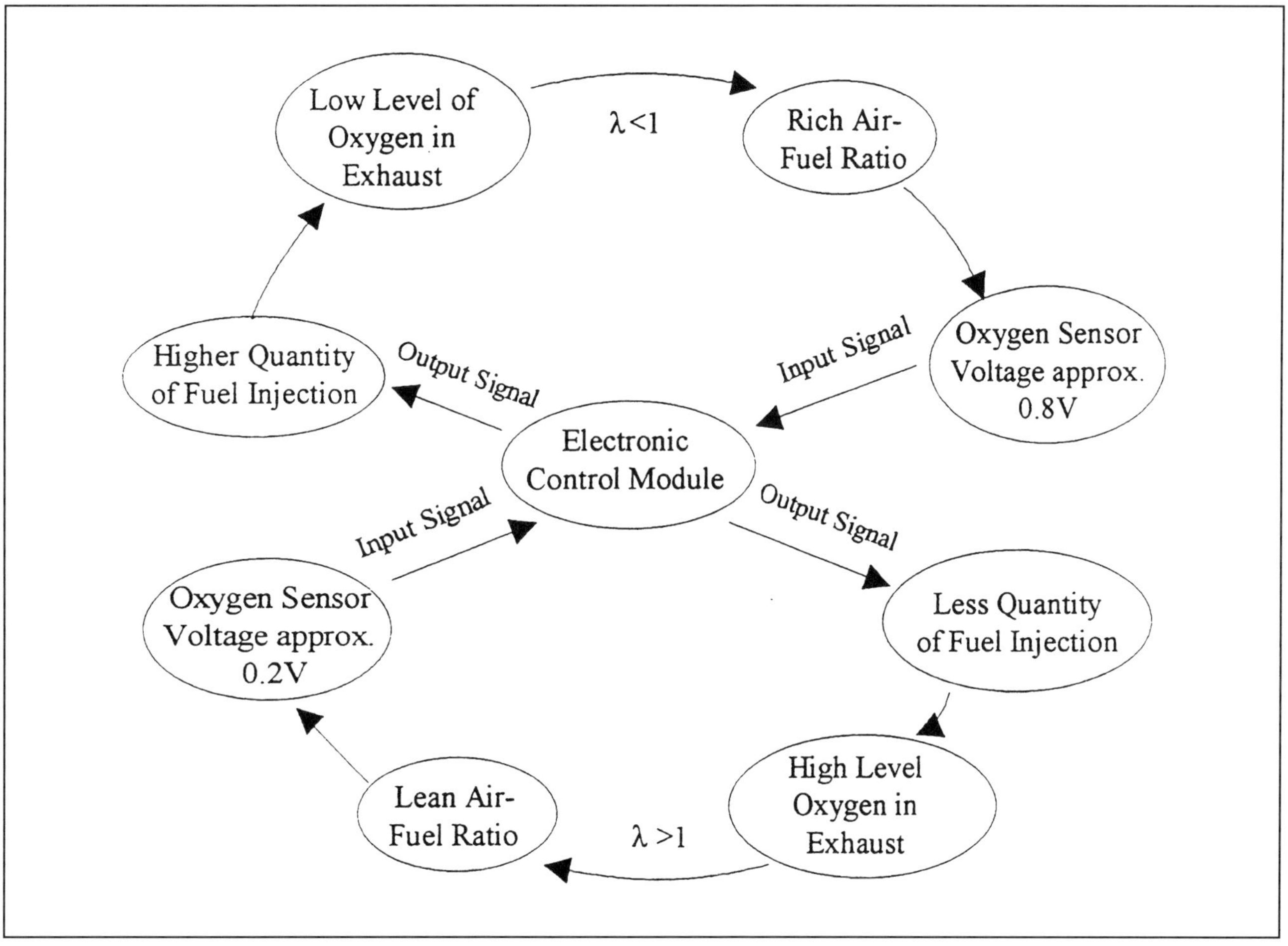

Methods To Reduce Emissions

If the oxygen content outside the sensor is different from the oxygen content in the exhaust system an electrical current is produced. This current is used to measure the difference of the oxygen content on both side of the sensor. The engine control module evaluates the signal and initiates the correction.

The oxygen sensor requires an operating temperature of at least 300°C (572°F) and is therefore also supplied as a heated oxygen (three-wire or four wire) sensor for faster response after a cold start.

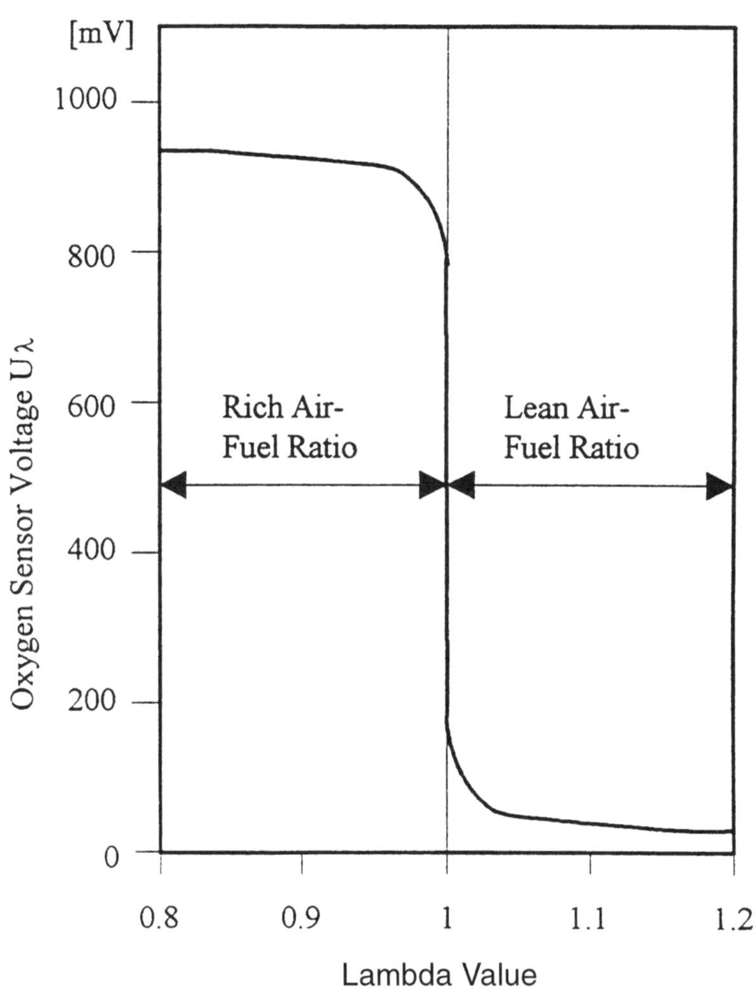

Secondary Air Injection

By injecting additional air into the hot exhaust gas in the exhaust system, it makes after-burning of unburned hydrocarbons (HC) and carbon monoxide (CO) possible and their conversion to water (H_2O) and carbon dioxide (CO_2).

For systems with oxidation catalytic converters, the fresh air is injected in front of the converter to supply sufficient oxygen for the oxidation of HC and CO (see also **Oxidation Catalytic Converter**). The control of the air supply is done today by an electrically-controlled solenoid valve.

In some systems, secondary air injection is used to shorten the heat-up phase of the catalytic converter after a cold start. After a cold start there is a high proportion of unburned fuel in the exhaust gas. The secondary air causes an after-burning of the fuel which brings the converter quickly to operating temperature.

Exhaust Gas Recirculation (EGR)

In exhaust gas recirculation, a portion of the exhaust gas is diverted via a connecting line into the air intake. An EGR valve in the line controls the amount of re-circulated exhaust gas. On later cars, a temperature sensor also measures the temperature of the recirculated gas which can be used as an additional control value.

The recirculated exhaust gas causes a direct reduction of the oxygen content in the fuel/air mixture and a reduction of the temperature in the combustion chamber because of the high temperature absorption of the exhaust gas. This causes the combustion temperature to be lowered and with that a reduction of NOx emission by up to 60%.

Too much recirculated exhaust gas causes an increase of HC and CO emissions and affects the combustion negatively to the point of misfiring and poor running. The amount of recirculated exhaust gas for a 4-cycle engine is therefore limited to approximately 3-5%.

Crankcase Ventilation

Combustion gases escaping between pistons and cylinders (blow-by gases) enter the crankcase and cause a pressure increase as well as a thinning of the engine oil. To prevent this from happening, the crankcase must be vented.

In older systems, the blow-by gases together with the oil vapors were vented to the outside air which lead to higher HC entering the atmosphere. In newer systems the gases from the crankcase are fed back into the intake system and are burned again.

A crankcase ventilation valve opens to the intake system when there is slight pressure in the crankcase. When the engine is not running the valve is closed to prevent the gas from entering the intake system.

Evaporative Emission (EVAP) Canister System

The evaporative emission (EVAP) canister system prevents highly volatile fuel vapors in the fuel tank system from entering the atmosphere. The center piece of the EVAP canister system is the EVAP canister, which is filled with activated charcoal.

Activated charcoal has the ability to absorb fuel vapors, to store them and to regenerate itself when the vapors are passed on. The EVAP canister is therefore a maintenance-free component, as long as the controlling EVAP purge valve (vacuum and frequency controlled) and the connecting lines are functioning properly.

At very low temperature it is important to check whether the vent opening at the bottom of the canister is free of ice and dirt.

The EVAP canister and the fuel tank are connected by a hose in the engine compartment. When the engine is not running, the vapors from the fuel tank are fed to the EVAP canister and are stored there. When the engine is started, a second hose leads the vapors to the intake manifold to be burned in the engine.

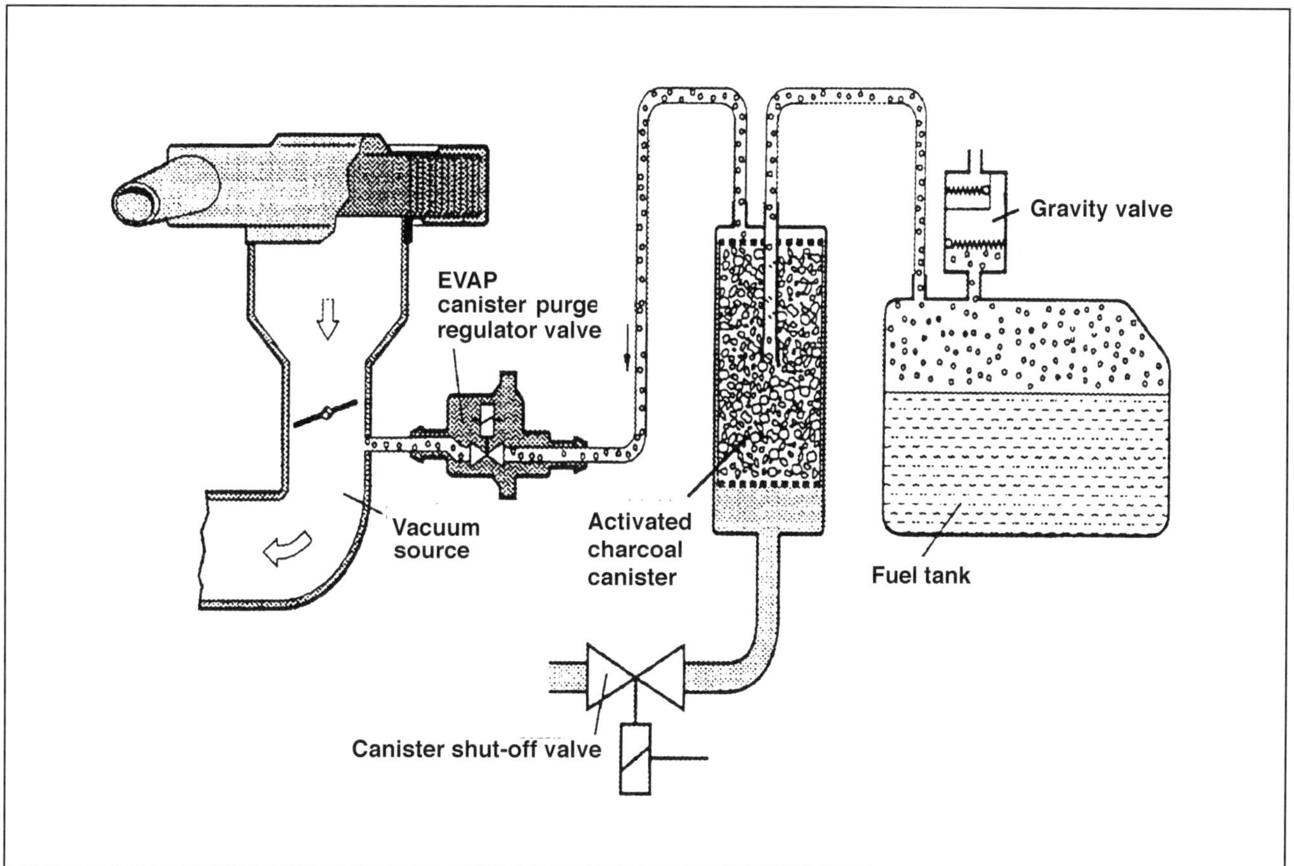
EVAP
canister purge
regulator valve
Gravity valve
Vacuum
source
Activated
charcoal
canister
Fuel tank
Canister shut-off valve

Notes

Appendix C

Diagnostic Trouble Codes (DTCs)

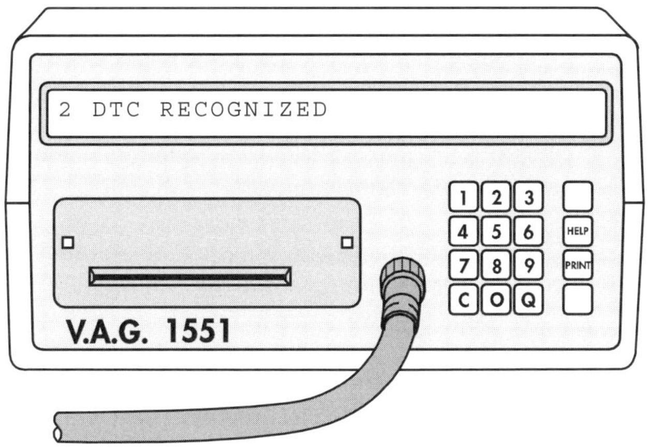

0021139

GENERAL

All engine management systems covered by this manual have the ability to monitor the operation of certain components and functions. If a monitored component fails or its signal is not correct, a record is stored in the ECM as a fault or **D**iagnostic **T**rouble **C**ode (DTC).

There are two methods of retrieving stored DTCs. The first method is through a process known as Blink Code. Blink code retrieval allows DTCs to be read by counting the number of times that a **L**ight **E**mitting **D**iode (LED) test light or the **M**alfunction **I**ndicator **L**ight (MIL) flashes or blinks. This method represents Volkswagen's first effort into onboard or self diagnostics. It does not require the use of a scan tool but also only provides limited information. Not all DTCs can be retrieved using this method and other parts of the system are not accessible. Retrieval of blink codes varies with vehicle type and system and not all vehicles support blink code access. For this reason and because of the very limited nature of the information, blink code retrieval information is outside the scope of this manual.

The second method of retrieving stored DTCs is through a process known as Rapid Data. Rapid Data retrieval allows DTCs to be read by a suitable scan tool through the use of a digital data stream. The digital data stream allows 2-way communication between the scan tool and the appropriate electronic control unit. Retrieval of DTCs is accomplished through Function 02 on the VAG 1551/1552 as outlined in the appropriate engine code chapters.

DTC Structure

Most Diagnostic Trouble Codes have two identifying tags. One tag is the 4-digit Blink Code and the other tag is the 5-digit VAG Code.

All DTCs have a VAG Code which details specific fault parameters that cause that particular DTC to be stored. Many VAG Codes also have a corresponding Blink Code and some VAG Codes have multiple Blink Codes.

When using the DTC tables, the following points should be considered:

- Tables are compiled from all VAG information available since the inception of permanent fault memory. They contain a wide range of DTCs that will not apply to every vehicle or system.
- Exact wording of the text for each DTC will vary slightly depending on the ECM software version and the scan tool software version.
- Other vehicle systems use the same format for recording malfunctions. These other systems often have codes that fall into gaps in the ECM code table. For example, a left front ABS wheel speed sensor malfunction carries Blink Code 1233 and VAG Code 00283. The following tables list only those DTCs that are accessible through the ECM. The above noted DTC, therefore, is not included because it can only be accessed through the ABS control module.
- Some VAG Codes are not listed as having a corresponding Blink Code. Actual on-vehicle experience has shown that in several cases Blink Codes are in fact present. These instances are noted by the format (xxxx?).

DTC Tables

The following tables are sorted first by the 5-digit VAG Code because most data will be retrieved with this information listed first. Some early scan tool software and/or systems may show Blink Code data listed first and therefore, a second table is included with data sorted by the 4-digit Blink Code.

DTCs Sorted by 5 Digit VAG Code

VAG Code	Blink Code	VAG 1551/1552 Scan Tool Display
	0000	Read out end
00000	4444	No DTC registered
00281	1231	Vehicle Speed Sensor (G68*), incorrect signal Vehicle Speed Sensor (G68*), no signal (* Note: scan tool displays G68 in error, actual component is G54, G22, or G21)
00282	1232	Throttle Position Actuator (V60), implausible signal
00310	1414	Temperature Sensor 1 for Catalyst (G20), open/short circuit to positive Temperature Sensor 1 for Catalyst (G20), short to ground
00312	1422	Temperature Sensor 2 for Catalyst (G132), open/short circuit to positive Temperature Sensor 2 for Catalyst (G132), short to ground
00313	1423	Catalyst, incorrect signal
00512	2114	Camshaft Position Sensor (G40), not at reference mark
00513	2111	Engine Speed Sensor (G28), no signal Engine Speed Sensor (G28), incorrect signal Engine Speed Sensor (G28), mechanical malfunction
00514	2112	Crankshaft Position Sensor (G4), no signal Crankshaft Position Sensor (G4), mechanical malfunction
00515	2113	Camshaft Position Sensor (G40), no signal Camshaft Position Sensor (G40), open/short circuit to B+ Camshaft Position Sensor (G40), short circuit to ground (gnd) Camshaft Position Sensor (G40), faulty Camshaft Position Sensor (G40), signal to positive Camshaft Position Sensor (G40), signal to ground Camshaft Position Sensor (G40), mechanical malfunction Camshaft Position Sensor (G40), faulty basic setting
00516	2121	Closed Throttle Position Switch (F60), short circuit to ground, Closed Throttle Position Switch (F60), open/short circuit to positive (+) Closed Throttle Position Switch (F60), signal to ground Closed Throttle Position Switch (F60), signal to positive
00517	2123	Wide Open Throttle Switch (F81), short to ground
00518	2212	Throttle Position Sensor (G69), open/short circuit to B+ Throttle Position Sensor (G69), open/short circuit to ground (gnd) Throttle Position Sensor (G69), short circuit to ground Throttle Position Sensor (G69), short circuit to B+ Throttle Position Sensor (G69), implausible signal Throttle Position Sensor (G69), no signal Throttle Position Sensor (G69), signal too high Throttle Position Sensor (G69), signal too low
00519	2222	Manifold Absolute Pressure Sensor (G71), no signal Manifold Absolute Pressure Sensor (G71), incorrect signal Manifold Absolute Pressure Sensor (G71), short circuit to positive Manifold Absolute Pressure Sensor (G71), open/short circuit to ground Manifold Absolute Pressure Sensor, signal too high Manifold Absolute Pressure Sensor, signal too low Manifold Absolute Pressure Sensor, control difference
00520	2232	Volume Air Flow Sensor (G70, G19), open/short circuit to ground Volume Air Flow Sensor (G70, G19), open/short circuit to positive (+)

DTCs Sorted by 5 Digit VAG Code

VAG Code	Blink Code	VAG 1551/1552 Scan Tool Display
00521	2242	CO Fuel Trim Potentiometer (G74), no signal CO Fuel Trim Potentiometer (G74), open/short circuit to positive (+) CO Fuel Trim Potentiometer (G74), short circuit to ground
00522	2312	Engine Coolant Temperature Sensor (G62), short circuit to ground Engine Coolant Temperature Sensor (G62), open/short circuit to positive (+) Engine Coolant Temperature Sensor (G62), implausible signal Engine Coolant Temperature Sensor (G62), signal to positive Engine Coolant Temperature Sensor (G62), signal to ground
00523	2322	Intake Air Temperature Sensor (G42), short circuit to ground, Intake Air Temperature Sensor (G42), open/short circuit to positive (+) Intake Air Temperature Sensor (G42), no signal Intake Air Temperature Sensor (G42), signal to positive Intake Air Temperature Sensor (G42), signal to ground
00524	2142	Knock Sensor 1 (G61), no signal Knock Sensor 1 (G61), open/short circuit to B+ Knock Sensor 1 (G61), open/short circuit to ground (gnd) Knock Sensor 1 (G61), incorrect signal
00525	2342	Oxygen Sensor (G39), no signal Oxygen Sensor (G39), short circuit to B+, Oxygen Sensor (G39), short circuit to ground (gnd) Oxygen Sensor (G39), incorrect signal Oxygen Sensor (G39), signal to positive Oxygen Sensor (G39), signal to ground
00527	2412	Intake Air Temperature Sensor (G72 or G42), short circuit to ground Intake Air Temperature Sensor (G72 or G42), open/short circuit to B+
00528	2223	Barometric Pressure Sensor (F96), open/short circuit to positive Barometric Pressure Sensor (F96), short circuit to ground
00529	2122	RPM information missing
00531	2233	Mass Air Flow Sensor (G70), open/short circuit to positive
00532	2234	Voltage Supply B+, incorrect signal Voltage Supply B+, signal too large Voltage Supply B+, signal too small
00533	2231	Idle speed (Idle Air Control) regulation, adaptation limit not reached Idle speed (Idle Air Control) regulation, adaptation limit exceeded
00534	2234	Voltage Supply B+, signal too large Voltage Supply B+, signal too small
00535	2141	First knock regulator (Sensor), incorrect signal First knock regulator (Sensor), regulation limit exceeded
00536	2143	Second knock regulator (Sensor), regulation limit exceeded
00537	2341	Oxygen Sensor (G39), control limit exceeded Oxygen Sensor Control, adaptation limit exceeded Oxygen Sensor Control, adaptations limit not reached Oxygen Sensor Control, signal to positive
00539	2311	Fuel temperature Sensor (G81), short circuit to ground Fuel temperature Sensor (G81), open/short circuit to positive

DTCs Sorted by 5 Digit VAG Code

VAG Code	Blink Code	VAG 1551/1552 Scan Tool Display
00540	2144	Knock Sensor 2 (G66), no signal Knock Sensor 2 (G66), open/short circuit to ground (gnd) Knock Sensor 2 (G66), incorrect signal
00542	2211	Needle Lift Sensor (G80), incorrect signal Needle Lift Sensor (G80), input open
00543	2214	RPM upper limit exceeded RPM signal too high
00544	2224	Maximum boost pressure exceeded Maximum boost pressure exceeded, incorrect signal
00545	2314	Engine/trans, electrical connection Engine/trans, short circuit to ground (gnd)
00546	2132	Data line faulty
00549	2243	Consumption signal, short circuit to B+
00550	2244	Injection start control, control difference
00552	2323	Volume Air Flow Sensor (G19), no signal
00553	2324	Mass Air Flow Sensor (G70), incorrect signal Mass Air Flow Sensor (G70), open/short circuit to B+ Mass Air Flow Sensor (G70), short circuit to ground (gnd) Mass Air Flow Sensor (G70), signal too high Mass Air Flow Sensor (G70), signal too low
00554	2331	Oxygen Sensor Control 2, adaptation limit exceeded Oxygen Sensor Control 2, adaptation limit not reached
00555	2332	Oxygen Sensor 2 (G108), no signal Oxygen Sensor 2 (G108), short circuit to B+, Oxygen Sensor 2 (G108), short circuit to ground (gnd) Oxygen Sensor 2 (G108), incorrect signal
00558	2343	Mixture control adjustment, lean limit exceeded
00559	2344	Mixture control adjustment, rich limit exceeded
00560	2411	Exhaust Gas Recirculation Vacuum Regulator Solenoid Valve (N18), mechanical malfunction Exhaust Gas Recirculation Vacuum Regulator Solenoid Valve (N18), incorrect signal Exhaust Gas Recirculation system, short circuit to ground Exhaust Gas Recirculation system, implausible signal
00561	2413	Mixture control adjustment, adaptation limit exceeded Mixture control adjustment, adaptation limit not reached Mixture adaptation, adaptation limit (multiplicative) exceeded Mixture adaptation, adaptation limit (multiplicative) undershot Mixture adaptation, adaptation limit (additive) exceeded Mixture adaptation, adaptation limit (additive) undershot
00575	2221	Manifold absolute pressure, control difference
00577	2141	Knock regulation cyl. 1, regulation limit exceeded
00578	2141	Knock regulation cyl. 2, regulation limit exceeded
00579	2141	Knock regulation cyl. 3, regulation limit exceeded

DTCs Sorted by 5 Digit VAG Code

VAG Code	Blink Code	VAG 1551/1552 Scan Tool Display
00580	2141	Knock regulation cyl. 4, regulation limit exceeded
00581	2141	Knock regulation cyl. 5, regulation limit exceeded
00582	2141	Knock regulation cyl. 6, regulation limit exceeded
00585	2411	EGR Temperature Sensor (G98), short circuit to ground (gnd)
00586	(2441?)	EGR system control, impossible signal EGR system control, incorrect signal
00587	na	Adjustment limit mixture regulator lean, Adaptation limit exceeded, Adjustment limit mixture regulator rich, Adaptation limit not reached
00609	4332	Ignition Output 1, short circuit to B+ Ignition Output 1, open/short circuit to positive Ignition Output 1, short circuit to ground Ignition Output 1, output does not operate
00610	4332	Ignition Output 2, short circuit to B+ Ignition Output 2, open/short circuit to positive Ignition Output 2, short circuit to ground Ignition Output 2, output does not operate
00611	4332	Ignition Output 3, short circuit to B+ Ignition Output 3, open/short circuit to positive Ignition Output 3, short circuit to ground Ignition Output 3, output does not operate
00624	na	A/C interruption, mechanical malfunction
00625	na	Vehicle speed signal, incorrect signal
00640	3434	Heated Oxygen Sensor Relay (J278), short circuit to B+ Heated Oxygen Sensor Relay (J278), open/short circuit to ground (gnd)
00668	na	Battery positive voltage, (B+), terminal 30, signal too low
00671	na	Cruise Control Switch (E45), undefined switch position
00689	4431	Air leak in intake air system, mechanical malfunction
00703	na	Closed Throttle Position Switch (F60), impossible signal
00740	na	Cyl. 1 Crankshaft position Sensor, no signal
00741	na	Brake pedal position monitoring, incorrect signal
00758	1344	Secondary Air Injection System (AIR), short circuit to B+ Secondary Air Injection System (AIR), open/short circuit to ground (This code has no reference in any material supplied by the manufacturer. The publisher has listed it here as the result of field testing.)
00765	1412	Modulating Piston Displacement Sensor (G149)
00777	3131	Throttle Position Sensor (G79), short circuit to positive Throttle Position Sensor (G79), incorrect signal
00824	3424	Fault lamp trigger, short circuit to B+ Fault lamp trigger, open/short circuit to ground (gnd)

DTCs Sorted by 5 Digit VAG Code

VAG Code	Blink Code	VAG 1551/1552 Scan Tool Display
01025	na	Malfunction Indicator Light faulty, short circuit to B+ Malfunction Indicator Light faulty, open/short circuit to ground (gnd)
01087	na	Basic setting not performed
01208	na	Data record changed
01235	4313	Secondary Air Injection Solenoid Valve (N112), short circuit to B+ Secondary Air Injection Solenoid Valve (N112), open/short circuit to ground (gnd)
01237	4321	Fuel Cut-Off Valve (N109), mechanical malfunction Fuel Cut-Off Valve (N109), open/short circuit to ground
01241	4331	EVAP Canister Purge Solenoid Valve (N115), open/short circuit to B+ EVAP Canister Purge Solenoid Valve (N115), open/short circuit to ground (gnd)
01242	4332	Final stage in control module, mechanical fault/malfunction Final stage in control module, open/short circuit to positive Final stage in control module, incorrect signal
01243	4333	Intake Manifold Change-Over Valve (N156), open/short circuit to ground Intake Manifold Change-Over Valve (N156), short circuit to positive Intake Manifold Change-Over Valve (N156), output does not operate
01247	4343	EVAP Canister Purge Regulator Valve (N80), open/short circuit to B+ EVAP Canister Purge Regulator Valve (N80), open/short circuit to ground (gnd) EVAP Canister Purge Regulator Valve (N80), output does not operate EVAP Canister Purge Regulator Valve (N80), signal to positive EVAP Canister Purge Regulator Valve (N80), signal to ground
01249	4411	Injector, cyl. 1 (N30), short circuit to B+ Injector, cyl. 1 (N30), open/short circuit to ground (gnd) Injector, cyl. 1 (N30), output does not operate Injector, cyl. 1 (N30),signal to negative Injector, cyl. 1 (N30), signal to positive
01250	4412	Injector, cyl. 2 (N31), short circuit to B+ Injector, cyl. 2 (N31), open/short circuit to ground (gnd) Injector, cyl. 2 (N31), output does not operate Injector, cyl. 2 (N31), signal to negative Injector, cyl. 2 (N31), signal to positive Injector, cyl. 2 (N31), incorrect signal
01251	4413	Injector, cyl. 3 (N32), short circuit to B+ Injector, cyl. 3 (N32), open/short circuit to ground (gnd) Injector, cyl. 3 (N32), output does not operate Injector, cyl. 3 (N32), signal to negative Injector, cyl. 3 (N32), signal to positive
01252	4414	Injector, cyl. 4 (N33), short circuit to B+ Injector, cyl. 4 (N33), open/short circuit to ground (gnd) Injector, cyl. 4 (N33), output does not operate Injector, cyl. 4 (N33), signal to negative Injector, cyl. 4 (N33), signal to positive
01253	4421	Injector, cyl. 5 (N83), short circuit to B+ Injector, cyl. 5 (N83), open/short circuit to ground (gnd) Injector, cyl. 5 (N35), output does not operate Injector, cyl. 5 (N35), signal to negative Injector, cyl. 5 (N35), signal to positive

DTCs Sorted by 5 Digit VAG Code

VAG Code	Blink Code	VAG 1551/1552 Scan Tool Display
01254	4422	Injector, cyl. 6 (N84), short circuit to B+ Injector, cyl. 6 (N84), open/short circuit to ground (gnd) Injector, cyl. 6 (N30), output does not operate
01257	4431	Idle Air Control Valve (N71), open/short circuit to ground, Idle Air Control Valve (N71), short circuit to positive (+) Idle Air Control Valve (N71), mechanical malfunction Idle Air Control Valve (N71), signal to negative Idle Air Control Valve (N71), signal to positive
01259	4433	Fuel Pump Relay (J17), short circuit to B+
01262	4442	Wastegate Bypass Regulator Valve (N75), short circuit to positive Wastegate Bypass Regulator Valve (N75), open/short circuit to ground
01264	4311	Secondary Air Injection Pump Relay (J299), short circuit to B+ Secondary Air Injection Pump Relay (J299), open/short circuit to ground (gnd)
01265	4312	EGR Vacuum Regulator Solenoid Valve (N18), open/short circuit to ground (gnd) EGR Vacuum Regulator Solenoid Valve (N18), short circuit to B+
01268	4113	Quantity Adjuster (N146), control difference
65535	1111	ECM, malfunctioning

DTCs Sorted by 4 Digit Blink Code

Blink Code	VAG Code	VAG 1551/1552 Scan Tool Display
0000		Read out end
1111	65535	ECM, malfunctioning
1231	00281	Vehicle Speed Sensor (G68*), incorrect signal Vehicle Speed Sensor (G68*), no signal (* Note: scan tool displays G68 in error, actual component is G54, G22, or G21)
1232	00282	Throttle Position Actuator (V60), implausible signal
1344	00758	Secondary Air Injection System (AIR), short circuit to B+ Secondary Air Injection System (AIR), open/short circuit to ground (This code has no reference in any material supplied by the manufacturer. The publisher has listed it here as the result of field testing.)
1412	00765	Modulating Piston Displacement Sensor (G149)
1414	00310	Temperature Sensor 1 for Catalyst (G20), open/short circuit to positive Temperature Sensor 1 for Catalyst (G20), short to ground
1422	00312	Temperature Sensor 2 for Catalyst (G132), open/short circuit to positive Temperature Sensor 2 for Catalyst (G132), short to ground
1423	00313	Catalyst, incorrect signal
2111	00513	Engine Speed Sensor (G28), no signal Engine Speed Sensor (G28), incorrect signal Engine Speed Sensor (G28), mechanical malfunction
2112	00514	Crankshaft Position Sensor (G4), no signal Crankshaft Position Sensor (G4), mechanical malfunction

DTCs Sorted by 4 Digit Blink Code

Blink Code	VAG Code	VAG 1551/1552 Scan Tool Display
2113	00515	Camshaft Position Sensor (G40), no signal Camshaft Position Sensor (G40), open/short circuit to B+ Camshaft Position Sensor (G40), short circuit to ground (gnd) Camshaft Position Sensor (G40), faulty Camshaft Position Sensor (G40), signal to positive Camshaft Position Sensor (G40), signal to ground Camshaft Position Sensor (G40), mechanical malfunction Camshaft Position Sensor (G40), faulty basic setting
2114	00512	Camshaft Position Sensor (G40), not at reference mark
2121	00516	Closed Throttle Position Switch (F60), short circuit to ground, Closed Throttle Position Switch (F60), open/short circuit to positive (+) Closed Throttle Position Switch (F60), signal to ground Closed Throttle Position Switch (F60), signal to positive
2122	00529	RPM information missing
2123	00517	Wide Open Throttle Switch (F81), short to ground
2132	00546	Data line faulty
2141	00535	First knock regulator (Sensor), incorrect signal First knock regulator (Sensor), regulation limit exceeded
2141	00577	Knock regulation cyl. 1, regulation limit exceeded
2141	00578	Knock regulation cyl. 2, regulation limit exceeded
2141	00579	Knock regulation cyl. 3, regulation limit exceeded
2141	00580	Knock regulation cyl. 4, regulation limit exceeded
2141	00581	Knock regulation cyl. 5, regulation limit exceeded
2141	00582	Knock regulation cyl. 6, regulation limit exceeded
2142	00524	Knock Sensor 1 (G61), no signal Knock Sensor 1 (G61), open/short circuit to B+ Knock Sensor 1 (G61), open/short circuit to ground (gnd) Knock Sensor 1 (G61), incorrect signal
2143	00536	Second knock regulator (Sensor), regulation limit exceeded
2144	00540	Knock Sensor 2 (G66), no signal Knock Sensor 2 (G66), open/short circuit to ground (gnd) Knock Sensor 2 (G66), incorrect signal
2211	00542	Needle Lift Sensor (G80), incorrect signal Needle Lift Sensor (G80), input open
2212	00518	Throttle Position Sensor (G69), open/short circuit to B+ Throttle Position Sensor (G69), open/short circuit to ground (gnd) Throttle Position Sensor (G69), short circuit to ground Throttle Position Sensor (G69), short circuit to B+ Throttle Position Sensor (G69), implausible signal Throttle Position Sensor (G69), no signal Throttle Position Sensor (G69), signal too high Throttle Position Sensor (G69), signal too low
2214	00543	RPM upper limit exceeded RPM signal too high

DTCs Sorted by 4 Digit Blink Code

Blink Code	VAG Code	VAG 1551/1552 Scan Tool Display
2221	00575	Manifold absolute pressure, control difference
2222	00519	Manifold Absolute Pressure Sensor (G71), no signal Manifold Absolute Pressure Sensor (G71), incorrect signal Manifold Absolute Pressure Sensor (G71), short circuit to positive Manifold Absolute Pressure Sensor (G71), open/short circuit to ground Manifold Absolute Pressure Sensor, signal too high Manifold Absolute Pressure Sensor, signal too low Manifold Absolute Pressure Sensor, control difference
2223	00528	Barometric Pressure Sensor (F96), open/short circuit to positive Barometric Pressure Sensor (F96), short circuit to ground
2224	00544	Maximum boost pressure exceeded Maximum boost pressure exceeded, incorrect signal
2231	00533	Idle speed (Idle Air Control) regulation, adaptation limit not reached Idle speed (Idle Air Control) regulation, adaptation limit exceeded
2232	00520	Volume Air Flow Sensor (G70, G19), open/short circuit to ground Volume Air Flow Sensor (G70, G19), open/short circuit to positive (+)
2233	00531	Mass Air Flow Sensor (G70), open/short circuit to positive
2234	00532	Voltage Supply B+, incorrect signal Voltage Supply B+, signal too large Voltage Supply B+, signal too small
2234	00534	Voltage Supply B+, signal too large Voltage Supply B+, signal too small
2242	00521	CO Fuel Trim Potentiometer (G74), no signal CO Fuel Trim Potentiometer (G74), open/short circuit to positive (+) CO Fuel Trim Potentiometer (G74), short circuit to ground
2243	00549	Consumption signal, short circuit to B+
2244	00550	Injection start control, control difference
2311	00539	Fuel temperature Sensor (G81), short circuit to ground Fuel temperature Sensor (G81), open/short circuit to positive
2312	00522	Engine Coolant Temperature Sensor (G62), short circuit to ground Engine Coolant Temperature Sensor (G62), open/short circuit to positive (+) Engine Coolant Temperature Sensor (G62), implausible signal Engine Coolant Temperature Sensor (G62), signal to positive Engine Coolant Temperature Sensor (G62), signal to ground
2314	00545	Engine/trans, electrical connection Engine/trans, short circuit to ground (gnd)
2322	00523	Intake Air Temperature Sensor (G42), short circuit to ground, Intake Air Temperature Sensor (G42), open/short circuit to positive (+) Intake Air Temperature Sensor (G42), no signal Intake Air Temperature Sensor (G42), signal to positive Intake Air Temperature Sensor (G42), signal to ground
2323	00552	Volume Air Flow Sensor (G19), no signal

DTCs Sorted by 4 Digit Blink Code

Blink Code	VAG Code	VAG 1551/1552 Scan Tool Display
2324	00553	Mass Air Flow Sensor (G70), incorrect signal Mass Air Flow Sensor (G70), open/short circuit to B+ Mass Air Flow Sensor (G70), short circuit to ground (gnd) Mass Air Flow Sensor (G70), signal too high Mass Air Flow Sensor (G70), signal too low
2331	00554	Oxygen Sensor Control 2, adaptation limit exceeded Oxygen Sensor Control 2, adaptation limit not reached
2332	00555	Oxygen Sensor 2 (G108), no signal Oxygen Sensor 2 (G108), short circuit to B+, Oxygen Sensor 2 (G108), short circuit to ground (gnd) Oxygen Sensor 2 (G108), incorrect signal
2341	00537	Oxygen Sensor (G39), control limit exceeded Oxygen Sensor Control, adaptation limit exceeded Oxygen Sensor Control, adaptations limit not reached Oxygen Sensor Control, signal to positive
2342	00525	Oxygen Sensor (G39), no signal Oxygen Sensor (G39), short circuit to B+, Oxygen Sensor (G39), short circuit to ground (gnd) Oxygen Sensor (G39), incorrect signal Oxygen Sensor (G39), signal to positive Oxygen Sensor (G39), signal to ground
2343	00558	Mixture control adjustment, lean limit exceeded
2344	00559	Mixture control adjustment, rich limit exceeded
na	00587	Adjustment limit mixture regulator lean, Adaptation limit exceeded, Adjustment limit mixture regulator rich, Adaptation limit not reached
2411	00560	Exhaust Gas Recirculation Vacuum Regulator Solenoid Valve (N18), mechanical malfunction Exhaust Gas Recirculation Vacuum Regulator Solenoid Valve (N18), incorrect signal Exhaust Gas Recirculation system, short circuit to ground Exhaust Gas Recirculation system, implausible signal
2411	00585	EGR Temperature Sensor (G98), short circuit to ground (gnd)
(2441?)	00586	EGR system control, impossible signal EGR system control, incorrect signal
2412	00527	Intake Air Temperature Sensor (G72 or G42), short circuit to ground Intake Air Temperature Sensor (G72 or G42), open/short circuit to B+
2413	00561	Mixture control adjustment, adaptation limit exceeded Mixture control adjustment, adaptation limit not reached Mixture adaptation, adaptation limit (multiplicative) exceeded Mixture adaptation, adaptation limit (multiplicative) undershot Mixture adaptation, adaptation limit (additive) exceeded Mixture adaptation, adaptation limit (additive) undershot
na	00624	A/C interruption, mechanical malfunction
na	00625	Vehicle speed signal, incorrect signal
3131	00777	Throttle Position Sensor (G79), short circuit to positive Throttle Position Sensor (G79), incorrect signal

DTCs Sorted by 4 Digit Blink Code

Blink Code	VAG Code	VAG 1551/1552 Scan Tool Display
3424	00824	Fault lamp trigger, short circuit to B+ Fault lamp trigger, open/short circuit to ground (gnd)
3434	00640	Heated Oxygen Sensor Relay (J278), short circuit to B+ Heated Oxygen Sensor Relay (J278), open/short circuit to ground (gnd)
na	00668	Battery positive voltage, (B+), terminal 30, signal too low
na	00671	Cruise Control Switch (E45), undefined switch position
na	00703	Closed Throttle Position Switch (F60), impossible signal
na	00740	Cyl. 1 Crankshaft position Sensor, no signal
na	00741	Brake pedal position monitoring, incorrect signal
na	01025	Malfunction Indicator Light faulty, short circuit to B+ Malfunction Indicator Light faulty, open/short circuit to ground (gnd)
na	01087	Basic setting not performed
na	01208	Data record changed
4113	01268	Quantity Adjuster (N146), control difference
4311	01264	Secondary Air Injection Pump Relay (J299), short circuit to B+ Secondary Air Injection Pump Relay (J299), open/short circuit to ground (gnd)
4312	01265	EGR Vacuum Regulator Solenoid Valve (N18), open/short circuit to ground (gnd) EGR Vacuum Regulator Solenoid Valve (N18), short circuit to B+
4313	01235	Secondary Air Injection Solenoid Valve (N112), short circuit to B+ Secondary Air Injection Solenoid Valve (N112), open/short circuit to ground (gnd)
4321	01237	Fuel Cut-Off Valve (N109), mechanical malfunction Fuel Cut-Off Valve (N109), open/short circuit to ground
4331	01241	EVAP Canister Purge Solenoid Valve (N115), open/short circuit to B+ EVAP Canister Purge Solenoid Valve (N115), open/short circuit to ground (gnd)
4332	01242	Final stage in control module, mechanical fault/malfunction Final stage in control module, open/short circuit to positive Final stage in control module, incorrect signal
4332	00609	Ignition Output 1, short circuit to B+ Ignition Output 1, open/short circuit to positive Ignition Output 1, short circuit to ground Ignition Output 1, output does not operate
4332	00610	Ignition Output 2, short circuit to B+ Ignition Output 2, open/short circuit to positive Ignition Output 2, short circuit to ground Ignition Output 2, output does not operate
4332	00611	Ignition Output 3, short circuit to B+ Ignition Output 3, open/short circuit to positive Ignition Output 3, short circuit to ground Ignition Output 3, output does not operate
4333	01243	Intake Manifold Change-Over Valve (N156), open/short circuit to ground Intake Manifold Change-Over Valve (N156), short circuit to positive Intake Manifold Change-Over Valve (N156), output does not operate

DTCs Sorted by 4 Digit Blink Code

Blink Code	VAG Code	VAG 1551/1552 Scan Tool Display
4343	01247	EVAP Canister Purge Regulator Valve (N80), open/short circuit to B+ EVAP Canister Purge Regulator Valve (N80), open/short circuit to ground (gnd) EVAP Canister Purge Regulator Valve (N80), output does not operate EVAP Canister Purge Regulator Valve (N80), signal to positive EVAP Canister Purge Regulator Valve (N80), signal to ground
4411	01249	Injector, cyl. 1 (N30), short circuit to B+ Injector, cyl. 1 (N30), open/short circuit to ground (gnd) Injector, cyl. 1 (N30), output does not operate Injector, cyl. 1 (N30),signal to negative Injector, cyl. 1 (N30), signal to positive
4412	01250	Injector, cyl. 2 (N31), short circuit to B+ Injector, cyl. 2 (N31), open/short circuit to ground (gnd) Injector, cyl. 2 (N31), output does not operate Injector, cyl. 2 (N31), signal to negative Injector, cyl. 2 (N31), signal to positive Injector, cyl. 2 (N31), incorrect signal
4413	01251	Injector, cyl. 3 (N32), short circuit to B+ Injector, cyl. 3 (N32), open/short circuit to ground (gnd) Injector, cyl. 3 (N32), output does not operate Injector, cyl. 3 (N32), signal to negative Injector, cyl. 3 (N32), signal to positive
4414	01252	Injector, cyl. 4 (N33), short circuit to B+ Injector, cyl. 4 (N33), open/short circuit to ground (gnd) Injector, cyl. 4 (N33), output does not operate Injector, cyl. 4 (N33), signal to negative Injector, cyl. 4 (N33), signal to positive
4421	01253	Injector, cyl. 5 (N83), short circuit to B+ Injector, cyl. 5 (N83), open/short circuit to ground (gnd) Injector, cyl. 5 (N35), output does not operate Injector, cyl. 5 (N35), signal to negative Injector, cyl. 5 (N35), signal to positive
4422	01254	Injector, cyl. 6 (N84), short circuit to B+ Injector, cyl. 6 (N84), open/short circuit to ground (gnd) Injector, cyl. 6 (N30), output does not operate
4431	01257	Idle Air Control Valve (N71), open/short circuit to ground, Idle Air Control Valve (N71), short circuit to positive (+) Idle Air Control Valve (N71), mechanical malfunction Idle Air Control Valve (N71), signal to negative Idle Air Control Valve (N71), signal to positive
4431	00689	Air leak in intake air system, mechanical malfunction
4433	01259	Fuel Pump Relay (J17), short circuit to B+
4442	01262	Wastegate Bypass Regulator Valve (N75), short circuit to positive Wastegate Bypass Regulator Valve (N75), open/short circuit to ground
4444	00000	No DTC registered

Appendix D
Glossary

GLOSSARY

ATDC — **A**fter **T**op **D**ead **C**enter; The position of the piston after it reaches the uppermost position in the cylinder. Expressed as degrees of crankshaft rotation.

a/t — **a**utomatic **t**ransmission.

BTDC — **B**efore **T**op **D**ead **C**enter; The position of the piston before it reaches the uppermost position in the cylinder. Expressed as degrees of crankshaft rotation.

C — **C**elsius; Metric temperature scale displayed on most scan tools. 0°C is the freezing point for water; 100°C is the boiling point.

Chassis — Shortened version of the VIN consisting of the model year, assembly plant, and 6 digit serial number (SH071871). Sometimes includes vehicle type (70SH071871).

CTP — **C**losed **T**hrottle **P**osition. Position of throttle plate in the rest or closed position.

DLC — **D**ata **L**ink **C**onnector. Interface connection that allows scan tool connection to vehicle systems for data transfer. All Volkswagen vehicles covered by this manual use one of the two types of DLCs illustrated below. The dual DLCs illustrated on the left were used from model year 1990 through early 1994. The 16-pin DLC on the right was phased in during the 1994 model year and is found on all newer vehicles.
Some older vehicles may use DLCs that are blue or red in addition to the black and white DLCs. The red DLC is used for diagnostics on Cabriolets with airbags. Blue connectors are used by systems that have blink code capabilities. Both of these systems are outside the scope of this book.

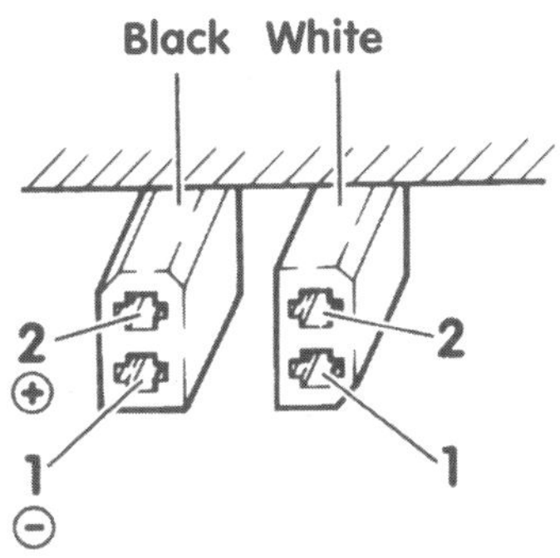

0021138

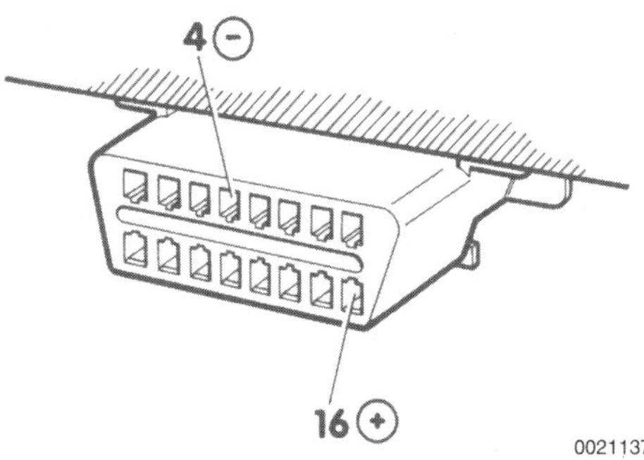

0021137

Glossary

DTC	**D**iagnostic **T**rouble **C**ode. Malfunction information stored electronically within the engine control module.
ECU	**E**lectronic **C**ontrol **U**nit. General term for any system controller. Example include (but are not limited to), **E**ngine **C**ontrol **M**odule (ECM), **T**ransmission **C**ontrol **M**odule (TCM), and Airbag Control Module.
EMS	**E**ngine **M**anagement **S**ystem
F	**F**ahrenheit; Temperature scale commonly used in the United States. 32°F is the freezing point for water; 212°F is the boiling point.
ft-lb (lb-ft)	Foot pound. Measurement of torque, used mainly when tightening fasteners or as an expression of engine output. Also expressed in Nm.
kg/H	**k**ilo**g**rams per **H**our; measurement of air flow.
km/H	**k**ilo**m**eters per **H**our; measurement of vehicle speed. Also expressed as kph.
ISC	**I**dle **S**peed **C**ontrol, also known as DIS (Digital Idle Speed Control). Engine idle speed control by means of small corrections to ignition timing.
J1930	Society of Automotive Engineers (SAE) standard covering consistent naming of EMS components. Component names in this manual follow this convention.
LEERLAUF	Idle or closed throttle position (CTP).
mbar	millibar; measurement of pressure. 1000 mbar equals approximately 14.5 psi (atmospheric pressure). Values less than 1000 mbar indicate vacuum in the system. Values greater than 1000 mbar are boost.
mg/H	**m**illi**g**rams per **H**our; measurement of flow or mass.
mph	**m**iles **p**er **h**our; measurement of vehicle speed.
mA	**m**illi**A**mp; 1/1000 of an Ampere.
ms	**m**illi**S**econd; 1/1000 of a second.
m/t	**m**anual **t**ransmission.
MY	**M**odel **Y**ear.
Nm	**N**ewton-**m**eters; Measurement of torque, used mainly when tightening fasteners or as an expression of engine output. Also expressed in lb-ft.
NTC	**N**egative **T**emperature **C**oefficient. A temperature sensor whose resistance decreases as temperature increases. All Engine Coolant Temperature Sensors and Intake Air Temperature Sensors covered by the manual are NTCs.
n.OT	n.o.T; "nach oberem Totpunkt", (After Top Dead Center, ATDC). The position of the piston after it reaches the uppermost position in the cylinder. Expressed in degrees of crankshaft rotation.
Observed value	Actual reading as shown on a scan tool during testing on subject vehicle.

Program Card — Operating instructions (software) that adapt a scan tool to a specific vehicle type or system. Also used to update scan tools with additional functions. Program cards usually have data stored on computer chips and are designed in such a way as to be removable (see below).

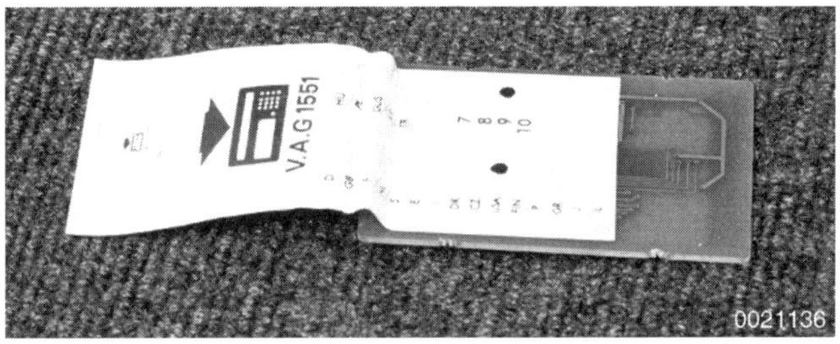

RPM (rpm) — **R**evolutions **P**er **M**inute; measurement of crankshaft speed.

Scan Tool — An electronic device connected by cable to the vehicle's Data Link Connector that allows interface between an operator and an ECU for diagnostic purposes. A scan tool reads data from the appropriate ECU and allows the operator to send data back to the ECU. Computer programs are also available to effectively turn a laptop or desktop computer into a scan tool with similar functions.

TEILLAST — Part throttle.

Tier 1 — Generally, a minimum national exhaust emission standard covering certain types of hydrocarbons (HC), carbon monoxide (CO), and oxides of nitrogen (NO_X).

WOT — **W**ide **O**pen **T**hrottle (full throttle). Position of throttle plate at full open position.

V — **V**olts.

Vehicle type — Two digit designation used to identify a particular vehicle class. Used in the VIN and as reference in some shortened chassis numbers.

Type	Models	Model Years
1G	Golf/Jetta/GTI (A2)	1991-1992
1H	Golf/Jetta/GTI (A3)	1993-1995
15	Cabriolet (A1)	1991-1993
1E	Cabrio (A3)	1995
30	Fox	1991-1993
31	Passat (B3)	1990-1994
3A	Passat(B4)	1995
50	Corrado	1991-1992
70	Eurovan (T4)	1992-1993

Glossary

VIN	**V**ehicle **I**dentification **N**umber. Unique 17 digit alpha-numeric designation assigned to all US specification Volkswagens at the time of assembly. Required by United States law since MY 1981 to identify specific vehicle attributes (WV2EE070XSH071871). Some partial VINs contain the letter Z in several positions. The letter Z is assigned to a body in production before final driveline and trim configurations are established. When these parameters are determined, the Zs are replaced with the appropriate letter or number and plates and stickers are attached to the vehicle. Many non-North American markets retain this production number containing Zs as the only vehicle identification.
VOLLAST	Full throttle or wide open throttle (WOT).
v.OT	v.o.T; "vor oberem Totpunkt", (Before Top Dead Center, BTDC). The position of the piston before it reaches the uppermost position in the cylinder. Expressed in degrees of crankshaft rotation.
/min	revolutions per minute (rpm); measurement of crankshaft speed.
/sp	sporadic fault. A DTC that was registered at one point, but may not be currently present.
∠	Angle (symbol).
°	Degrees (symbol).
λ	Lambda (symbol). Greek letter used to denote the air factor in the air/fuel ratio of 14.7:1.
%	Percentage (symbol).